Fortune or Failure

Missed Opportunities and Chance Discoveries

Alexander Kohn

Basil Blackwell

Copyright © Alexander Kohn 1989

First Published 1989

Basil Blackwell Ltd
108 Cowley Road, Oxford, OX4 1JF, UK

Basil Blackwell, Inc.
3 Cambridge Center
Cambridge, Massachusetts 02142, USA

British Library Cataloguing in Publication Data
A CIP catalogue record for this book is available from the British Library.

Library of Congress Cataloging in Publication Data
Kohn, Alexander.
    Fortune or failure : missed opportunities and chance discoveries /
· Alexander Kohn.
        p.   cm.
    Bibliography: p.
    Includes index.
    ISBN 0–631–16087–6
    1. Serendipity in science.   2. Creative ability in science.
3. Research.   I. Title.
Q172.5.S47K64   1989
500—dc20

Typeset in 10/12pt Baskerville
by Hope Services, Abingdon, Oxon.
Printed in Great Britain by
Billing and Sons Ltd., Worcester

Contents

Acknowledgements		x
Introduction		1
1	Discoveries in Physics: Electricity and Radioactivity	10
	The twitching frog's muscle (Galvani and Volta)	10
	A class experiment discovers electromagnetism	11
	A flash of insight and the induction motor	14
	X-rays – luminescence in the darkness	15
	A cloudy day helps in the discovery of radioactivity	22
2	From Atomic Nuclei to the Universe	26
	Masers, lasers and the 'big bang' theory	26
	Mössbauer's recoilless nuclear resonance	31
	New planets of Herschel, Adams and Leverrier	36
3	The Role of Chance in Chemistry and Biochemistry	41
	Erroneous concepts lead to the discovery of oxygen	41
	Berzelius, Wöhler and urea	45
	Perkin and the aniline dyes	46
	A dye or a drug?	47
	Why clonidine?	49
	Wrong rice and Vitamin B	50
	All sorts of switches – Hokin's hokum	51
4	Chance and Disappointment in Microbiology	56
	Chance favours none but the prepared mind	56
	Is there latent typhus?	57
	Puerperal fever and frustrated Semmelweiss	59
	'A slot machine – a broken test tube'	60
	The forgotten transformation	66

Hydrogen bromide and the genetic code 70
Polymorphism, Australia antigen and hepatitis 71

5 The Discovery of Penicillin – Design or Chance? 76

6 Antibiotics 97
Undiscovered antibiotics 97
Waksman's hesitations 103
Frogs and magainins 105

7 What Changes Our Behaviour? 110
From laughing gas to ether and chloroform 110
Local anaesthesia – it all started with cocaine 115
Endorphins – Thomas Mann's prophecy 117
Chance and tranquillizers 119
Psychedelic drugs and the cure of mental disturbances 121
Psychoneuro-immunology 124
The Portuguese man-of-war and anaphylaxis 126

8 Medical Discoveries 130
Night driving and discovery 130
What makes us sleep? 131
Schäfer did not believe it 133
The discovery of radioimmunoassay 134
How to stop bleeding: from citrate to heparin 136
How to freeze cells and keep them alive 138
Tap water leads by mistake to discovery 139
Papain and rabbits' floppy ears 140

9 The Incredible Story of Insulin 147
Banting and Best 152
Epilogue 156

10 What Do We Call a Fact? 163
The thought collective and a scientific fact 163
The role of lateral or divergent thinking 170

11 Personal Epilogue 175

Table of Missed Discoveries 179
Additional Reading 180

Name Index   181
Subject Index   187

Figures

1 Model for X-rays   18
2 A recoil model for gamma radiation   34
3 Schematic representation of the biochemical events involved
   in stimulation by choline and secretion in the salt gland   54
4 The experiment proposed by W. Szybalski   65
5 Comparison of Fleming's and Hare's experiments with
   Penicillium and staphylococci   81
6 Diagram of the pancreas   148
7 An enigmatic arithmetical series   164
8 Two faces in profile or a wine glass?   165
9 An old woman or a young girl?   165

Plates

1   Antoine Henri Becquerel (1852–1908)
2   Wilhelm Conrad Röntgen (1845–1923)
3   Arno A. Penzias and Robert W. Wilson
4   Rudolf Mossbauer
5   Gerhard Domagk
6   Christiaan Eijkman
7   Lowell Hokin
8   Salvador E. Luria
9   Elena Nightingale
10 Waclaw Szybalski
11 Baruch S. Blumberg
12 Sir Alexander Fleming
13 Lord Florey, 1952
14 Ernest Chain
15 Selman Waksman
16 Carl Koller (1857–1944)
17 Rosalyn S. Yalow
18 John Pappenheimer
19 Frederick Grant Banting (1891–1941)
20 C. H. Best
21 Ludwik Fleck

The seeds of great discoveries are constantly floating around us, but they only take root in minds well prepared to receive them.

Joseph Henry

Discovery needs luck, invention, intellect; one will not do without the others.

von Goethe

... and with due respect to Goethe's genius I might add: But patience, hope and expectation play an important part.

Helmut Stähle

Experiment is the sole interpreter of the artifices of Nature.

Leonardo da Vinci

Je ne cherche pas; je trouve!

Pablo Picasso

Scientific discovery depends on four G's – Geld, Geduld, Geschick, Glück.

Paul Ehrlich

Unless we are prepared to pose our questions anew we are unlikely to think beyond the first question we have formulated.

G. F. Kneller

To know a lot helps to discover new things, but it also has a gradually immobilizing effect.

Man cannot create science out of nothing. What man could do in creating science was to discover something hidden in Nature.

Invention and discovery always have something of the nature of the unpredictable.

Failure is the mother of success.

Hideki Yukawa

Remain seekers, cultivate in the garden of your souls that plant of
curiosity that will yield satisfying fruit.

J. Dible

In physical sciences the discovery of new facts is open to any
blockhead with patience and manual dexterity and acute senses.

William Rowan Hamilton

I thank God I was not made a dexterous manipulator; the most
important of my discoveries have been suggested by my failures.

Humphrey Davy

No great discovery is ever made without a bold guess.

Isaac Newton

I have the result, but I do not yet know how to get it.

Johann K. F. Gauss

He who cannot see that which he finds shall never find that which
he seeks.

Simon Roman

All the inventions that the world contains,
Were not by reason first found out, nor brains;
But pass for theirs who had the luck to light
Upon them by mistake or oversight.

Samuel Butler

Acknowledgements

I wish to express my sincere thanks to Dr Bernard Dixon for his interest and moral support; to Professors L. Hokin, S. E. Luria, W. Szybalski, R. Yalow and to Dr Elena Nightingale for providing me with insight into their work; to Dr Shai Shoham, and Professors H. J. Lipkin (of the Weizmann Institute), S. Rosenwaks (of Ben Gurion University) and John Yudkin (in London) for their critical assistance; to Professors Volker Neuhoff and Rudolf Rott, Dr Ion Gresser and Dr Mario Pezella for help in tracing old texts for me; and especially to Romesh Vaitilingam (at Basil Blackwell) for his help in preparing this book for publication.

I also greatly appreciate the assistance of the Wellcome Museum of Medical History, the Nobel Foundation, the Royal Society of Chemists, the US Instititute of Physics, the Department of Pathology at Oxford University and the Waksman Institute of Microbiology for supplying me with many of the photographs reproduced in this book. I also thank Drs B. Blumberg, E. Nightingale, J. R. Pappenheimer and R. S. Yalow for photographs. Help from Dr David Katz, of the Israel Institute for Biological Research, in preparing some of the sketches, is gratefully acknowledged. I thank Mrs Galina Segal, a librarian at the Weizmann Institute, Israel, for her assistance.

I am grateful to the following for permission to reproduce photographs: AT & T Bell Laboratories (Penzias and Wilson); the Niels Bohr Library, American Institute of Physics (Becquerel and Röntgen); the Nobel Foundation (Domagk and Eijkman); the Sir William Dunn School of Pathology, Oxford (Florey); the Waksman Institute of Microbiology, Israel (Waksman); the Wellcome Institute, London (Banting, Best, Fleming and Koller); to Rudolf Mössbauer, Lowell Hokin, Salvador Luria, Elena Nightingale, Waclaw Szybalski, Baruch S. Blumberg, Rosalyn S. Yalow and John Pappenheimer for photographs of themselves; to Daniel Chain for that of his father, Ernest Chain. Ludwik Fleck's photograph is my own.

Introduction

The word 'serendipity' was coined by Horace Walpole in 1754 and was based on the tale 'The three Princes of Serendip' (Serendip=Ceylon=Sri Lanka). Walpole's definition of the word was: 'Making discoveries by accident and sagacity, of things which they were not in quest of'. The faculty of making happy and unexpected discoveries in the course of scientific investigation is therefore also termed serendipity. The famous American physicist, Joseph Henry, recognized that 'the seeds of great discovery are constantly floating around us, but they take root only in minds well prepared to receive them', a statement which is a paraphrase of the famous dictum of Louis Pasteur: 'Chance favours the prepared mind.' Hideki Yukawa, the Japanese Nobel laureate in physics, stated: 'Invention and discovery always have something of the nature of the unpredictable.'[1]

Only a few understand the meaning of what they see, and make a discovery. To make a discovery, said Albert Szent-Gyorgyi, means to see what everyone has seen, but to think something special about it. Discovery often means simply the uncovering of something which has always been there, but was hidden from the eye by the blinkers of habit. Dr P. E. Pattle of the Chemical Defence Research Establishment at Porton Down has stated: 'Some authors refer to a discovery based on observation which was not what was actually being investigated as "chance" or "accidental" discovery. This is *never* true. Observations are made because the observer is on the lookout for something strange.'

Among those who could have made a discovery, but did not, are many who missed the opportunity, either because they did not fully appreciate the importance of their results, or because they were too timid to insist on the correct, but novel, interpretation of their findings which ran against the accepted paradigm. Missed opportunities are also the result of the background, the education and the environment of the scientist as well as of his or her preoccupations, bias and goals. Winston Churchill said that men occasionally stumbled over the truth, but that most of them picked themselves up and hurried off as if nothing had happened. There have also been those who simply made their discoveries too early, when the communal thinking of the scientific community was not yet ready to accept the new idea and its explanation. It is not only the discoverer's ability to observe what chance has presented to him. He has to be able to judge the importance of the observation, to have not only the prepared mind, but also a flexible mind. Thus chance can either speed up the work in progress or change the goals of the scientist involved.

Scientists prefer to be seen as having meticulously planned their experiments in order to arrive at confirmation of their hypotheses rather than to be regarded as discoverers. When young scientists at the beginning of their careers report findings and results that have a considerable impact on the advancement of science, they seldom admit that chance has led to their achievements. When a scientist reaches the summit of his career and does not need to worry about his future advancement or fame, he is more often than not willing to admit how chance has influenced his career.

Accidents do not happen to scientists who trust that chance will provide them with inspiration. 'They come rather to him who, while continuously busy with the work of research, does not close his attention from matters outside his principal aims and immediate objective but keeps it alert to what unexpected observation they may have to offer.' Sir Henry Dale did not believe that any research work or any discovery of importance was made without a great deal of hard, systematic and conscientious work.[2]

In the following chapters I shall describe both aspects: missed discoveries of scientists who, in spite of their devotion and persistence, made no discovery after all, and those who made the discoveries without having any specific intention of making them. Although I describe in this book some examples of serendipitous discoveries in the fields of physics and mathematics, the text is biased towards biology and medicine, the fields in which my professional interests and abilities lie. Thus I shall not discuss the interesting story of a broken crystal leading Hauy to develop the crystallographic theory, or the detection of the polarization of light by the French mathematician E. L. Malus. I shall not dwell on errors that played an essential role in the discovery of some fundamental principles, such as, for instance, Kepler's formulation (1609) of the three laws governing the motion of planets in the solar system. Kepler originally had an erroneous conception and it was only the realization that his calculation differed by eight minutes from Tycho Brahe's actual observation that led him to the correct solution. Knowing how meticulous Brahe was, Kepler wrote: 'These 8 minutes which we dare not neglect will give us means of reforming the whole of astronomy.'[3]

I shall also omit myths that explain some important scientific discoveries, such as the story of Archimedes' 'Eureka' when he grasped that the volume of water displaced in his bathtub was equal to that of his body, Newton's discovery of the laws of gravity, presumably the outcome of his watching a falling apple, or the discovery of the steam engine by James Watt from his observation of the lid of a boiling kettle. Another myth, which has been recently laid to rest, is that concerning Kekulé's discovery of the structure of benzene, which he himself attributed to a dream he had while snoozing in front of a fire when he saw snakes wriggling in a circle.[4] This book should be viewed as an assembly of commentaries rather than as excerpts from the history of science.

'The question of true authorship of a discovery confronts the historian of science with an extremely difficult and complex problem, often obscured by questions of vanity, of personal rivalries and even of chauvinism.'[5] It is a fact that many discoveries are made almost simultaneously by different scientists. This indicates that great discoveries are made when the general level of science is such as to make them inevitable. Examples are provided by the discoveries, by Fermat and Descartes, of analytical geometry, by Leibniz and Newton of infinitesimal analysis, by Lobatchevski, Bolyai and Gauss of non-Euclidean geometry, by Abel and Jacobi of elliptic functions, by Ting and Richter of the J/PSI meson, etc. (The story of how Burton Richter, with his team of over thirty people, working at the Stanford Linear Accelerator Center, and Samuel C. C. Ting at MIT, with twelve collaborators, simultaneously, but independently, discovered the J/PSI meson in November 1974 and were jointly awarded the Nobel Prize in 1976 is aptly described by Gilbert Shapira in his book on serendipity.)[6]

'Although it is common knowledge that sometimes chance is a factor in the making of a discovery the magnitude of its importance is seldom realized and the significance of its role does not seem to have been fully appreciated or understood.'[7] Nearly all the great discoveries in chemotherapy have been made as a result of a false hypothesis or due to a so-called chance observation.

Maurice Wilkins, the recipient of the Nobel Prize for 1962 (with Watson and Crick) wrote in 1988:[8]

Scientists like to succeed. They like to get the results they hope for, to be recognized for what they have done. But they also know that the greatest success may come from something unexpected, including failure. For example, the failure of Michelson and Morley to detect ether drift was a magnificent failure which upset classical physics and helped advance Einstein's revolutionary ideas.

Another Nobel Prize winner, François Jacob, said in his Nobel Lecture in 1965:

> ... when I entered research in 1950, I was fortunate enough to arrive at the right place at the right time. At the right place, because there, in the attics of the Pasteur Institute, a new discipline was emerging in an atmosphere of enthusiasm, lucid criticism, nonconformism, and friendship. At the right time, because then biology was bubbling with activity, changing its way of thinking, discovering in microorganisms a new and simple material, and drawing closer physics and chemistry. A rare moment, in which ignorance could become a virtue.[9]

Some discoveries appear not to have been made because their discoverers did not publish them, and they remained in notebooks or manuscripts. One such discovery, of the pulmonary blood circulation, made in the thirteenth century, remained unknown for 700 years.

During the reign of Marcus Aurelius, Roman Emperor in the second century AD, there lived a Greek physician Galen, a gifted anatomist: his teaching of animal and human anatomy prevailed for more than fourteen centuries. Knowing that blood had to pass somehow from the left half of the heart to the right half, Galen claimed the existence of pores, too small to be seen, in the muscular partition between the two halves. This view was still supported by Andreas Vesalius, a Flemish physician and anatomist in the sixteenth century.

The discovery of the pulmonary blood circulation from the right heart ventricle through the lungs and back to the left ventricle, was attributed for centuries to Michael Servetus (1553) and then to Realdo Colombo (1559). But this discovery was actually made in the thirteenth century by Ibn-al-Nafis, al Qurashi, the physician to the ruling Baybars al-Zahir in Cairo.

In 1242 Ibn-al-Nafis wrote four medical commentaries on *Kitab al Qanum*. In the first of these books, *Sharh al Qanum*, he contradicted Galen's teaching that there was a direct connection between the two parts of the heart. He wrote:

> There is no connection between the two sides. It must therefore be that when the blood has become thin, it is passed into the arterial vein [the

pulmonary artery] to the lung, to be dispersed inside the substance of the lung and to mix with air. The finest parts of the blood are then strained, passing into the venous artery [the pulmonary vein] reaching the left of the two cavities of the heart, after mixing with the air and becoming fit for the generation of pneuma.[10]

There was no follow-up to this discovery for the next 300 years. Were it not for the finding of Islamic manuscripts (including those of al-Nafis) in 1952 in Cambridge and then in Stanford, the real discoverer of the pulmonary circulation would have remained anonymous, and Servetus and Colombo would be the only ones remembered.

There are many examples of unrecognized discoveries in the last two centuries. Cavendish's results of his experiments in electrostatics became known, or rather rediscovered, only by Coulomb and Faraday. Similarly Gauss's elliptic functions were rediscovered later. Jean Frederick Joliot and Irène Curie, who were awarded the Nobel Prize in 1935 for the discovery of artificial radioactivity, forfeited the discovery of the neutron to Chadwick and that of the positron to David Anderson. The famous French mathematician Henri Poincaré, with much wider mathematical background, had mastered all the elements of the principle of relativity before Einstein, but he dared not publish his thoughts and their consequences.[11] The laser was first constructed by Gordon Gould, but it took him almost thirty years to obtain recognition from the US Patent Office because his invention was recorded only in his notebooks (see chapter 2 below).

There were also discoveries that were not appreciated as such, because they encountered hostility and opposition from well-known contemporary scientists. The most serious enemy of discovery and scientific attainment based on a new idea is dogma and authority; the accepted dogma of today may be the error of tomorrow.

Robert Mayer, co-discoverer of the principle of the conservation of energy, went mad because his work was not recognized. So did Ignaz Semmelweiss, who discovered how to prevent puerperal fever (see chapter 4 below).

Einstein did not receive the Nobel Prize for his theory of relativity, although he was nominated ten times between 1910 and 1922 by most of the outstanding physicists of the time. It was not until 1922 that he was awarded the prize for 1921 for 'his services to theoretical physics and especially for his discovery of the law of the photoelectric effect'.[12] In his message to Einstein, Professor C. Aurivillius, the secretary of the Swedish

Academy of Sciences, added: 'but without taking into account the value which will be accorded your relativity and gravitation theories after these are confirmed in the future'.[13]

Amazingly, one may find in the *Nobel Lectures* a transcript of Einstein's lecture to the Nordic Assembly of Naturalists at Gothenburg, given on 11 July 1923. It was entitled 'Fundamental ideas and problems of the theory of relativity'. At the end of the text there is a remark: 'The lecture was not delivered on the occasion of the Nobel Prize award, and did not, therefore, concern the discovery of the photoelectric effect'![14]

Belated recognition for important discoveries was awarded to George Mendel forty years after his publication that laid the foundations of modern genetics. In more recent times, the discovery of tumour-producing viruses in cell-free filtrates of chicken sarcoma by Peyton Rous at the Rockefeller Institute in 1913 was met with sheer disbelief. It took over fifteen years for the idea that viruses cause cancer to become established. During that period scientists used to say, 'Rous has either a hole in his filter or a hole in his head.' It took over fifty years for the scientific community, represented by the Nobel foundation, to recognize the import-ance of Rous's discovery, and to award him the prize in 1966. At that time Rous was eighty-seven years old. Another belated recognition and a Nobel Prize were given to Barbara McClintock 'for the discovery of mobile structure in the genetic mass'[15] in 1983. She had made the discovery of 'jumping genes' in maize some forty years earlier, while working com-pletely on her own at the Carnegie Institute of Washington in Cold Spring Harbor. She published her results in the *Proceedings of the National Academy of Science* in 1950 under the title, 'The origin and behavior of mutable loci in maize'[16] but – as M. Asburner, of the Department of Genetics at the University of Cambridge, said – 'it was so far out that no one could relate it to anything anyone at the time knew about the genome.'[17]

The men who for decades were credited with inventing the first electronic computers, such as the Colossus built by Alan M. Turing and M. H. A. Newman (1943) and the ENIAC (Electronic Numerical Integrator and Computer) built by John W. Mauchly and J. Prosper Eckert (1945), were in fact not the first. The credit should actually go to John V. Atanasoff, a physicist at the University of Iowa, who designed and built two small electronic computers in 1937 and between 1939 and 1942, with his graduate student Clifford E. Berry, produced a larger machine known as the Atanasoff–Berry Computer (ABC). Unfortunately he did not take out a patent on this invention and his recognition after more than forty years came about only when the Sperry Rand Corporation (the owner of the ENIAC patent) sued Honeywell for violation of the anti-trust regulations. In their defence Honeywell showed that parts of the ENIAC patent were derived from the ABC and from information given to Mauchly by Atanasoff. The court declared the patent invalid. The whole story of Atanasoff's work leading to the invention and his belated recognition as the inventor was not described until two books were published in 1988.[18]

These, then are examples of what I would call 'communal blindness'. The existing paradigm would not accept these 'new facts'.

Some famous scientists (e.g. Dumas, Berthelot), with advancing age, held theories that became dogmas and would not allow any criticism to the extent that they had the power to suppress progress dictated by a new unpopular theory. An example of such suppression is provided in the discovery by Ignaz Semmelweiss of the means of prevention of puerperal fever in the middle of last century (see chapter 4 below).

The idea of preventing smallpox by vaccination is generally attributed to Edward Jenner of Berkeley, Gloucestershire, who in 1790 injected the fluid obtained from a pox lesion in a hog to his ten-month-old son. Later he used similar fluid from a pock lesion on the hand of a milkmaid (cowpox) for the inoculation of James Phipps who developed the typical vaccination reaction and became immune to later infection through the agency of smallpox. Jenner was not really original in his idea. Vaccination had been suggested even earlier in France, but nothing had come of it because the idea was condemned by theologians at the Sorbonne as well as by English clergy at Canterbury.[19] Even earlier, in 1721, Dr Zabdiel Boylston, of Boston, had inoculated his son with variola material, believing it would protect him from smallpox. He was attacked by the clergy because smallpox was considered at that time to be 'a judgement of God on the sins of the people . . . and to avert it is to provoke Him'.[20]

When Jenner, the father of vaccination, asked the Royal Society for permission to present his findings and ideas there, the answer was: 'He ought not to risk his reputation by presenting to the learned body anything which appeared so much at variance with established knowledge, and withal so incredible.'[21] In 1798 Jenner was also attacked by the Anti-vaccination Society, and in 1803 at Cambridge Dr Ramsden claimed that the practice of vaccination was prohibited by God's law. The negative attitude of the Catholic Church to vaccination reached the extreme when in 1885 there was a smallpox epidemic in Montreal. The Catholic population, having refused vaccination, suffered terribly, while the Protestants, who had been vaccinated, escaped the epidemic almost entirely.[22]

In 1845, when J. J. Waterston submitted a paper on the molecular theory of gases to the Royal Society, it was rejected as utter nonsense, to be rediscovered by Joule and James Clerk Maxwell forty-five years later.

In the field of physics it was Robert Millikan, the recipient of the 1923 Nobel Prize for physics, who claimed that cosmic rays were photons, even in the face of overwhelming contrary evidence provided by Jacob Clay and Arthur Holly Compton. Millikan obstinately defied the bulk of scientific opinion. In 1929, when asked by reporters whether cosmic rays were not charged particles, he answered: 'You might as well sensibly compare an elephant and a radish.'[23] In the pursuit of his wrong hypothesis on cosmic rays Millikan continued to accumulate data measuring the intensity of cosmic rays everywhere on earth, in the oceans, and in the atmosphere, and these data eventually led to the discovery of the positron.[24]

In a letter of 8 July 1901 to Jost Winteler concerning the difficulties he had with his Ph.D. thesis, Einstein wrote: "The stupor of authority is the greatest enemy of truth.'[25]

NOTES TO INTRODUCTION

1 Yukawa, H. 1966: *Creativity and Invention. A Physicist Looks at East and West*. Tokyo, New York, San Francisco: Koshanada International Ltd.: 123.
2. Dale, H. 1948: Accident and opportunities in medical research. *British Medical Journal*, 2: (1948): 455.
3 Taton, R. 1957: *Reason and Chance in Scientific Discovery*. London: Hutchinson and Co.
4 Kohn, A. 1988: *False Prophets. Fraud and Error in Science and Medicine* (revised edn). Oxford: Basil Blackwell.
5 Taton, *Reason and Chance*: 107.
6 Shapira, G. 1986: *A Skeleton in the Darkroom. Stories of Serendipity in Science*. San Francisco: Harper and Row: 79.
7 Beveridge, W. I. B. 1957: *The Art of Scientific Investigation* (3rd edn). London: Heinemann Ltd.: 31.
8 Wilkins, M. 1988: Fortunate failures I don't regret. *Scientist*, 2/3: 14.
9 Jacob, F. 1965: Genetics of the bacterial cell. *Nobel Prize Lectures 1965*. New York: Elsevier: 219.
10 Iskandar, A. Z. 1974: Ibn–al Nafis. In C.C. Gillespie (ed.), *Dictionary of Scientific Biography*. New York: Scribner and Sons.
11 Koestler, A. 1964: *The Art of Creation*. London: Hutchinson and Co. Ltd. (Pan Books): 236.

12 *Nobel Lectures: Physics 1901–1921* 1967: New York: Elsevier: 477.

13 Pais, A. 1982: *Subtle is the Lord*, ch. 30: How Einstein got the Nobel Prize. New York: Dover Publications.

14 *Nobel Lectures* 1967: 482f.

15 *Nobel Lectures: Physiology and Medicine* 1983: New York: Elsevier: 28.

16 McClintock, B. 1950: The origin and behavior of mutable loci. *Proceedings of the National Academy of Science, USA*, 36: 344.

17 Cherfas, J. and Connor, S. 1983: How restless DNA was tamed. *New Scientist*, 100 (1979): 79.

18 Burks, A. R. and Burks, A. W. 1988: *The First Electronic Computer: The Atanasoff Story*. Madison: University of Michigan Press.
   Mollenhoff, C. R. 1988: *Atanasoff: Forgotten Father of the Computer*. Ames: Iowa State University Press.

19 Williams, G. 1960: *Virus Hunters*, chs 1–4. New York: A. A. Knopf: 13–44.

20 Pyke, M. 1982: *The Science Myth*. London: J. Murray: 101.

21 White, A. D. 1960: *A History of the Warfare of Science with Theology in Christendom*. (reprint of 1896 edn). New York: Dover: ii. 56–7.

22 Ibid.: 58.

23 Kevles, D. J. 1979: Robert A. Millikan. *Scientific American*, 240/1: 121.

24 Ibid.: 118f.

25 Stachel, J. 1987: *The Collection of Papers of Albert Einstein*, vol. 1. *The Early Years*. Princeton: Princeton University Press.

1

Discoveries in Physics: Electricity and Radioactivity

The twitching frog's muscle (Galvani and Volta)

Luigi Galvani was Professor of Anatomy at the University of Bologna in the middle of the eighteenth century. At that time one of the rages of a well-equipped physical laboratory was the Leyden jar, a device for storing static electricity. Galvani had Leyden jars in his laboratory too; he was experimenting with frogs' muscles. On one occasion while the calf muscles of a frog were suspended on a metallic support, and a spark was produced during a discharge of a Leyden jar near by, Galvani observed that the frog's muscles contracted vigorously. This also happened when during the electric discharge the muscles, stretched on a wooden board, were touched with a metal scalpel that had a bone handle. The fact that electric current could make a living frog's muscles twitch was not surprising, but the observation of the contraction of a muscle from a dead frog was novel and demanded some explanation. Galvani assumed that the electrical discharge in the air somehow affected the muscle. In a paper in 1792 he wrote:

> . . . we discovered that the whole matter was to be attributed to the question of which different part of the scalpel we were holding with our fingers; the scalpel had a bone handle and, if this handle were held in the hand when a spark was produced, no movements [of the frog's muscle] resulted, but they did result when the fingers were placed either on the metal blade or on the iron nails securing the blade of the scalpel.[1]

Galvani next set up an experiment in which, during a thunderstorm, he laid a frog's muscles, suspended on brass hooks and resting against iron lattice, against the laboratory window. Galvani noted that whenever there was lightning the muscles twitched, but, more surprisingly, they also twitched whenever the brass hooks and the iron lattice simultaneously touched the muscle. Galvani's interpretation of this finding was that electricity was generated in the muscle itself, and he called this effect 'animal electricity', thus making an important observation which might have led him to the conclusion that two different metals touching an animal tissue produce electricity. However, he failed to reach this conclusion.

Alessandro Volta, however, who was already Professor of Physics at Como at the age of twenty-nine, understood Galvani's phenomenon and proved his conclusions wrong. Volta showed that the source of the electricity that made the muscle twitch was not in the muscle, but in the metals. In 1794 he demonstrated that an electric current would flow between two metals even without the muscle. In 1800 Volta built an apparatus made of two bowls filled with salt solution, dipped a bar of copper in one of them and a bar of zinc in the other, and then connected the two by an arc (a piece of conducting wire), showing that an electric current would flow through the wire. Volta thus invented an electric battery, which was then improved, to become the 'Voltaic pile'. Galvani, who died in 1798, knew of Volta's experiments, but he stuck to his theory and died a disappointed man. Nevertheless the terms 'Galvanic electricity', Galvanization and Galvanometer attest his priority in a discovery that he himself did not understand. So Galvani survives in galvanometer and Volta in volt (for electric potential).

Once the secrets of electric current had apparently been mastered, scientists experimented to show the connection between electricity and heat and light. Coulomb had apparently proved in the 1780s that electricity and magnetism were two entirely different phenomena and therefore that conversion of one to another was impossible.

A class experiment discovers electromagnetism

The story of the missed discovery of electromagnetic induction by Ampère begins with Oersted[2]. Hans Christian Oersted, a Danish physicist, finished his studies in chemistry and physics at the University of Copenhagen and was appointed professor there in 1806. Electricity being the 'hot' topic of science at the beginning of the nineteenth century, Oersted experimented with electric current. His concept of electricity was that it consisted of a conflict of negative and positive aspects of magnetism. When the conflict occurred in a wire, heat was produced; when the wire was very thin the conflict produced light. In one of his seminars on 'Electricity, Galvanism and Magnetism', held in the spring of 1820, Oersted held a classroom demonstration. He connected the two ends of a Galvanic pile with wires, with one section made of thin platinum wire which would glow when current flowed through it. Another section of the wire was laid over a compass. When a current was passed through the wire the magnetic needle of the compass would move in a direction at an angle to the wire (or current). When the current was reversed, the needle would move in the opposite direction. Oersted describes his experiment:

> The preparations for the experiment were made but for some accident having hindered [me] from trying it before the lecture, [I] intended to defer it to another opportunity; yet during the lecture, the probability of its success appeared stronger, so that [I] made the first experiment in the presence of the audience. The magnetic needle, though included in a box, was disturbed; but as the effect was very feeble, and must, before its law was discovered, seem very irregular, the experiment made no strong impression on the audience.[3]

By the summer of 1820 Oersted had written a short paper entitled 'Experimenta circa effectum conflictus electrici in acum magneticum', sent to the major scientific journals in Europe[4] in which he clearly stated that a current-carrying wire was surrounded by a circular magnetic field. His announcement of this experiment to the French Academy of Science in 1820 caused a tremendous stir. From contemporary literature it appears that this statement had an effect similar to that encountered in our century with the announcement of nuclear fission.

André Marie Ampère, a French mathematician and physicist, immediately repeated Oersted's experiment. Ampère, born in 1775, was Professor of Physics at the École Centrale in Burgen–Bresse, Inspector-General of a university, Assistant Professor of Astronomy at the University of Paris and finally held a chair in experimental physics at the Collège de France. By 1820 he had achieved a certain reputation as a mathematician and chemist. When Oersted's discovery was communicated to the Academy of Science (4 September 1820), Ampère repeated his experiments and within a week reported the so-called 'right-hand rule'. If one puts the right hand, palm down, along the curved wire carrying an electric current, with the fingers pointing in the direction of the current (which at that time was wrongly believed to move from positive to negative poles), then the magnetic needle will be deflected in the direction of the thumb. Ampère also realized that a coil of wire in the shape of a spring (a 'solenoid') would behave like a magnet when an electric current was flowing through it. He summarized his results by stating: (a) Two electric currents attract each other when they are moving parallel to each other in the same direction, and repel each other when they are moving in opposite directions; they can therefore cause a wire loop to swing. (b) There is a similarity between the interaction of the two electric currents and Oersted's experiment.

Ampère was also interested in a related phenomenon, namely, whether a magnetic field would produce an electric current in a closed circuit. His first experiments failed because, as we now know, a fixed magnetic field does not induce a current. It was not until 1822 that Ampère, in collaboration with Auguste de la Rive, carried out the following experiment. They made a ring of a strip of copper and suspended it by a thin silk thread. Inside this ring they had a flat coil of wire, parallel to the ring, and then brought a magnet near to the wire. They noticed that whenever a current was set up in the coil, or when it was broken, the copper ring would move. Ampère attributed the movement of the ring at the breaking of the circuit to the effect of the torsion of the suspending thread, and not (as Farady demonstrated later) to a change in the magnetic field.

Ampère's own description of the experiment is rather confused according to modern concepts: he claims to have demonstrated:

1 The equality of the absolute value of the attraction and repulsion which is produced when a current flows first in one direction, then in the opposite direction in a fixed conductor which is left unchanged as to its orientation and at the same distance from the body on which it acts.
2 The equality of actions exerted on a mobile rectilinear conductor by two fixed conductors situated at equal distances from the first of which one is rectilinear and the other bent or contorted in any way whatsoever . . .
3 A closed circuit of any form whatsoever cannot move any portion of conducting wire forming an arc of a circle whose center lies on a fixed axis about which it may turn freely and which is perpendicular to the plane of the circle of which the arc is a part.[5]

Taton[6] finds that 'this astonishing blindness in so great a man was probably due to the fact that he was expecting to find a permanent induction current.' This expectation probably also led to the failure of other scientists, Ampère's contemporaries.

Devons, of Barnard College in New York, built in his laboratory an apparatus as described by Ampère. By performing an experiment according to his description, Devons obtained results indicating that Ampère

either had not done the experiment as he described it or else had failed to
see the dramatic effects of the current on the copper ring.[7]

When Faraday published his discovery of induction and electromagnetism, Ampère expressed his appreciation of this discovery in a letter to his
friend de la Rive in 1833:

> It is to Faraday that we owe the discovery of all the laws of currents
> produced by influence, it is he who was the first to recognize that these arise
> not only at the moment when one sets up or interrupts the current in a coil,
> but also when the influence is brought closer or is removed; in such a way
> that when one produces the inducing current or brings it closer the in-
> stantaneous [induced] current is in a contrary sense to that obtained when
> the inducing current is destroyed or else moved away.
>   ... M. Faraday's discovery was one of the most important of the century ...
> which has crowned the edifice others have built.[8]

'Unfortunately', Ampère had written to de La Rive in 1831, 'neither of
us thought of analysing this phenomenon.'[9]

A flash of insight and the induction motor

Practically all modern electric motors are designed to run on alternate
current, but in 1873 only direct-current motors and dynamos of the
Gramme and Fontain type were in use. The transmission of current via
commutators and brushes in these motors was a very messy affair.

The simplest type of electric motor consisted of a soft iron bar revolving
between two electromagnets. On the axle of such a bar there was a simple
switch, made of a ring of two metal parts separated by insulating material.
During the revolution, fixed carbon brushes, through contact with these
metal half-circles, transmit the electric current through the electromagnetic
coils from the source of the direct current. Since a coil or a loop carrying
current will move around an axis of one pole of a magnet, in the modern
induction motor the current is supplied to an electromagnet made of two
coils wound in the opposite direction around the two halves of the rotor.
When the current flows through these coils it creates a magnetic field
which, by interacting with the permanent magnet bracketing the rotor,
causes the rotor to rotate. The advantage of this sort of motor is that it
uses an alternating current. There is no contact between the electromagnet
and the rotor.

The first motor of this kind, capable of running on alternating current
(the induction motor), was invented by Nikola Tesla in 1888.[10]

Tesla was born in 1856 in Croatian Yugoslavia. He studied at the Polytechnic College in Graz and later at the University of Prague. Even as a student, he had put forward the idea of building a motor without a commutator, but his suggestion was greeted with ridicule. The idea of an induction motor came to Tesla suddenly, out of the blue, while he was walking in the park with his friend Antony Szigety and reciting some verses from *Faust*: '. . . an idea came like a lightning flash. In an instant I saw it all, and drew with a stick on the sand the diagrams which were illustrated in my fundamental patents in May 1888, and which Szigety understood perfectly.'[11]

In 1882 Tesla worked for the Edison Company in Paris. In 1884 he went from there to the United States, equipped only with 4 cents, a letter of recommendation to Thomas A. Edison and a book of poetry. He worked for a year under the guidance of Edison on direct-current dynamos (Edison did not like the idea of induction motors at all). In 1888 he obtained the patent for the invention and sold it to Westinghouse. His idea was then utilized first in building the electric works at Niagara Falls and harnessing their energy. It then spread to the whole industry.

Tesla was also the inventor of the so-called Tesla coil, the air-core transformer, high-frequency devices, and a machine which under a potential of 1,000,000 volts produced 130-feet-long sparks. It was Tesla who predicted wireless communication before Marconi. Later in life he became a mystic and died in poverty.

Tesla's story is not a story of chance discovery. It is included here because he described how the idea of an induction motor came to him in a flash of inspiration, which seems to have been the outcome of the subconscious occupation of his mind with the problem of making electric motors simpler and less messy.

X-rays – luminescence in the darkness

New experiments demand replication before they are accepted as facts.

At the end of the nineteenth century many physicists were experimenting with the Crookes tube. The evacuated chambers developed by Geissler in 1855 had been improved by Sir William Crookes in 1875 to the extent that he could use them to study radiation and luminescence. The apparatus, called a Crookes tube ever since, consisted of a negatively charged cathode embedded in an evacuated glass tube. Crookes found that radiation emitted from the cathode (cathode rays) travelled in straight lines, as was evidenced by sharp shadows produced at the end of the tube when variously shaped objects were put in its path. He also noted that he could deflect these rays by a magnet. He understood that the cathode rays were charged particles and he thought of them as a fourth state of matter. He encountered disbelief and hostility among fellow scientists and it took some two decades before J. J. Thomson proved that Crookes was right. Crookes almost discovered X-rays. He observed that some of the photographic plates enclosed in his containers became fogged during the running of the Crookes-tube experiments, but he allowed this opportunity to slip through his fingers. He also almost discovered isotopes in 1900, when he found that uranium salt in solution could be treated to produce a precipitate that was radioactive, while the solution itself lost this property. In 1903 Crookes invented the spinthariscope, on which, by scintillation, a zinc-sulfide screen would record the hits of charged atomic particles.

The next milestone on the way to the discovery of X-rays was the modification of the Crookes and Hittorf cathode-ray tube by Philip Lenard, Professor of Physics at the University of Heidelberg. At the end of this tube, opposite the cathode, at the suggestion of the German physicist, Heinrich, he inserted a very thin (0.00026 cm.) aluminium window. The stream of charged atomic particles was propelled by a potential of 6,000 volts to strike the aluminium window. In 1894 Lenard observed that some 8 cm. outside the window there appeared a glow on a paper coated with platinum cyanide.[12] Lenard interpreted this as indicating a flow of 'streaming electricity', but he did not follow up this observation. Two other scientists who missed the discovery of X-rays were A. W. Goodspeed and W. N. Jennings in Philadelphia. In 1890, while demonstrating a Crookes tube, they noticed a blackening of their photographic plates, but did not follow up this observation either. The ball now passed to Röntgen.

After a professorship in Giessen, Wilhelm Conrad Röntgen became Professor of Physics at the University of Würzburg in 1888. During the years 1887–91 Röntgen had a Ph.D. student, Ludwig Zehnder, who later became his friend. According to Ernest Krafft,[13] Zehnder participated in some of Röntgen's experiments with a Hittorf vacuum tube. To eliminate interference from the light emanating from the cathode, he covered the tube with black cloth. When he turned the current on, he noticed a flash on a remote zinc-sulfide screen, but the vacuum was immediately lost and the incident forgotten.

Lenard's experiment caught Röntgen's attention and in 1895, when Röntgen was fifty years old, he tried to replicate it. Lenard was kind enough to send the aluminium foil for the window. Röntgen had a modified

Crookes tube constructed, but it was not leak proof and he was not able to obtain the desired vacuum (0.01 mm. mercury pressure) in it. Röntgen thought that he could repeat the experiment with an all-glass tube by applying a higher voltage, hoping that the cathode rays propelled at the higher voltage would be able to penetrate the glass wall of the vessel. He used a Ruhmkorff induction coil which produced the necessary voltage, a current of 20 amperes and a spark 6 cm. long. In order to observe any glow outside the tube Röntgen did two things: first he wrapped the tube in black paper so that there would be no interference from light emitted inside the tube, and second, he prepared a piece of cardboard coated with barium platinocyanide, which was known to glow when struck by radiation. This he planned to place at the 'target' end of the tube.

On 8 November 1895 Röntgen set up the experiment in a completely darkened room. The Crookes tube was wrapped in thin, black cardboard. When he applied voltage to generate the cathode rays, he noticed a glow at the end of the table, which he soon identified as the piece of cardboard coated with the fluorescent crystals. The glow would appear when the tube was energized by the application of high voltage and would disappear when the Ruhmkorff coil was switched off. Röntgen understood that the fluorescence was somehow connected with the operation of the cathode-ray tube. By bringing the fluorescent cardboard disc nearer to the tube, he eventually established that the strongest glow occurred at the spot where the cathode rays struck the glass of the tube. Since the glow was also apparent at a considerable distance from the tube, Röntgen realized that he was encountering some new type of ray, different from the electrons Lenard had been studying. He was also amazed to observe that even when the cardboard disc was turned so that it faced the hypothetical rays with its uncoated side, the coated side still continued to glow. This could only mean that the new rays penetrated not only some 2 m. of air, but also the few millimetres of the cardboard. Röntgen then placed various objects in the path of the rays. The rays penetrated even two decks of cards, a 1,000-page book and thick blocks of wood, but were stopped by some metals: a 1.5-mm.-thick lead foil would stop the rays. 'If the hand is held between the discharge tube and the screen, the darker shadow of the bones is seen within the slightly dark shadow-image of the hand itself.'[14]

At this stage Röntgen was sure that the cathode-ray tube was producing invisible radiation, which could cause fluorescent crystals to glow. He called the new radiation X-rays.

During the next seven weeks, without telling anybody, Röntgen experimented with various tubes and materials. He found that water, rubber or

Figure 1 Model for X-rays
When a drum is struck by a flying ball, the ball flies back and is affected by
gravity. At the same time a sound wave is produced which spreads in all
directions and is not affected by gravity. The 'cathode rays' of Crookes and
Lenard are electrons (= balls) which are affected by magnetic fields. When
they strike a metal, X-rays (gamma rays), equivalent to sound waves in this
sketch, are produced. They are about one-thousandth of visible light waves.

aluminium let the X-rays through, whereas gold, platinum and lead did
not. Repeating Crookes's experiment with magnets, Röntgen also concluded that these rays were not charged atomic particles because they
could not be deflected or bent by a magnetic field.   As his next step
Röntgen decided to use photographic plates instead of fluorescent crystals,
because working with luminescence required darkness and adaptation
and was a considerable strain. Photographic plates would provide more
objective evidence for the existence of X-rays. So he placed photographic
plates wrapped in black paper in the path of the X-ray beam. When
developed, the plates showed a black spot where the beam struck. This
finding permitted Röntgen to continue his experiments in daylight. To
protect his photographic plates from undesired exposure, he kept the stock
of plates in another room. He now also arranged his laboratory so that it
contained a lead-shielded booth, with a window of wood or black paper
through which he could expose the plates to X-rays emitted by a tube

situated outside the booth. At the same time the booth served as a darkroom, where he could develop his plates on the spot. Unknown to Röntgen, this lead-shielded booth protected him from the X-ray radiation damage that others later suffered.

In one of his first experiments with photographic plates Röntgen put into the path of the X-rays a wooden box with metal balance weights which he held in his hand during the exposure. In the developed plate Röntgen saw not only the white weight-shaped outline.

> I possess [he wrote] photographs of the shadow of the profile of a door that separates the room in which, on one side, the discharge apparatus was placed, on the other the photographic plate; the shadow of the bones of the hand; the shadow of a covered wire wrapped on a wooden spool . . .[15]

For the next experiment Röntgen enlisted the help of his wife, Anna Bertha, asking her to place her hand in front of the plate while the tube was emitting X-rays. On the developed plate there was a clear image of the bones of his wife's palm with an even stronger image of the gold wedding ring on her middle finger.

Röntgen worked steadily and with intense enthusiasm for the next three weeks. At the end of December he reported accurate, concise results of these investigations to the Würzburg Physico-medical Society, and in the first week of 1896 published his findings in the *Proceedings of the Würzburg Physico-Medical Society*.[16] (At that time he was also Rector of the University.)

At the same time he sent printed copies of his report to his colleagues and other scientists in Berlin, Paris, Vienna and London. Within a few weeks Röntgen's experiments were known all over Europe and the United States. No scientific discovery has ever produced such a thrill or dramatic effect. Radiographs of hands appeared in medical and lay literature throughout the world. The *Vienna Press* stated:

> At the present time we wish only to call attention to the importance this discovery would have in the diagnosis of diseases and injuries of bones if the process can be developed so that not only the human hand can be photographed, but the details of the bone can be shown without the flesh. The surgeon then could determine the extent of complicated bone fracture *without the manual examination which is so painful to the patient*: he could find the position of a foreign body such as a bullet or a piece of shell much more easily than has been possible heretofore and *without any painful examination* with a probe.[17]

Being a modest, dedicated, honest and enthusiastic scientist, Röntgen would not permit the commercial exploitation of his discovery, even though he had been offered 'millions' by an American firm.[18] He believed that his discoveries belonged to humanity and should not be hampered by patents, licences and contracts. He did not patent his discovery, but he did receive many honours, including the Nobel Prize.

In 1894 Röntgen had said in his rectorial address:

> Nature often allows amazing miracles to be produced which originate from the most ordinary observations, and which are, however, recognized only by those who are equipped with sagacity and research acumen, and who consult experience, the teacher of everything.
>
> Only gradually has the conviction gained importance that the experiment is the most powerful and the most reliable lever enabling us to extract secrets from nature, and that the experiment must constitute the final judgement as to whether an hypothesis should be retained or be discarded. If the result does not agree with reality, it must necessarily be wrong, even though the speculations which led to it may have been highly ingenious . . .
>
> Yet the investigator . . . must consider the possibility . . . that his work will be superseded by others within a relatively short time, that his methods will be improved and that the new results will be more accurate and that the memory of his life and work will gradually disappear.[19]

In his speech Röntgen also quoted Werner von Siemens, the great technical engineer:

> The intellectual life gives us at times perhaps the purest and the highest joy of which the human being is capable. If some phenomenon which has been shrouded in obscurity suddenly emerges into the light of knowledge, if the key to a long-sought mechanical combination has been found, if the missing link of a chain of thought is fortuitously supplied, this then gives the discoverer the exultant feeling that comes with a victory of the mind, which alone can compensate him for all the struggle and effort, and which lifts him to a higher plane of existence.[20]

These words, uttered two years after Röntgen's discovery, were indeed prophetic. At the same time they summarize well what any serious scientist must have felt at any time.

On the second anniversary of the discovery, which coincided with the Röntgens' silver wedding anniversary, he wrote to Zehnder,[21] thanking him for his presents and adding: 'As far as the X-ray tubes are concerned, they continue to be as moody and unpredictable as women.'

For the first six years after the discovery until the receipt of the Nobel Prize in 1901, Röntgen was acknowledged as the undisputed discoverer of X-rays. Later, however, many scientists and laymen began to claim priority. Zehnder wrote to Röntgen: 'What do you say that even your great admirer, Lenard, has, at last, turned against you, and now claims to be the true discoverer of the X-ray?'[22]

Philip Lenard was only one among many scientists (including Crookes himself) who must also have produced X-rays in their experiments with the Crookes tube, but the hints that they had did not lead them to their discovery. Röntgen's contribution was, first, to realize that something unusual was happening when cardboard, coated with fluorescent crystals, began to glow in the darkness of the laboratory, and secondly to follow this observation carefully and systematically. Röntgen was the first with the sagacity and the ability to establish the source of this new radiation. During the first few years after his discovery he was to become world-famous, but had to face a number of detractors who tried to minimize the importance of his discovery. He once said: 'It is almost as if I had to apologize for having discovered X-rays.'[23]

Röntgen himself did not speculate on the potential value of X-rays (except perhaps for simple surgical procedures), but within a week of the discovery, Hugo Münsterberg was to write: 'The value of such a method for medical diagnosis is clear . . . It will be a matter for the future to learn whether the rays have a psychophysiological effect' *(Science* 3. 161, 1896). Two months later, in the same volume of *Science* (3. 334), Henry Cattell predicted that in addition to surgical uses, X-rays might be used to detect flaws in metals and to kill bacteria.

How rapidly the news of Röntgen's discovery spread is well recorded in the report given by Dr James F. Brailsford in a lecture at the University of Birmingham on 5 December 1945. The day after the New Year announcement of the discovery of X-rays, Brailsford and his colleague, John Hall Edwards, decided to repeat Röntgen's experiment. Edwards was an accomplished photographer, who by 1896 had already won twenty-four medals for photography. Brailsford and Edwards managed to 'scrounge' an induction coil and a Crookes tube and set up the apparatus. They put a purse containing coins and keys on to a well-wrapped photographic plate, and set the machinery going for a long period. The plate, when developed, showed the coins and the keys. On 12 February 1896 they obtained an X-ray picture of Dr Ratcliffe's hand with a piece of needle stuck in it and reported this in the *Mosley Society Journal* (3/1, 1896). Later they helped Dr J. H. Clayton of Queen's Hospital in Birmingham to remove a needle that stuck into a woman's hand, by providing him with an X-ray photograph of the injured hand. Hall Edwards became a radiographer at the General Hospital and later an operator in a mobile unit in South Africa during the Boer War. He paid a heavy price for his work with X-rays, developing cancer in his fingers, which had to be amputated.

Within the year 1896 extraordinary advances in the use of X-rays were made: practically all the specialized techniques pertaining to X-rays known today were developed at that time. It is an intriguing fact that in July 1896 an X-ray photograph was used in a court in Nancy in support of a claim by a patient who had had his arm set for a fracture, whereas the X-ray showed that there was no fracture, but just a dislocation. The court found the operating doctor guilty.

It did not occur to scientists at the time that X-ray radiation, and the radioactive materials discovered later, had injurious effects on living tissue. X-rays turned out to be not only a blessing, but also a curse. Radiation of the scalp, which was found to cure ringworm, also caused hair loss and cancer of the thyroid gland. Many doctors who operated the first X-ray machines without any protection suffered burns, lost fingers and hands, and developed cancers and died. Later on, X-rays and radio-active radiations were understood to be injurious. This fact was accidentally discovered by Becquerel, who had carried a sealed glass tube in his pocket for ten days. It contained a solution of radioactive barium chloride. He noted a red mark shaped like the tube on his skin under the pocket. This then developed into a wound which took several months to heal. Though there were other similar isolated warnings of the dangers of exposure to X-rays and radioactive materials, it took another twenty years before the health hazards of these radiations were fully understood.

A cloudy day helps in the discovery of radioactivity

Was the discovery of radioactivity really due to Henri Becquerel, and should the credit for the discovery be given only to him?

Becquerel was a son of a scientist, Alexander Becquerel, who studied luminescence and photochemistry. Following in the steps of his father, Henri was interested in the luminescence that appeared at the end of a cathode-ray tube. In 1896 he already knew of Röntgen's discovery of X-rays and thought that the luminescence and X-rays were somehow connected. In his Nobel Prize lecture in 1903 he said:

At the beginning of 1896, on the very day that news reached Paris of Röntgen's experiments and of the extraordinary properties of the rays emitted by the phosphorescent walls of the Crookes tubes, I thought of carrying out research to see whether all phosphorescent material emitted similar rays. The results of the experiment did not justify this idea, but in this research I encountered an unexpected phenomenon.[24]

In his laboratory Becquerel had some uranium salts which would emit light in the darkness after being exposed to sunlight. In one of his experiments, he exposed to sunlight a photographic plate wrapped in thick black paper. The plate remained white (unexposed) when chemically developed. But when he put a sheet of uranium salt (a double salt of sulphate and potassium) on to a similar plate, wrapped in black paper and protected by a sheet of aluminium, and then exposed it to sunlight for several hours, he found that the image of the salt layer on the wrapping paper appeared on the plate.[25]

From this experiment he concluded that the sun had caused the uranium salts to emit some sort of radiation which penetrated the paper and blackened the emulsion on the plate. On 26 February 1896 Becquerel had some wrapped plates, with uranium salt on them, waiting to be exposed to sunlight, but the sun did not shine for several days. On 1 March he nevertheless developed the plates, to find that the image of the salt appeared in the photographic emulsion. He now understood that the plates were blackened by something emitted by the uranium salt without any need for sunlight.

. . . ces radiations, dont les effets ont une grande analogie avec les effets produits par les radiations étudiées par MM. Lenard et Röntgen, seraient des radiations invisibles émises par phosphorescence, et dont la durée de persistance serait infiniment plus grande que la durée de persistance des radiations luminescentes émises par ces corps.[26]

The next step was to perform the whole experiment in complete darkness. Again the plates, exposed to uranium salts for five days, were blackened in the presence of uranium. Becquerel concluded that uranium salts emitted some radiation which penetrated the black paper and affected the photographic plate. In another experiment he caused the rays from the uranium salt to pass through a 2mm.-thick aluminium sheet as well as cause a discharge of a gold-leaf electroscope. The radiation therefore consisted of charged particles, later identified as alpha particles. During the year after this discovery, Becquerel reported a series of experiments to the French

Academy of Science. These experiments convinced him of the existence of a new type of radiation, which he called *rayons uraniques*. He determined that the source of the radiation was the element uranium, that the intensity of radiation from the same sample did not diminish with time, that various metals absorbed this radiation and that it was different from X-rays because it could be reflected and refracted.

The question that might be posed today is why Becquerel decided to develop the plates, although he knew that they were not exposed to sunlight. The 'accident' here was the result of his involvement in radiation effects.

Becquerel's discovery was not accepted as bona fide by all contemporary physicists. In a speech in 1948 Sir Henry Dale remembers that when John William Strutt (later Lord Rayleigh) reported Becquerel's discovery to the Undergraduate Science Club in Cambridge,

> One of us who was later to become world famous in theoretical physics and astronomy said: 'Why, Strutt if this story of Becquerel's were true it would violate the law of conservation of energy'. At that time such a statement was an expression of quite reasonable orthodoxy. Strutt replied: 'Well, all I can say is 'so much the worse for the law of conservation of energy' because I am quite sure that Becquerel is a trustworthy observer.'[27]

To return to the question we put at the beginning of this story, whether Becquerel was the actual discoverer: the answer is that he was preceded, by thirty years, by Niepce de St Victor, who was one of the pioneers of photography.[28] In 1847 St Victor produced the first photographic emulsion from silver iodide grains held together by a mixture of albumen and starch. In 1867 he noticed some 'fogging' plates separated by several layers of paper from luminescent uranium salts. He did not follow up this observation, though he thought that luminescence was somehow involved, but he missed an important discovery because he did not check his ideas with an experiment.

The St Victor–Becquerel sequence reminds us of the Galvani–Volta one, but whereas Galvani was honoured for a discovery, though he did not understand it, Niepce de St Victor remains known only as the father of photography.

NOTES TO CHAPTER 1

1 Galvani, A. 1792: On the effect of electricity on the muscles. In J. F. Fulton,

Selected Readings in the History of Physiology. Springfield, Ill.: C. C. Thomas, 1930: 593.

2 Meyer, K. (ed.) 1920: *The Scientific Life and Works of H. C. Oersted.* Copenhagen: A. F. Hoechst & Son: 69

3 Gillespie, C. C. (ed.) 1970: *Dictionary of Scientific Biography*, vol. 10. New York: Scribner & Sons: 185

4 Ibid.

5 Ibid.: 1. 39.

6 Taton, R. (ed.) 1961: *Science in the Nineteenth Century.* London: Thames & Hudson.

7 Devons, S. [n.d.]: *Notes on the Development of a History of Physics, laboratory and selected experiments.* History of Physics Lab., New York: Barnard College: 82.

8 Taton (ed.), *Science in the Nineteenth Century*: 195.

9 Ibid.: 190.

10 Hunt, I. and Draper, W. W. 1977: *Lightning in His Hand. The Life Story of Nikola Tesla.* New York: W. S. Heinemann.

11 Gillespie, *Dictionary of Scientific Biography*, 13. 266.

12 Lenard, P. 1894: Über Kathodenstrahlen in Gasen von atmosphärischen Druck und im äussersten Vacuum. *Wien Annalen*, 51: 225.

13 Krafft, E. 1973: W. C. Röntgen. His friendship with Ludwig Zehnder. *New York State Journal of Medicine*, 73: 1002.

14 Röntgen, W. C. 1895: Eine neue Art von Strahlen. *Sitzungsberichte der physikalischen medizinischer Gesellschaft.* Würzburg: 132.

15 Ibid.: 134.

16 Ibid.

17 Brailsford, J. F. 1946: Röntgen's discovery of X-rays. Their application to modern surgery. *British Journal of Radiology*, 19: 455.

18 Ibid.: 456.

19 Ibid.: 454.

20 Ibid.: 454.

21 Kraft, *Röntgen*: 1005.

22 Ibid.: 1007.

23 Brailsford, Röntgen's Discovery of X-rays: 460.

24 Becquerel, A. H.: On radioactivity, a new property of matter. *Nobel Lectures. Physics 1901–1921*: 52.

25 Becquerel, H. 1896: Sur les radiations invisibles émises par les corps phosphorescents. *Comptes rendus de l'Académie des Sciences*, 122: 503.

26 Ibid.: 501.

27 Dale, H. 1948: Accident and opportunism in medical research. *British Medical Journal*, 2: 451.

28 Sutton, C. 1986: Serendipity or sound science. *New Scientist*, 27 Feb.: 30–1.

2

From Atomic Nuclei to the Universe

Masers, lasers and the 'big bang' theory

The problem of attributing a discovery to a specific person or a group of scientists is not simple. Most of us assume that recognition for a discovery, whether in the form of the Nobel Prize or in any other form, identifies the discoverer. This is not so in reality. In some rare cases the Nobel Prize is awarded to people who have originated a new and fruitful idea, but in most cases it is given to those who conducted the experiments that led to the discovery. The recognition of the contribution of Watson and Crick in Cambridge to unravelling the structure and function of DNA was for their theoretical model, which did not prove to be correct and fruitful until later.

In this chapter I shall describe two discoveries in physics where the scientists who set the theoretical predictive background for a discovery were not honoured by a Nobel Prize, and the prize went to experimenters who proved the theory to be correct (in one case without even knowing that they had proved it).

In 1978 the Nobel Prize in physics was given to Arno A. Penzias and Robert W. Wilson for their radiotelescopic observation of the residual background radiation thought to have remained after the 'big bang' start of the universe. The idea that the universe started as a 'cosmic egg' which exploded in a 'big bang' to produce all the galaxies and stars that are continuously flying apart had already been conceived in 1927 by Abbé Georges Lemaître, a Belgian astronomer. This idea was later picked up by the Russian–American physicist, George Gamow. From the known data on the so-called redshift, indicating the spreading of the universe, the relative abundance of elements and their isotopes and the decay periods of the latter (log relative abundance is a linear function of nuclear binding energy and of atomic weight), Gamow calculated the age of the universe and the fact that primordial matter was made of neutron gas and neutron fluid.[1] He postulated that this original huge explosion of primordial matter, which occurred some 15 billion years ago and which generated a temperature of some 10 billion degrees, would lead to the formation, from elementary particles, of lighter chemical elements (later coalescing into heavier elements), as well as to a tremendous amount of radiation of all wave lengths. As the universe expanded, the temperature of the radiation should have gone down. In 1948 R. A. Alpher and R. C. Herman predicted[2] that if the 'big bang' origin of the universe was correct, then from the known rate of expansion and the expected drop of temperature of radiation, the temperature should now have fallen to about 5° Kelvin (i.e. above absolute zero).

Almost fifteen years after the publication of this theoretical prediction a dramatic change occurred – in the years 1963–4. At the beginning of the 1960s scientists and engineers at the Bell Laboratories in Holmdel, New Jersey, constructed a radiotelescope from a 20-foot horn reflector antenna coupled to a radiometer driven by a ruby travelling wave (7 cm.) maser cooled to 4° K. This instrument was constructed for communication, by microwaves, with the ECHO satellites and later with the TELSTAR satellites. But when the Europeans went ahead in communications with TELSTAR, the Bell project was dropped, and the exquisite radiotelescope became free for use in the studies of Arno A. Penzias.

Penzias, a member of a German Jewish family, escaped the Nazi regime and arrived in the United States in 1940. He graduated from Columbia and, under the guidance of Professor Charles Hard Townes, obtained his Ph.D. for constructing a maser amplifier for use in radio astronomy. When he joined the Bell Laboratories he planned to study, by radiotelescope, the noise coming from the Milky Way. In 1963 Penzias was joined by a Caltech physicist, Robert W. Wilson. 'This stroke of good fortune came at the right moment', as Penzias wrote in his Nobel Prize lecture.

Penzias and Wilson first measured extraterrestrial radiation at 31 cm. and were planning to convert the antenna to a 21 cm. wavelength (characteristic of the radiation of atomic hydrogen). In order to calibrate the telescope, they first decided to measure the radiation at the wavelength of 7 cm. because at this wavelength the noise from space should have eliminated all local sources of radio noise. They would thus have a baseline against which to measure the radio noise from intergallactic space. Their calculation showed that the background radiation should have been equivalent to about 2.3° K from the earth's atmosphere and about 1° K from the noise attributable to the antenna itself.

In May 1964 they pointed the antenna to the zenith and carried out measurements. The temperature of the recorded 7-cm. radiation was 7.5° K, that is, about 4.2° K higher than expected. This result led them to consider all sorts of possibilities to account for the discrepancy. In the course of examining these possibilities they turned a pair of nesting pigeons out of the horn of the antenna! All this was no use. The 7.5° K was recorded from all directions, independent of the time of day and of the year. It was clear that it was not coming from the sun or the galaxy. Wilson relates in his Nobel Prize lecture:[3]

> The sequence of events which led to the unravelling of our mystery began one day when Arno was talking to Bernard Burke of MIT about other matters and mentioned our unexplained noise. Bernie recalled hearing about theoretical work of P. J. E. Peebles in R. H. Dicke's group in Princeton on radiation in the Universe. Arno called Dicke who sent a copy of Peebles' preprint. The Princeton group was investigating the implications of an oscillating universe with an extremely hot condensed phase. This hot bounce was necessary to destroy the heavy elements from the previous cycle so each cycle could start fresh. Although this was not a new idea, Dicke had the important idea that if the radiation from this hot phase were large enough, it would be observable. In the preprint, Peebles, following Dicke's suggestion calculated that the universe should be filled with a relic blackbody radiation at a minimum temperature of 10° K . . .
> Shortly after sending the preprint, Dicke and his co-workers visited us in order to discuss our measurements and see our equipment. They were quickly convinced of the accuracy of our measurements. We agreed to a side-by-side publication of two letters in the *Astrophysical Journal* – a letter on the theory from Princeton[4] and one on our measurement of excess antenna temperature from Bell Laboratories.[5] Arno and I were careful to exclude any discussion of the cosmological theory of the origin of the background radiation from our letter because we had not been involved in that work. We thought, furthermore, that our measurement was independent of the theory and might outlive it. We were pleased that the mysterious noise appearing in our antenna had an explanation of any kind, especially one with such significant cosmological implications.[6]

In 1978 Penzias and Wilson obtained the Nobel Prize in Physics 'for the discovery of microwave cosmic radiation' or, as the representative of the Nobel Committee poetically said, 'cold light from the birth of the Universe'.[7]

The discovery of chemical lasers is also interesting. When an external energy, such as radiation, is applied to start a chemical reaction (defined as the making or breaking of a chemical bond), free energy may be produced. This free energy can be utilized for the 'inversion' of a critical population (i.e. bringing more molecules to an excited state than to a lower one) and this in turn results in laser action.

What is the laser?

As early as 1951, Charles Hard Townes at the Bell Laboratories had calculated that molecules had various fashions of vibration, some of which would be equivalent to radiation in the microwave region. So, for instance, the 'vibration' frequency of ammonia is 24 billion per second, which is equivalent to a microwave with a wavelength of 1.25 cm. So when a cloud of ammonia molecules is irradiated with waves at 1.25 cm., some molecules struck by this radiation would emit an equal radiation wave, and this in turn by striking yet another molecule, would cause it to give up its energy as radiation. This starts a cascade reaction resulting in an avalanche of microwaves, and in the end all the energy originally used to excite the ammonia molecules would be converted into radiation at 1.25 cm. In 1953 on the basis of his prediction, Townes and his students constructed a gadget he called MASER (Microwave Amplification of Stimulated Emission of Radiation). Later, together with A. L. Schawlow, Townes showed that masers could also be made to operate in optical and infra-red regions. They described a maser with potassium vapour:

> . . . using a resonant cavity of centimeter dimensions, having many resonant modes, maser oscillation at these wavelengths can be achieved by pumping with reasonable amounts of incoherent light . . . When the walls of the cavity are made highly reflecting and it has a suitable small angular aperture, then extremely monochromatic and coherent light is produced[8]

In 1960 T. H. Maiman constructed another device in which a pink ruby rod would produce a burst of coherent (i.e. very narrow) beam of red light, with light waves all of the same wavelength and phase. In pink ruby, ionized chromium ions excited by intense light at 5,500 Å lose energy through a non-radiative transitional state, and decay by emitting red light. This was called LASER (Light Amplification of Stimulated Emission or Radiation). Maiman demonstrated the first laser on 16 May 1960 at the Hughes Research laboratories in Malibu, California.[9] The first lasers were physical in the sense that the stimulating energy was supplied to them by radiation.

Maiman was not really the first to develop a laser. The person who did it was Gordon Gould, a graduate student in physics at Columbia University.

In 1957, being familiar with optics, he developed the idea of a gas-discharge laser and wrote it down in his notebook, officially recording it in November 1957. In this notebook Gould actually coined the word LASER. He then left Columbia to work with a commercial company.[10] This company used Gould's idea to obtain a contract with the Department of Defense and by doing so put a seal of secrecy on the project. Gould did not apply for a patent for his laser until 1959. By that time, however, Townes and Schawlow had patents for 'optical masers' and in 1964 Townes won the Nobel Prize together with the Soviet scientists, Alexander Prokhorov and Nicolai Basov.

In 1970 Gould decided to start a fight for his patent (which was refused at first). He was assisted in this by the Refac Technology Development Corporation. By 1979 most of his patents (the original one being divided into parts) were granted by the US Patent and Trademark Office. Gould's patents were then acquired by the Patlex Corporation in California and now, as a result of a court decision in Florida in November 1987, laser producers have to pay a 5-per-cent royalty for the use of the patent.[11] Gould's reaction to this development was: 'That's the kind of irony I like.'[12]

As for chemical lasers, the person whose mind was the hatching ground for this idea was Kurt E. Shuler, Professor of Theoretical Chemistry at La Jolla, California. In the period 1950–65 Shuler had studied the rotational, vibrational and electronic excitation of product molecules resulting from the chemical reaction involving combustion. He published some fifty papers on these subjects.

In 1965 Shuler, together with K. A. Brueckner and W. R. Bennett, organized a symposium on chemical lasers, which at that time existed as a concept only. In this symposium Shuler presented a paper[13] co-authored with his junior colleagues T. Carrington and J. C. Light, in which they summed up what was then known about the chemical reactions that might lead to excited products. Shuler listed six reactions that involved dissociative excitation transfer, twelve exchange reactions leading to vibrational excitation and fifteen reactions producing electronically excited products. Many of these reactions have since been shown to yield operational chemical lasers. At the same symposium J. C. Polanyi, in his paper on vibrational-rotational population inversion, predicted the possibility of a chemical laser, and laid the theoretical background for it.[14]

Following this conference, George Pimentel at Berkeley and a graduate student actually found and applied the precise conditions predicted by John Polanyi, and produced chemical lasers.

Today lasers are used on a grand scale for a variety of purposes: cutting metals, surveying, communication in space and through optical fibres, radar, the detection of pollutants in the atmosphere, compact disc players, high speed printers, bar-code readers, and in many medical applications in therapy and surgery, not to speak of classified military usages.

The names of Gould and Shuler are rarely mentioned as being the first discoverers, but while Gould will enjoy quite a large income from the royalties that are being awarded to him only now, Shuler continues with his modest academic life.

Mössbauer's recoilless nuclear resonance

One of the very important chance discoveries of modern physics has a very provocative name: recoilless nuclear resonance absorption of gamma radiation. This discovery was made by Rudolf Mössbauer, a doctoral student of Professor Heinz Maier Leibniz at the Max Planck Institute in Heidelberg in the years 1955–8. In 1961 Mössbauer shared the Nobel Prize in physics with Robert Hofstadter. The importance of Mössbauer's discovery lay in its becoming a basis for investigations in solid state and chemical physics. The events associated with Mössbauer's early experiments that led to the great discovery are like a scientific fairy tale.

In his thesis, Mössbauer investigated the absorption of gamma rays into matter, or in technical terms 'nuclear resonance scattering of gamma rays emitted by an isotope of Iridium ^{191}Ir'.

Since Mössbauer's experimental results involved quantum physics, it may be necessary to explain the type and the rationale of his experiments by simpler concepts of classical mechanics.

More than a hundred years ago Stokes observed that some solids, liquids and gases, when irradiated by light, would absorb this radiation and re-emit it as resonant fluorescence: that is, the light emitted was of the same wavelength as that which elicited it (e.g. the yellow fluorescence of sodium vapour). Resonance is generally known as an acoustic phenomenon: sound waves from a vibrating piano string induce resonant vibrations in another string tuned to the same note, but not in one tuned to a neighbouring one. The physical explanation of resonant fluorescence is that the incidental light causes the absorbing atoms to move from a ground state (G) to an excited state (E). When the absorbing atoms return from E to G they emit fluorescent light.

In 1929 Richard Kuhn suggested that in nuclear physics the emission of gamma rays by radioactive atoms would also be associated with resonant absorption by similar atomic nuclei, analogously with optical resonance, the difference between optical and nuclear radiation being only in the much shorter wavelength of the gamma rays. He postulated that gamma rays emitted by an oscillating nucleus (the source), when absorbed by another nucleus (the absorber) of the same kind, would set up a similar vibration in it, a resonant vibration. But if the inherent natural vibrations of the source and the absorber nuclei differ, there will be no resonance. The vibration frequency is proportional to the energy of the emitted gamma rays.

In the case of the iridium isotope used by Mössbauer the energy of the emission of gamma rays is equivalent to 129,000 electron volts and a half-life of 10^{-9} seconds.

When the nuclei of atoms emit gamma rays, they recoil, like a gun that has fired a bullet, the size of the recoil depending on the ratio of the masses of the emitted gamma rays and that of the nucleus. The energy of the gamma ray and its wavelength depend on the size of the recoil. Because of this recoil the gamma rays emerge with less than the maximum available energy. So such a photon is not absorbed by the target nucleus at the original natural frequency of the emitter. The amount of energy carried away by the photon equals the difference of energy between the excited and the ground states of the emitting nucleus. The energy of the emitted quantum of radiation is thus too small for the inverse process of resonant absorption. So the recoil causes a lengthening in the wavelength of the emitted rays (the Doppler effect).

In 1951 P. B. Moon and others devised an ingenious experiment. To compensate for the loss of energy due to recoil (and change of wavelength) he moved the radioactive source towards the absorber at a speed calculated to offset the effect of the recoil (to counteract the Doppler effect), thus proving that recoil existed and could be offset by quite simple means. Similar experiments with rotating discs and centrifuges were performed by others.

This was the state of affairs when Mössbauer started his experiments in Heidelberg. He himself constructed all the necessary apparatus for this type of gamma-ray experiment. His colleagues saw him pacing the corridor by night. When questioned, he explained that it was easier to carry out the experiments at night, and that he preferred to be in the corridor in order to avoid radioactive radiation in his laboratory.

Mössbauer calculated that if there was a shift between the emission wavelength, a temperature change should have affected it, by either improving or worsening the shift. He decided to cool the source and the absorber in liquid air.

In his Nobel Prize lecture he said:

> The simultaneous cooling of the source and of the absorber with liquid air led to inexplicable results for which I first blamed the effect associated in some way with the cooling of the absorber. In order to eliminate these unwanted side effects, I finally left the absorber at room temperature and cooled only the source. In very tedious experiments . . . a small decrease in the absorption in respect to the value at room temperature was in fact obtained – a result consistent with my expectations.[15]

In a second series of experiments, in an attempt to explain the side effects due to simultaneous cooling of both the source and the absorber, 'a strong increase in the absorption clearly manifested itself when the absorber was cooled. *This result was in complete contradiction to the theoretical expectations*' (my italics).[16] Mössbauer was surprised by his own results; other physicists simply did not believe them. Mössbauer's theoretical expectation rested on the assumption that the momentum of the recoil would be transmitted only to the absorbing atoms and their immediate neighbours, and not to the whole crystal.

Thus Mössbauer understood that the atomic nuclei were bound in the crystal and that the recoil was taken up by the mass of the crystal, just as a cannon anchored to a concrete base offsets its recoil. The cooling of the crystal would reduce its recoil energy. A useful description of a recoil model may be provided by the personification of gamma radiation as a human being jumping off a small boat (figure 2A). If he jumps on to solid ground or a pier, he loses some of his energy by making the boat he jumps off recoil. His total energy is thus the sum of that which carries him on to the pier, and that which made the boat recoil. If Mr Gamma jumps from one boat into another, neither being anchored, then there will be a double loss of recoil energy, which is the sum of the energy that makes one boat move backwards and the other forwards (figure 2B). But if the boats are made immobile by being frozen in solid ice in a lake, then Gamma's jump will conserve all its energy (figure 2C).[17]

Another simple explanation has been provided by Harry J. Lipkin (of the Weizmann Institute):

> A downhill skier uses the Mössbauer effect without realizing it. Newton says that the force of gravity on the skier is directed downwards. But the skier moves forward as well as downward. Newton says that if a skier moves

Figure 2   A recoil model for gamma radiation
The boat represents an atom, the person jumping a gamma ray, and the
water (or ice) the crystal.

forward when there is no external force in the forward direction, something else must recoil backwards in order to conserve momentum. The motion of the object recoiling backwards has kinetic energy, and this energy must be supplied from somewhere. Mössbauer pointed out that you can forget about recoil if the recoiling object is very heavy, much heavier than the object going forward. Then the skier goes forward, the earth goes backwards. But the earth is so heavy that it easily takes up the skier's momentum with an imperceptibly tiny recoil. This 'recoil free' motion is the Mössbauer effect.[18]

According to the quantum theory, the absorption or emission of a quantum by a nucleus in a crystal should be taken up in two forms: translational and internal energy. The increase in translational energy is negligible because of the enormous mass of the crystal as compared to the mass of the nucleus. The increase in internal energy, however, can be absorbed only in discrete amounts (quanta) by their harmonic oscillations, meaning that there could not be any change at all in their state either. Indeed, Mössbauer's calculations indicated that in his experiment nuclear transitions could occur with the high probability of no change in the crystal lattice state or of energy loss due to recoil. Thus the term 'recoilless' was born, meaning that the entire excitation energy was carried away by the emitted quantum, and the same was true for absorption.

The final proof that Mössbauer had correctly interpreted this result was his reversal of Moon's experiment. Having achieved resonant conditions by 'setting' the radioactive nuclei in a crystal and holding them at a very low temperature, he argued that, if he moved the absorber in relation to the source, the resonance would now disappear (through the Doppler effect). Mössbauer mounted the source on to a turntable moving at its edge at a few centimetres per second, with the absorber held stationary, and showed that while a maximum resonance effect was observed when both were stationary, the movement of the source destroyed the resonance according to predicted calculations. The accuracy of this experiment was such that absorption effects of the order of 1 per cent were observed.[19]

Mössbauer's experiment (called the Mössbauer effect) also made it possible to perform an experiment measuring the effect of gravity on light in the laboratory rather than by astronomical observations. According to Einstein's theory, the wavelength of electromagnetic radiation (visible light or gamma rays) should increase under the influence of the gravitational field. Therefore if a beam of gamma rays were to be shot downwards from a tall building to its basement, its wavelength should increase by an incredibly small amount. This increment could be detected by Mössbauer's experiment with exquisite accuracy and sensitivity. A gamma ray emitted by a crystal-bound isotope (held in liquid air or helium), if gravitationally modified, should produce a measurable drop in the absorption by a similar crystal exposed to the ray. An experiment of this type was actually performed in 1960 in England and in the United States, verifying Einstein's predictions[20].

Mössbauer made the discovery because he did not discard his unexpected results. 'His greatness can be shown by the fact that he did not ignore the small peculiar singularity in his gamma-ray counting system, instead he made an effort to understand this effect fully.'[21]

New planets of Herschel, Adams and Leverrier

Friedrich William Herschel, from Hanover in Germany, emigrated to England in 1757, where he became William Herschel and in 1766 an accomplished organist and music teacher in Bath. In time he was to become the most famous astronomer of the century. In 1772 he brought to England his sister Caroline, who, like him, was an amateur astronomer and a devoted lens-grinder. Together as a team the brother and sister made the best lenses then available and constructed the best telescopes. By 1776 he had built a telescope of 20-foot focal length, with a 12-inch mirror. Herschel started to publish his astronomical observations in 1774. They included descriptions of moon mountains, sun spots, variable stars, etc.[22]

On 13 March 1781, while surveying the entire visible sky, Herschel came upon a celestial object that looked more like a disc than a point of light. He assumed therefore that he had discovered a comet and reported it as such. Upon continued observation of this 'comet' he noted that it had sharp outlines and did not look fuzzy, as a comet should. He calculated the trajectory of this new object as being in an orbit outside the planet Saturn and realized that he had discovered a new planet, the first to be discovered in historical time outside the seven known from antiquity. Herschel named the new planet *Georgium sidus* (George's Star). Other astronomers tried to name the new planet after Herschel, but it finally received the name of Uranus. In 1787 Herschel discovered that Uranus had two satellites (Titania and Oberon) and erroneously thought that the planet had four additional satellites. The discovery of Uranus was widely acclaimed, and in 1781 Herschel was elected to the Royal Society and nominated as King George's private astronomer.

In stellar astronomy Herschel's first major discovery was of a planetary nebula, 'a curious nebula, or what else to call it I do not know . . .' He continued the study of nebulae and eventually catalogued 1,500. His other discoveries included double stars (some 850!). These were the first objects outside the solar system shown to circle each other and to behave in accordance with Newton's laws of gravity. But Herschel was not infallible. He also held the view that the sun was a cold star with light and heat stemming from its fiery atmosphere. For him sun spots were holes through which the cold body of the sun could be observed. On the other hand, his theory that stars are formed by the condensation of matter in nebulae was later fruitfully exploited.

Herschel made another unexpected, but important, discovery, namely that of infra-red radiation from the sun. He tested the colour spectrum of sunlight with a thermometer and noticed that the largest increase in temperature occurred beyond the visible red part of the spectrum. He understood that there was a new type of radiation in this invisible part of the spectrum. On balance, Herschel occasionally made some mistakes, mostly conceptual, but his many astronomical discoveries certainly make him an outstanding astronomer.

Herschel's Uranus presented the astronomers with a problem. Its motion did not follow the gravitational predictions of Newton's theory exactly. Uranus was 1.5 minutes of arc away from its calculated expected position.

John Couch Adams, the son of a poor farmer, studied mathematics at Cambridge. In 1843, as an undergraduate, he calculated the motion of Uranus and came to the conclusion that the discrepancy between the observed and the calculated position of this planet must be due to another, more distant planet (which, as it turns out, was observed by Cambridge astronomers, but not recognized as such). He presented his data to his superior, George Bidell Airy, the Astronomer Royal, but he ignored Adams's information.

On the other side of the English Channel, Urbain Jean Joseph Leverrier was, by the age of thirty-four, an astronomer at the École Polytechnique in Paris. He was studying another planet, Mercury, and was concerned with the anomalies observed in its motion (which, *nota bene*, were not resolved until 1915 with the advent of the general theory of relativity). The perihelion of Mercury (the point in its orbit at which it most closely approaches the sun) was 40 seconds of the arc in advance of the position predicted by Newton's theory of gravitation. Leverrier therefore postulated the existence of another planet, which he named Vulcan, that should be some 19 million miles away from the sun. (No such planet exists.) This prediction of Leverrier's, though wrong, was highly esteemed and he was made a member of the Paris Academy of Science in 1846.[23]

Dominique Arago (whom we have already encountered in his involvement with the electromagnetic experiments), who had advised Leverrier to work on Mercury, also suggested that he should turn his attention to the planet discovered by Herschel, Uranus. Leverrier thus proceeded to calculate the size and position of a hypothetical planet that would cause the deviation observed in the orbit of Uranus. He had no idea that such calculations had already been made by Adams. Armed with his calculations, Leverrier approached Johnann W. Galle, the German astronomer at the Berlin Observatory, and suggested that he should look for the predicted planet. Galle, who had a detailed map of the part of the sky where the new planet should have been located, actually found it on 23 September 1846. The new planet was named Neptune and the person credited with its discovery is Leverrier. Adams, who did the same calculations and actually predicted the existence of Neptune, had lost his chance of the discovery because of the small-mindedness of his superior, the Astronomer Royal. Sir John Herschel (William Herschel's son), then President of the Royal Astronomical Society, knowing the true story, intervened on behalf of Adams, and so he eventually received his share of the credit.

How can a mistaken hypothesis lead to a discovery? At the beginning of the century, when the existence of cosmic rays had been established, the famous American physicist Robert Millikan claimed that the cosmic rays were photons, and this in the face of overwhelming evidence to the contrary and in spite of the weighty scientific opinions of Jacob Clay, Walther Bothe, Thomas A. Johnson and Arthur H. Compton. In 1929, when asked by reporters whether cosmic rays were in fact charged particles, Millikan answered: 'You might as well sensibly compare an elephant and a radish.'[24] Following up his mistaken hypothesis, Millikan continued to accumulate data measuring the intensity of cosmic rays everywhere on earth and in the atmosphere. His data, though assembled on the basis of an incorrect hypothesis, led to the discovery of the positron by Karl David Anderson in 1932. In the course of his studies on cosmic rays with the aid of a specially devised cloud chamber, Anderson studied photographs of tracks in this sort of chamber. He saw tracks that looked exactly like those of an electron, but they curved the wrong way, and were compatible with the assumption that the track had been made by an electron carrying a positive charge. Anderson's discovery preceded a similar one made later by Patrick M. S. Blackett and Joliot Curie.

NOTES TO CHAPTER 2

1 Gamow, G. 1948: The evolution of the Universe, *Nature*, 162: 680.
2 Alpher, R. A. and Herman, R. C. 1949: *Physical Reviews*, 75: 1333.
3 Wilson, R. W. 1978: The cosmic microwave background. In *Les Prix Nobel 1978*. Stockholm: Almquist and Wiksell International: 126.
4 Dicke, R. H., Peebles, P. J. E., Roll, P. G. and Wilkinson, D. T. 1965: Cosmic black body radiation. *Astrophysical Journal*, 142: 414.
5 Penzias, A. A. and Wilson, R. W. 1965: A measurement of excess antenna temperature at 4080 Mc/s. *Astrophysical Journal*, 142: 420.
6 Wilson, The cosmic microwave background: 126.
7 Ibid.: 22.
8 Maiman, T. H. 1960: Stimulated optical radiation in ruby. *Nature*, 187: 493.
9 Hecht, J. 1985: Laser, the answer that found many questions. *New Scientist*, 106 (1456): 12.
10 Ibid.: 12.
11 Hecht, J. 1987: Laser pioneer receives belated recognition – and a patent. *New Scientist*, 116 (1587): 28.
12 Ibid.: 29.
13 Shuler, K. E., Carrington, T. and Light, J. C. 1965: Nonequilibrium chemical excitation and chemical pumping of lasers. In *Applied Optics*, suppl. 2: *Chemical Lasers*, ed.: K. E. Shuler and W. C. Bennett.
14 Polanyi, J. C. 1961: Proposal for an infra-red maser dependent on vibrational excitation. *Journal of Chemical Physics*, 34: 347.
15 Mössbauer, R. 1962: Recoilless nuclear resonance absorption of gamma radiation. *Science*, 137: 731–8.
16 Ibid.: 733.
17 Gonser, U. 1975: From a strange effect to Mössbauer spectroscopy. In U. Gonser (ed.) *Topics in Applied Physics*, vol. 5. *Mössbauer Spectroscopy*. New York: Springer Verlag.
18 Lipkin, H. J. 1987: Adventures on two frontiers in science with Hans Frauenfelder. *Proceedings of the International Symposium on the Frontiers of Science*. University of Illinois, May 1987.
19 Mössbauer, Recoilless nuclear resonance absorption: 736.
20 De Benedetti, S. 1960: The Mössbauer Effect. *Scientific American*, 202/4: 72.
21 Gonser, From a strange effect: 2.

22 Hoskins, M. 1986: William Herschel and the making of modern astronomy. *Scientific American*, 254/2: 90.

23 Asimov, I. 1964: *Biographical Encyclopedia of Science and Technology.* Garden City, NY: Doubleday & Co.: 265.

24 Kevles, D. J. 1979: Robert A. Millikan, *Scientific American*, 240/1: 118.

3

The Role of Chance in Chemistry and Biochemistry

Erroneous concepts lead to the discovery of oxygen

It is now commonplace knowledge that the air we breathe contains a mixture of gases, of which nitrogen comprises almost four-fifths, followed by about one-fifth of oxygen, with minute proportions of other gases such as CO_2, argon, xenon, etc.

The discovery of oxygen is credited to Joseph Priestley and Antoine Lavoisier. Scientists like the Englishman John Mayow, the Russian Mikhail Lomonosov or the Swede Karl Wilhelm Scheele, who preceded Priestley and Lavoisier in this discovery, are practically unknown. They are the heroes of missed opportunities.[1]

In the eighteenth century the accepted interpretation of combustion was based on the phlogiston theory (from the Greek *Phlogiston*, 'inflammable'), a theory proposed around 1700 by Georg E. Stahl, a German chemist. Stahl claimed that combustible objects contained 'phlogiston' which was lost during the process of burning. What was left therefore (e.g. ash, in the case of wood) would not be able to burn any more. With insight he also connected rusting (calcination, in the language of those days) with the process of loss of phlogiston. So calx (a general name for metal oxide) was phlogiston-less metal. The scientists of the eighteenth century assigned to air the role of carrier in the burning process. When a metal ore (lacking phlogiston) was heated with charcoal (which contained phlogiston) the phlogiston would pass through the air from the charcoal to the ore and produce pure metal.

The situation was not quite so simple. There was a problem, namely that of weight. While rusting (calcination), interpreted as loss of phlogiston, was accompanied by a gain in weight, the burning of charcoal was associated with loss of weight, though in both cases phlogiston was lost.

How does one get out of such a dilemma? Throughout the ages scientists have solved some of the riddles and problems by giving them names. If you don't understand a phenomenon, give it a name. This makes everyone feel that they understand the process. In the case of the contradictory results obtained with the concept of phlogiston, the invented name was *levity*, as the converse of gravity. So gain of weight during the loss of phlogiston was explained by levity.

As early as 1674 John Mayow in England knew from his experiments with candles burning and small animals that some part of the air, necessary for life or for combustion, was removed by fire or respiration, and he called that part 'nitro-aerial spirits'.

In the second half of the eighteenth century (1742–86) there lived in Sweden a well-known chemist-apothecary, Karl Wilhelm Scheele. During his short life of forty-three years, which he devoted entirely to science, he discovered a large number of acids (such as tartaric, citric, lactic, malic, benzoic, oxalic and gallic); he prepared hydrogen fluoride, hydrocyanic acid, and hydrogen sulfide, and discovered the elements of chlorine, magnesium, barium, molybdenum, tungsten and nitrogen. But he is not credited with the discovery of even one of them, except perhaps of copper arsenite, which is called 'Scheele's green'. Despite his preparation of chlorine in 1770 he did not recognize it as an element: it took another thirty years before Davy was to identify chlorine as an element.

In 1771 Scheele made his most important discovery. He heated a number of substances, including mercuric oxide (calx) and obtained metallic mercury and some gas. He described this experiment in great detail in his book which, unfortunately for Scheele, was not published till 1797, because his publisher was not very efficient. By that time Joseph Priestley had already published the same experiment, so the credit goes to him.

Priestley, the son of a nonconformist preacher, was himself a Unitarian minister, rather daring in his beliefs, preaching against slavery, sympathizing with the French Revolution. In short, he was what we would today call a radical.

In 1776 he met Benjamin Franklin during his visit to England. Under his influence Priestley wrote a book on electrical research. He lived in Leeds, nextdoor to a brewery, where he had the opportunity to observe that the gas produced during fermentation extinguished flames. Priestley dissolved this gas (CO_2) (known at that time as 'fixed air') in water and found it to be acid. This finding led to the development of soda water (seltzer), and so Priestley may be called the father of the soft-drink industry.

Priestley studied gases, collecting them over mercury (rather than over water as was usual in those days). In 1774 he took some brick-red powder of calx, put it in a closed tube, heated it by concentrating sunlight with a lens on it and observed that droplets of pure mercury appeared at the top of the tube. A gas was formed permitting combustible materials to burn brightly. According to the accepted nomenclature, Priestley called this gas 'dephlogisticated air'. In March 1775 he found that mice caged in a glass bell filled with this dephlogisticated air felt 'light and easy'. He also noticed that plants restored used-up air (fixed air) to its original freshness, making it into dephlogisticated air. Thus without naming it properly or even understanding what was really going on, Priestley discovered oxygen.

Towards the end of his life Priestley ran into trouble. He practised his clerical profession in Birmingham, but because he became known as a sympathizer of the French Revolution, his house was burned down and he left England for the United States, where he died.

Following his findings with 'dephlogisticated air' Priestley went to France to consult with Antoine Laurent Lavoisier, whose fame as a chemist spread all over Europe. Lavoisier was a brilliant chemist who was guillotined by the French revolutionary court in 1794, at the height of his career at the age of fifty-one. Lavoisier's role in chemistry can be compared to that of Galileo in physics. He was one of the first chemists to recognize that accurate measurements (usually weights) of chemical reactants were essential for the understanding of processes. His main technique was the heating of substances in air. From 1772 onwards he would heat sulphur, phosphorus, etc. in air and weigh the products of the reactions to find that they usually weighed more than the original compound. This, however, was not the case when metals were heated in closed containers. When these were heated in air, 'rust' formed on their surface. This rust was heavier than the part of the metal that they replaced. Lavoisier found that the weight of the vessel with the air, the metal and the calx was the same before and after heating. This meant that the gain in weight of calx must have been due to something in the air that left the air and became part of the calx. If so, Lavoisier reasoned, the loss of this something from the air should reduce the pressure in the vessel, that is, it should produce a vacuum. In fact when he opened the vessel at the end of the reaction, air rushed in, indicating a partial vacuum.

Lavoisier interpreted these findings as meaning that the formation of calx was not due to a loss of phlogiston, but to the acquisition of something in the air, which he first named 'principe oxigine' ('begetter of acids') and later oxygen. In his experiments Lavoisier disposed of the

100-year-old phlogiston theory, and laid the basis for modern chemistry and the law of the conservation of mass.

In 1774 Priestley visited Lavoisier and told him about his experiments with mercury and dephlogisticated air. Lavoisier repeated Priestley's experiments and realized that the gas that formed upon the heating of mercury oxide provided a better medium for breathing and burning because it was undiluted by the other ingredients of air. He then announced that the air contained two gases, one that supported combustion (and breathing), which he called 'principe acidifiant' or oxygen (from the Greek to 'generate acid') and one that did not. This he called 'azote' ('no life'). Azote was later renamed nitrogen.

Priestley (or rather Scheele) had carried out the proper experiment to obtain oxygen, but he did not understand the actual chemical reaction. In contrast, Lavoisier knew exactly what was happening. If the Nobel Prize had existed in their lifetime they would have probably shared it.

There remains an ethical problem. The real discoverer of oxygen was Priestley (Scheele is a loser because he did not publish in time). Lavoisier, however, who correctly interpreted Priestley's findings, claimed the credit for the discovery, presumably not mentioning Priestley as the original experimenter. The truth is slightly different. In his *Expérience sur les respirations des animaux et sur les changements qui arrive à l'air en passant par leur poumon*, published in 1777, Lavoisier stated:

> . . . Dr Priestley has lately published a treatise in which he has greatly extended the bounds of our knowledge; and has endeavoured to prove, by a number of very ingenious, delicate and novel experiments, that the respiration of animals has the property of phlogisticating air in a similar manner to what is effected by the calcination of metals and many other chemical processes, and that the air ceases not to be respirable till the instant when it becomes surcharged, or at least saturated with phlogiston.[2]

In the next passage, however, Lavoisier 'found . . . the theory of this celebrated philosopher [Priestley] contradicts a great number of phenomena . . . I found myself led irresistibly by the consequences of my experiments to very different conclusions.'[3]

Tragically, till the end of his life Priestley would not part with his belief in phlogiston. As for Lavoisier, he is also credited with the discovery of hydrogen (in 1783), but the discovery was actually made in 1740 by the Russian genius Lomonosov. Lomonosov published his antiphlogistic views and suggested the law of conservation of mass well before Lavoisier.

Berzelius, Wöhler and urea

At the beginning of the nineteenth century there was a clear distinction between inorganic and organic chemicals. The similarity in the elemental composition of natural products and probably also the fact that, unlike mineral compounds, they were combustible, led to the belief that animal and vegetable substances were produced under the influence of a 'vital force' and that their formation was regulated by laws quite different from those regulating the formation of mineral substances. Compounds obtained from living organisms were designated 'organic', and it was thought impossible to prepare them artificially.

One of the main proponents of this belief was Jons Jakob Berzelius, a Swedish medical doctor turned chemist. In 1803 he published a textbook of chemistry, which was reprinted in five editions during his lifetime. In 1828 he had published a very accurate list of the atomic weights of elements and it was he who introduced the one- or two-letter codes for them. This code also gave expression to the structure of molecules made of the elements (e.g. H_2O, CO_2). His authority in chemistry became so great that his criticism or condemnation of works or theories of other chemists was the last word on the subject. One of Berzelius's beliefs was that an organic compound could not be synthesized in the laboratory from inorganic ones.

One of Berzelius's own ex-pupils, a German chemist named Frederick Wöhler (born 1800) was to explode this theory. Wöhler studied chemistry for some time with Berzelius and then taught it in a trade school in Berlin. In one of his laboratory experiments he heated a mixture of potassium cyanate with ammonium sulphate hoping to obtain ammonium cyanate. He found, however, that the product obtained was urea (which has the same general composition as ammonium cyanate) but with a different arrangement of atoms.

$$C\ N_2H_4O \rightarrow \begin{matrix} NH_2 \\ NH_2 \end{matrix}\!\!>\!C{=}O$$
urea

Urea was known at that time as a waste product of mammalians' bodies excreted in urine; that is, it was an organic compound which according to Berzelius could be produced only in living tissues. Wöhler wrote to Berzelius: 'I must tell you that I can prepare urea without requiring a kidney of an animal, a man or a dog.'[4]

In view of the existing paradigm about organic and inorganic compounds, this claim was not exactly correct, since one of the molecules from which Wöhler prepared urea was cyanate, which, as a molecule containing carbon, is considered to be an organic compound.

Berzelius accepted Wöhler's result as a proven fact and it became a turning-point in that it induced many chemists to try to synthesize organic molecules from inorganic ones.

Perkin and the aniline dyes

By the middle of the nineteenth century a large number of other organic substances had been successfully synthesized. One of the major challenges at that time was the synthesis of stable dyes for use in the giant European textile industry. The only dyes then available were dark-blue indigo, obtained from the indigo plant and from woad, and the red dyes obtained from the madder plant and from snails (alizarin).

The discovery of aniline dyes in 1856 is attributed to Sir William Henry Perkin, who was born in London and studied chemistry under August Hofmann (who in turn was a student of Justus von Liebig). Hofmann's researches were concerned with coal-tar and aniline compounds. When Perkin joined Hofmann at the Royal College of Chemistry in London at the age of seventeen, he tried to derive quinine from coal-tar chemicals, but he did not succeed. After all, the structure of quinine was at that time unknown and was not unravelled until a century later by Robert Burus Woodward. During the Easter vacation of 1856 Perkin mixed aniline – one of the coal-tar chemicals – with potassium bichromate. The outcome was a messy substance which would have been thrown out by an experienced chemist. Perkin, however, noted that the material had a purple tinge. He added alcohol to the mess, and a beautiful purple colour appeared in the extracting solution. Perkin immediately thought that this coloured extract would make a good dye for textiles.

Perkin then contacted Pillars of Perth, a Scottish firm engaged in dyeing textiles, sent them a sample of his extract, and was pleased and excited when they reported that the new dye would dye silk beautifully. Perkin patented his process for the preparation of the dye, left Hofmann and in 1857, financed by his father and brother, started a dye factory at Greenford near London. To his dismay Perkin found that one of the raw materials needed for his process was not available on the open market, so with his usual flair he worked out a synthesis using benzene and citric acid. He himself also devised the necessary equipment for large-scale production of the dye and within six months was already producing a dye named Aniline Purple. Interestingly, the main customers for this dye were not the English, but the French, who called it 'mauve' and made it the fashionable colour of the season. In 1869 Perkin synthesized alizarin, the red constituent of madder. But when he put in for a patent, he was disappointed to find that a German chemist, Heinrich Caro, had beaten him by a single day. In 1879 von Baeyer produced indigo and was awarded the Nobel Prize for it.

At the age of twenty-three Perkin was rich and famous. His discovery initiated the synthetic-dye industry. Although the new industry had started in Britain, it operated mainly in Germany up to World War I. Perkin left the industry in 1874 and became interested in perfumes. He was knighted a year before his death, in 1906.[5]

A dye or a drug?

The synthetic-dye industry is also closely associated with the discovery of the sulfonamides. This story, begun in 1908, is strewn with many missed opportunities and false leads, to be crowned eventually by accidental success, when in 1936 Gerhard Domagk demonstrated the extraordinarily lethal effects of protonsil on streptococcal infections.

The story begins with Paul Gelmo, a Ph.D. student who synthesized sulfanilamide at the University of Vienna in 1908. Basing his research on the observation that this compound combined well with wool and silk, Heinrich Hörlein, working (with Dressel and Kothe) at the IG Farben-industrie (the famous German dye factory) constructed new colour-fast dyes.[6] As a chemist he never even dreamed of using sulfanilamide as an anti-bacterial agent, and so they were used as dyes only.

Seven years later, however, the matter was taken up by Charles Heidel-berger at the Rockefeller Institute in New York. Prompted by the Director of the Institute, Simon Flexner, Heidelberger was searching for substances that would kill pneumococci and streptococci (pneumonia at that time was a fatal disease). One of the substances tested, optochin, a derivative of sulfonilamide, would kill bacteria in the test tube, but when injected into mice infected with the pathogens, it turned out to be more lethal than the disease itself. This experiment put an end to bacteriological research on sulfanilamide for the next twenty years. Heidelberger later remembered: the possibility

That so simple a substance [sulfanilamide] could cure bacterial infection by a mechanism other than direct killing of the microorganism never occurred to us. If it had, we might have saved hundreds of thousands of lives in the twenty years before Domagk, the Tréfouels, Nitti and Bovet made their discoveries.[7]

Back at the IG Farbenindustrie, in 1932 the chemists Klarer and Mietsch synthesized a red dye – protonsil, which was shown by Gerhard Domagk in 1935 to be a potent anti-bacterial agent. Domagk had trained as a medical doctor and joined IG Farbenindustrie in the late twenties where he studied the possible medical applications of various organic dyes synthesized by his firm. It was therefore quite understandable that as soon as protonsil was synthesized in 1932, Dogmagk discovered that it had a powerful effect on streptococcal infections in mice. In 1935, when his daughter became seriously ill with a streptococcal infection, Domagk ventured to inject her with large doses of protonsil, and she dramatically recovered. (Protonsil later saved the life of Frank D. Roosevelt, the son of the President of the United States.) In the next few years the Trefouels, Nitti and Bovet at the Pasteur Institute in Paris showed that the bactericidal properties of protonsil were due to the sulfanilamide part of the molecule, and that the rest of the molecule was superfluous.[8]

At the time of Domagk's discovery, Hörlein, who had patented sulfanilamide in 1909 and was the director of the medical division of IG Farbenindustrie, reported in the *Proceedings of the Royal Society of Medicine* that at the time Domagk discovered the anti-bacterial activity of protonsil, he himself had numerous azo compounds containing sulfanilamide ready to be tested specifically in streptococcal infections in mice.[9] But, alas, the historical credit goes to Domagk and not to Hörlein.

In his *Retrospectroscope*[10] J. H. Comroe thinks that IG Farbenindustrie rediscovered and tested sulfanilamide first, and then spent a few years disguising it, because by that time the original patent of 1909 had expired, and so they prepared a new, patentable red compound, protonsil.

As indicated before, protonsil had no direct effect on bacteria in the test tube. It is only when it is administered to a mammal that it breaks down into para-amino-benzene sulfonamide, the agent that kills bacteria.

Thus the circle, begun with Gelmo in 1908, aborted in 1915 in Heidelberger's laboratory and interrupted for twenty years, was triumphantly closed in the late thirties when Domagk was awarded the Nobel Prize for 1939 in medicine and physiology. Tragically, Domagk withdrew acceptance of the prize under the threat of imprisonment by Hitler and the Gestapo. It was not until 1947, with Germany in shambles, that Domagk went to Stockholm to receive his prize.[11]

Why clonidine?

As everyone knows, the common cold is associated with a runny nose and swelling of the nasal tissues due to swelling of the blood vessels there. The pharmaceutical industry has been very much interested in finding remedies at least against these symptoms. Helmut Stähle, working at C. H. Böhringer und Sohn, synthesized a series of analogues of imidazolines as possible vasoconstrictors (to reduce the swelling of the blood vessels). One of his compounds, a 2,6-dichloro derivative of imidazoline (later called clonidine) was given for trials to the Company's medical department. Dr M. Wolf, the physician in charge of trials on human subjects, decided to test it on his secretary, Mrs Schwandt, who happened to have developed a nasty cold. He instilled into her nose a solution of 0.3 per cent of clonidine. However, as Stähle relates there was some surprise and embarrassment when the lady fell asleep for twenty-four hours, and, when examined by the physicians, also had very low blood pressure.[12]

This unexpected finding led to the development of an anti-hypertensive drug, which later also became useful in the treatment of glaucoma and migraine. It also turned out to be a useful drug to improve the conditions of children suffering from the so-called Tourette syndrome, a rare and bizarre psychiatric disorder in children, characterized by incoordinate motor and psychic disturbances and compulsive actions (such as the repetition of obscene words). As it turned out, clonidine stimulated the central alpha adreno-receptors which are responsible for the activation of the peripheral sympathetic nervous system.

Another unexpected effect of clonidine was the stimulation of human growth hormone, with its effect on a decrease in secretion from all the secretory glands (especially the sweat gland).

If serendipity is defined as 'something extraordinary' that has not been searched or looked for, but has been detected by plain curiosity, meticulous observation, sagacity and lateral thinking, the clonidine story is a significant and pertinent example. Conceived as a vaso-constrictor, clonidine was delivered in due time as a centrally acting blood-pressure-lowering drug, and finally developed into a cure for several other diseases and symptoms.

These examples show that it is seldom that a scientist has made a discovery and understood its full implication. The process of understanding is usually a slow journey through the minds of many scientists, each adding a little bit until someone paints the final, comprehensive picture. The powers of human intellect, in fact, are much less outstanding than we are usually led to believe. 'Discovery only visits those who are working in the field over which it hovers, and who have both the prepared vision ready to recognize her gifts when they are bestowed, and mind and industry to put them to use.'[13]

Wrong rice and Vitamin B

Beri-beri, a disease affecting the nervous system, was first described in China some 600 years ago. The disease assumed epidemic proportions in Dutch East India, and in 1886 the Dutch Government dispatched a special commission comprising two scientists, Pickelharing and Winkler, and an army doctor, Christian Eijkman. At that time, the heyday of Koch and Pasteur, the paradigm for the study of epidemic disease was based on the assumption that disease was caused by bacteria, which should be isolated and studied. The team worked for two years in an attempt to isolate a bacterium, and finally settled (wrongly) on one. At that stage the two senior scientists returned to Holland, leaving Eijkman behind to put the finishing touches to the research. Eijkman, then thirty years old, worked for another two years. He became convinced that there was something wrong with the whole concept that beri-beri was an infectious disease. 'Attempts to induce the infection with material from infected birds or from birds which had died of the disease were inconclusive since all chickens, even those kept separate as controls, were affected. No specific microorganism or parasite was found.'[14]

Chance then intervened. Eijkman's experimental animals were chickens. The experimental, as well as the control, chickens had been affected by the disease from mid-July to the end of November, when the disease vanished. Eijkman investigated closely what had happened during this period. He found out from his laboratory keeper that there had been a change of cook at the military hospital (the hospital provided the food for both people and chickens) and that the new cook refused to let the cooked rice be used by 'civilian' chickens. So from June to November they were fed on polished rice purchased from outside.

This information led Eijkman to start deliberate feeding experiments to find out whether food had anything to do with the disease. He soon established that it was definitely caused by a diet of polished rice. Animals fed on such rice became ill within three to four weeks, whereas other chickens, fed on unpolished rice, remained healthy. The change of diet from polished to unpolished rice, or even just the material removed from the rice during the polishing, cured the sick chickens.

Did Eijkman interpret these results correctly? No, he did not. At first he thought that the disease was caused by a toxin, and that this toxin was neutralized by something present in the rice hulls. Finally, after consultation with Pickelharing, Eijkman did understand the true meaning of his discovery. This was a new principle of the causation of disease: the disease resulted from a lack of something in very minute quantities in the diet, something that did not *per se* have any calorific value.

This explanation matured during the next ten years and was finally formulated by Sir Frederick Hopkins, the English biochemist, on the basis of his own experiments in 1912. The missing 'something' was given the name 'vitamine' (vital amine) by Kasimir Funk, to be changed later to 'vitamin'. In the case of beri-beri the vitamin was B. In 1929 Eijkman and Hopkins shared the Nobel Prize for its discovery.

The discovery of Vitamin C in 1907 was also the result of unexpected results in an experiment planned for another purpose. The Norwegians Axel Holst and Theodor Frölich tried to produce beri-beri in guinea pigs by means of a suitable diet. They did produce a disease, but it turned out later to be scurvy, which was already known to occur in sailors on long sea voyages when they had no access to fresh food. This disease was not reproduced in animals before the chance observation of the Norwegians.

In 1928 Albert Szent Györgyi, a Hungarian American biochemist working in Hopkins's laboratory, was studying the reduction of substances in the adrenal cortex. From the adrenal glands he isolated a substance that was a good hydrogen carrier and named it hexuronic acid. Szent Györgyi then found that the same compound was present in fresh vegetables, such as cabbage, and in citrus fruits, but it took another four years before he realized that his hexuronic acid was actually Vitamin C. In 1932 Charles G. King reported the isolation of Vitamin C and showed that it was identical with the hexuronic acid. The vitamin was renamed ascorbic acid.

All sorts of switches – Hokin's hokum

Let us consider an electric switch that is operated by a key, such as the ignition switch in a car or that for a burglar alarm in the home. We all know that the switch cannot be turned on without the proper key (or magnetic card). Once the key is inserted and the switch activated, what happens next depends on the sort of mechanism connected to the switch, whether it is light, heat, motor, radio or an alarm. Once the switch is turned on, the relevant mechanism will operate (provided of course, that there are suitable connections).

Analogously, the cells in our organism perform different functions depending on which organ or tissue they are in. The muscles contract, the glands excrete, the white blood cells produce antibodies, the nerve cells conduct messages, etc. All these cells have on (or in) their surface receptors like the locks mentioned above: they need a key to be activated. Once a receptor is activated by its key, whether a hormone, a neurotransmitter or any other specific molecule, it transmits the signal received from its 'key' to the inside of the cells via the so-called second messengers. What are these second messengers? We shall make a digression here to explain the structure of cellular membranes which separate the inside of the cell from the outer environment whence the signals may come.

The cell membrane is basically a layer of fatty materials (phospholipids and cholesterol). In this layer are embedded various proteins or glycoproteins, some of which serve as the receptors, the recognition mechanisms, the locks, ready to interact with their specific keys, or signals. The attachment of the signal to the receptor has to be translated inside the cell into an activity, or inhibition, i.e. it has to switch on or off the specific properties of the host cells. Here another mechanism is needed for transmission, a sort of a clutch. This mechanism may be constructed from one of the two components of the membrane, the lipids or the proteins. Indeed such proteins are found in the membrane functioning as enzymes (e.g. adenylate cyclase, which upon activation converts adenosine triphosphate into cyclic AMP); there are also phospholipids, such as phosphatidylinositol, that are intimately involved in the transmission of signals. In every case these second messengers elicit a cascade of events (usually involving some phosphorylations) which make the cell act as it is programmed to do.

Where do the signals come from? Communication between the cells is based on chemical language. So hormones, released from one tissue, convey a specific message to another, often distant, tissue; neurotransmitters such as acetylcholine, released by nerve endings, stimulate the relevant muscles to contract or other nerve cells to 'fire'. Research in the last few decades has unravelled the molecular structure of most of the important signals that operate in the organism, as well as of some receptors. Advances have also been made in elucidating the action and function of the transducers, the second messengers. One of the second messengers extensively studied is cyclic adenylate monophosphate.

Another intriguing second messenger unravelled quite recently (1984–6) is the phospho–inositide (PI)-derived IP_3 and diglyceride. This second messenger was almost discovered by Hokin and Hokin in 1950 but theirs was a 'voice crying in the wilderness'. Even as late as 1970 the concept of the PI response was called 'Hokin's hokum and Michell's folly'.

Lowell E. Hokin did his Ph.D. thesis in Hans Krebs's laboratory, where he studied the role of ribonucleic acid (RNA) in protein synthesis. He learned from a report made by some Russian workers that during the hormonal stimulation of secretion in internal organs and glands, radioactive phosphorus would be incorporated into nucleoproteins (i.e. nucleic acids closely associated with proteins). Repeating some of these experiments, Hokin confirmed that ^{32}P was incorporated into RNA, but the quantitative data led him to suspect that some of the phosphorus might be taken up by phospholipids which form an important constituent of the cell membranes. The reason for this assumption was that the radioactive phosphorus incorporated during tissue stimulation by a hormone would also be found in ether extract of the tissue, and this indicated the involvement of lipids. Hokin made this observation shortly before returning from England to Canada. He took with him the tubes with the ether extracts and there, at Quastel's laboratory at McGill University in Montreal, he and his wife Mabel, a scientist in her own right, found that there was a lot of radioactivity due to phosphorus in the lipids of the pancreas (the stimulated organ). Upon closer examination, they established that the ^{32}P was only in phospholipids and not in RNA, as was previously believed. The actual proof for this finding was not published until 1953.[15] In 1955 the phospholipids involved were identified as phosphatidylinositol and phosphatidic acid. What was quite obvious, though not understood at that time, was that this uptake of radioactive phosphorus was connected with stimulation of the cells.

In 1964, when Hokin spoke at a Symposium on the Metabolism and Physiological Significance of Lipids, he proposed the existence of a phosphatidylinositol–phosphatidic acid cycle occurring during stimulation by acetylcholine of secretion in a salt gland of an albatross (see figure 3).[16] When the salt gland is stimulated, the enzyme phospholipase C breaks phosphatidylinositol down into diglyceride and phosphatidic acid.

After examining his early papers, dating from 1950, Hokin himself thinks that his interpretation of the phospholipid effects was somewhat naïve, because at that time very little was known about the main structural components involved in such a cycle, namely about the cell membrane. The actual structure of phosphatidylinositol was not elucidated till 1958–60 and the involvement of calcium ions in the cycle was not known until the late seventies, when Bob Michell showed that there was a link between

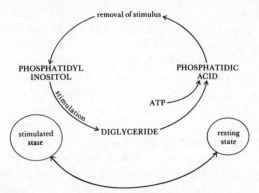

**Figure 3   Schematic representation of the biochemical events involved in
stimulation by choline and secretion in the salt gland**
Phosphatidylinositol–phosphatidic acid cycle proposed by the Hokins in
1964.
Source: M. R. Hokin and L. E. Hokin (1965): Interconversion of phosphatidyl
and phosphatidic acid involved in the response to acetylcholine in the salt gland.
In *Metabolism and Physiological Significance of Lipids*, ed. R. M. C. Dawson and D. N.
Rhodes. New York: John Wiley and Sons: 423–34.

receptor-activated PI and cellular calcium metabolism.[17] It was not until
the eighties that Berridge showed that IP$_3$ released intracellular stores of
calcium.

Now it is known that the function of second messengers involves IP$_3$
and two related inositol phosphates, that they mobilize calcium from the
internal stores of the cell and that the second messenger eventually activates
the protein kinase C, which in turn phosphorylates certain target proteins.[18]

Writing in *Trends in Pharmacological Sciences* in February 1987, Hokin
said:

> This is the story of the discovery of the phosphoinositide effect in the early
> 1950's, a 'discovery before its time' . . . If only we could have taken a
> glimpse into the future back then I would never have allowed an albatross to
> side-track me from continuing to investigate the true meaning of this
> fundamentally important phenomenon.[19]

NOTES TO CHAPTER 3

1 Asimov, I. 1964: *Biographical Encyclopedia of Science and Technology*. Garden
City, NY: Doubleday and Co.

2 Daumas, M. 1959: *Lavoisier. Théoréticien et expérimentateur.* Paris: Presses Universitaires de France: 79.
3 Ibid.
4 Asimov, *Biographical Encyclopedia*: 246.
5 Ibid.: 280f.
6 Hörlein, H. 1909: German Patent DRP 226239, 18 May.
7 Heidelberger, M. 1977: A 'pure' organic chemist's downward path. *Annual Reviews of Microbiology*, 31: 8.
8 Tréfouel, J., Tréfouel, T. J., Nitti, F. and Bouvet D. 1935: Activité du p-aminophénylsulhamide sur les infections streptococciques expérimentales de la souris et du lapin. *Comptes rendus des Séances de la Société de Biologie* (Paris), 120: 756.
9 Hörlein, H. 1935: The chemotherapy of infectious diseases caused by protozoa and bacteria. *Proceedings of the Royal Society of Medicine*, 29: 313.
10 Comroe, J. H. 1977: *Retrospectroscope*, Menlo Park, Calif.: Van Gehr Press: 67.
11 Liljestrad, G. 1962: The Prize in Physiology and Medicine. In *The Nobel Foundation, Nobel the Man and Prizes*. Amsterdam: Elsevier: 172–80.
12 Stähle, H. 1982: Clonidine. In E. S. Bindra and D. Lednicer (eds), *Chronicles of Drug Discovery*. New York: J. Wiley and Sons: 87.
13 Dibble J. H., 1952: Chance, design and discovery. *Postgraduate Medical Journal*, 29: 62.
14 Eijkman, C. 1965: Antineuritic vitamin and beri-beri. In *Nobel Prize Lectures in Physiology and Medicine 1922–1944*. Amsterdam: Elsevier: 199–207.
15 Hokin, L. E. 1953: Enzyme secretion and the incorporation of P^{32} into phospholipids of pancreas slices. *Journal of Biological Chemistry*, 203: 967.
16 Hokin, M. R. and Hokin, L. E. 1965: Interconversion of phosphatidyl and phosphatidic acid involved in the response to acetylcholine in the salt gland. In *Metabolism and Physiological Significance of Lipids*, ed. R. M. C. Dawson and D. N. Rhodes. New York: John Wiley and Sons: 423–34.
17 Michell, R. A. 1975: Inositol phospolipids and cell surface receptor function. *Biochimica and Biophysica Acta*, 415: 81.
18 Nishizuka, Y. 1986: Studies and perspectives of protein kinase C. *Science*, 233: 305.
19 Hokin, L. E. 1987: The road to the phosphoinositide-generated second messengers. *Trends in Pharmacological Science*, 8: 53.

4

Chance and Disappointment in Microbiology

Chance favours none but the prepared mind

The life of Louis Pasteur, the famous French chemist and microbiologist, is a long chain of astounding successes running from the discovery of Lævo- and dextro-rotatory crystals of tartaric acid, to the finding that micro-organisms use only one form of this compound, then to putrefaction, to the role of micro-organisms in fermentation and disease, and finally to the development of vaccines against bacterial and viral diseases.

Pasteur's career was formed to a certain extent by accident, or by a series of accidental circumstances. The fame that came to him was associated with his researches in microbiology and immunology, though his original scientific interest was in chemistry and crystallography. Pasteur discovered that there were two isomeric forms of tartaric acid, and that each of these forms rotated the plane of polarized light in an opposite direction. When the solution of these two forms cystallized, they were seen under a microscope as having mirror-like symmetry. A mixture of these two forms is called racemic. Pasteur reported:

> The fortunate idea came to me to orient my crystals with reference to a plane perpendicular to the observer, and then I noticed that the confused mass of crystals of paratartrate could be divided into two groups according to the orientation of their facets of asymmetry. In one group, the facet of assymetry nearer my body was inclined to my right with reference to the plane of orientation which I just mentioned, whereas the facet of asymmetry was inclined to the left in the other. The paratartrate appeared as a mixture of two kinds of crystals, some asymetric to the right, some asymetric to the left.[1]

Having made this discovery, Pasteur was so happy and excited that he rushed from his laboratory and exclaimed to one of his chemistry assistants:

'I have just made a great discovery . . . I am so happy that I am shaking all over.'[2]

On one occasion Pasteur observed a *Penicillium* mould growing in a racemic solution. He noted that the mould destroyed only the form rotating the polarized light to the right so that the solution eventually contained only the leftward-rotating tartrate. This extraordinary observation turned Pasteur's interest to fermentation, and so the next problem he was to study, as Professor of Chemistry at Lille, was the production of vinegar and the brewing of beer by fermentation. From his studies in this field he then turned to the investigation of diseases in wine and the role of micro-organisms in the process, and later to the diseases of the silkworm.

One of Pasteur's important contributions to microbiological science, the discovery that an attenuated strain of bacteria could be used for immunization, was the result of a chance observation. He was experimenting on the bacteria that cause cholera in fowls. He grew cultures of these bacteria on agar plates and slants in tubes. On one occasion, when he returned from a vacation, he found that his cultures of bacteria had died. He tried to revive them by inoculating the cultures into fresh fowls. As he expected, he failed to produce a disease in them, indicating that the bacteria were dead and unable to cause disease. Later he obtained new cultures of the same bacteria. He injected the fresh cultures into a new batch of fowls as well as into those that had been previously inoculated with the 'dead' cultures. The unexpected result was that the latter survived the infection while the former all died. One of Pasteur's collaborators present on this occasion recounted that Pasteur turned to him and said: 'Don't you see that these animals have been vaccinated?'

Pasteur had the intelligence to appreciate the value of this unexpected result and to understand that he had discovered a new method and principle of vaccination, which he then applied successfully to other diseases such as anthrax and rabies.

Pasteur also foresaw the antibiotic era, when he considered the elimination of the plant louse *Phylloxera* by a micro-organism, or when he predicted that rabbits could be destroyed by infecting them with the self-propagating agent of a lethal disease. His observation in 1857 that onion juice added to sugar solution prevented the development of yeast in it led him to remark: 'These facts justify the highest hopes for therapeutics.'[3]

Is there latent typhus?

Typhus fever exists in several forms. In Europe, the disease was known in

German as *Flecktyphus*, because of the characteristic spots appearing on the skin of the patients. On the American continent one of the manifestations of the disease was the Rocky Mountain Spotted Fever, and there are many other varieties of it.

Charles Jules Henri Nicolle, a French physician, who from 1902 was the director of the Pasteur Institute in Tunis, encountered epidemics of typhus there. He noticed that the disease spread in the general population as well as in the workers who came into contact with patients upon their admission to the hospital, but it did not spread in the hospital ward after the patients had been stripped of their clothing and properly washed with soap and water. Nicolle realized that the disease was transmitted by body lice hiding in the clothing. At that time the agent of the disease transmitted by lice could not be cultivated outside the human body on any known culture media. Nicolle tried to transmit the disease to guinea pigs, monkeys and chimpanzees by inoculating them with the blood of the sick patients.

Nicolle also made some interesting epidemiological observations. The people most sensitive to the disease were European immigrants to those areas in Tunis where the disease was found. The local adults were less sensitive. Though seriously ill, they usually escaped death. Next in line were children, who suffered only a mild disease, and they were followed by monkeys and chimpanzees, in which the infection produced hardly any effects. At the end of the line were guinea pigs: they showed no symptoms of the disease beyond a very small rise in body temperature. The disease could not be diagnosed in the guinea pigs without a thermometer. Nevertheless the blood of infected, symptom-free guinea pigs was infective to primates.

In his *Biologie de l'invention* Nicolle writes:

> Now, it happened occasionally that we discovered among our guinea pigs, inoculated with the same virus, some who had no fever at all. The first time that we discovered this we thought it was due to an accident in the inoculation or to the particular resistance of the inoculated animal . . . When the phenomenon kept recurring, we felt that our explanation was too superficial, and that it must be due to another specific reason.[4]

Nicolle then reasoned that since there was a graduation in the virulence of the agents across species, the lack of response in some guinea pigs should be an indication of a latent, unseen infection. From this conclusion he generalized that in other micro-organisms also there must be various degrees of virulence and therefore that some infections would be unrecognizable, but still essential in the epidemic transmission of the disease through apparently healthy individuals. Much later, in the early forties, when laboratory techniques were available for the study of the poliovirus, it was shown that in this disease the transmission was mainly through children who did not suffer from any paralysis.

One may say that in the course of events related to epidemiology, natural and experimental, and Nicolle's thinking in connection with them, chance was not involved, and that reaching the conclusion about latency was inevitable. In fact, when Nicolle saw the phenomenon of the latency of typhus in guinea pigs he actually misunderstood it, thinking it to be a result of faulty experimentation – due to a mistake in inoculation or some natural resistance to the disease in a given individual guinea pig. It was only when the phenomenon recurred that he applied his intuition, courage and discipline to arrive at the right conclusion and to prove it correct. Although in this case the discovery arose from an accidental observation, it was in fact the result of well-based intellectual effort on his part.

Puerperal fever and the frustrated Semmelweiss

In the middle of the last century puerperal fever was considered to be a scourge sent from God. Women about to give birth in hospital' were terrified by it, because they knew that it might end in death and that it was safer to give birth at home. The doctors speculated that the disease was due to food, smells or whatever.

By 1843 Oliver Wendell Holmes had recognized that the disease known as puerperal fever was caused by germs carried from patient to patient by physicians and midwives. This warning fell on deaf ears in America and was not heeded in Europe.[5] A Hungarian doctor, Ignaz Philip Semmelweiss, working in the obstetrical ward of a hospital in Vienna, observed that one of the laboratory assistants who cut himself during the dissection of a woman dead of puerperal fever became ill with symptoms resembling those of the dead woman, and died. He therefore thought that they had both died of the same cause. Another of Semmelweiss's observations was that deaths from puerperal fever were more frequent in wards attended by medical students who often used to come straight from the prosectorium (the dissection room) where they participated in the dissection of women dead of puerperal fever. In a period when the role of micro-organisms in producing disease was yet unknown, Semmelweiss interpreted his observations thus:

Puerperal fever is a resorption fever produced by the resorption of decomposed animal organic matter . . . this material is 'brought to the
individual from without, and that is the infection from without . . . The
carrier of the decomposed animal organic material is the examining finger,
the operating hand, the bedclothes, the atmospheric air, sponges, the hands
of midwives and nurses which come into contact with the excreta of sick
lying-in women or other patients, and then come again into contact with the
genitals of women in labour or just confined. These were the carriers of the
contagion, the pyaemia, a blood poisoning produced by what Semmelweiss
called decomposed animal-organic matter?[6]

These observations led Semmelweiss to report to the Medical Council
of Vienna his hypothesis that puerperal fever was due to blood poisoning
caused by lack of antiseptic precautions on the part of attending doctors
and students. He claimed that doctors and nurses dealing with women in
labour should wash their hands thoroughly between treating various
patients, because they might be carrying 'cadaveric material' acquired at
post-mortem examinations. He demanded further that the wards should
be disinfected by chlorination. On his own ward, where these precautions
were observed from 1847, the mortality from puerperal fever dropped
from 12 to 3 per cent and later even to 1 per cent.[7]

The leading obstetricians in Vienna, however, supported by the famous
Rudolf Virchov (the opponent of the germ theory of disease and of
Darwin's theory of evolution), not only ignored Semmelweiss's precepts,
but actively fought him, so that he had to leave the hospital where he
worked and return to Hungary. In 1861 he published a paper 'On the
aetiology, the concept and prophylaxis of puerperal fever' He wrote:

When I look back upon the past, I can only dispel the sadness that falls
upon me by gazing into that happy future when infection will be banished.
But if it is not vouchsafed to me to look upon that happy time with my own
eyes . . . the conviction that such a time must inevitably arrive sooner or
later will cheer my dying hour.[8]

Opposition to his ideas was such that he had to leave his post as Professor
at the University Hospital in Budapest. In 1865 he died in a lunatic
asylum, a victim of sepsis, from a dissection wound in his hand.

'A slot machine – a broken test tube'

In the late 1940s Salvador E. Luria, an Italian-born scientist (and a Nobel
Prize winner in 1969) was working during the summer vacation with Max

Delbrück on the genetics of bacteriophages (viruses that attack bacteria). At that time these were the only viruses that could be cultivated easily in bacterial cultures and therefore amenable to genetic analysis. A problem that intrigued Luria was based on the observation that when bacteria, such as *Escherichia coli* were infected with a suitable bacteriophage, they lysed, releasing masses of new and identical bacteriophages; amid this havoc there were some survivors that could be shown to be resistant to an attack from these bacteriophages. (The test was done by diluting the lysed culture and seeding its contents on a nutrient agar plate, where only the survivors would grow and produce visible colonies.) Luria wondered whether these mutant resistant bacteria arose as a result of the action of the infecting phage or whether they were the product of spontaneous mutation, that is, already present in the bacterial population in no way related to the infection.

In his autobiography Luria wrote:

> I struggled with the problem for several months, mostly in my own thoughts, and also tried a variety of experiments, none of which worked. The answer finally came to me in February 1943 in the improbable setting of a faculty dance at Indiana University, a few weeks after I had moved there as an instructor.
>
> During a pause in the music I found myself standing near a slot machine, watching a colleague putting dimes into it. Though losing most of the time he occasionally got a return. Not a gambler myself, I was teasing him about his inevitable losses, when he suddenly hit a jackpot, about three dollars in dimes, gave me a dirty look, and walked away. Right then I began giving some thought to the actual numerology of slot machines; in so doing it dawned on me that slot machines and bacterial mutations have something to teach each other.[9]

In order to be profitable to their owners, slot machines return to the players only, say, 90 per cent of the money put in, but they do so in a very uneven way. Most trials yield nothing, some very little, and still fewer trials produce a jackpot, which does not obey statistical randomness. 'The gambler who wins is the one who by chance hits the jackpot early.'[10]

Luria argued that if bacteria were made resistant with a certain low probability by contact with the infecting phage, the number of resistant 'individuals' would depend only on the total number of bacteria exposed to the phage. But if the resistant bacteria arose independently by mutation, they should be clustered in families made up of the original mutant and its descendants. Therefore, when a number of independent bacterial cultures are set up, and infected with phages, the number of resistant colonies in each culture should depend on which of the two hypotheses is correct. If it is the random contact of the phages with bacteria that makes some of them resistant, then the number of resistant cells in each tube should, according to a certain statistical distribution, known as the Poisson distribution, be more or less constant. But if the resistant cells arise as a result of spontaneous mutation, the number of them in each tube will depend on the time of appearance of the mutation before the bacteria encounter the infecting phage. In some cultures, therefore, the number of mutants will be greater and in others smaller. So if the mutation occurred just before the phage was put into the bacterial culture, there will be only one resistant colony stemming from the single available mutant. When the mutation has occurred n generations before testing with phage, there will be at least 2^n resistant mutants in the tube.

> Realizing the analogy between slot-machine returns and clusters of mutants was an exciting moment. I left the dance party as soon as I could . . . Next morning I went early to my laboratory, a room I shared with two students and eighteen rabbits. I set up the experimental test of my idea – several series of identical cultures of bacteria, each started with a very few bacteria. It was a hard Sunday to live through, waiting for my cultures to grow . . . Next day, Monday morning, each culture contained exactly one bilion bacteria. The next step was to count the phase-resistant bacteria in each culture. I proceeded to mix each culture with phage on a single test plate. Then I had again a day of waiting – but at least I was busy teaching. Tuesday was the day of triumph. I found an average of ten resistant colonies per culture, with lots of zeros and, as I hoped to find, several jackpots. I had also set up my control. I had taken many individual cultures and pooled them all together, then divided the mixture again into small portions and counted the resistant colonies in each portion. Complete success: this time the average number of resistant colonies was again about the same, but the individual numbers were distributed at random and there were no jackpots.[11]

These results fully supported the idea that the resistant bacteria originated by spontaneous mutation.

Luria was happy and elated and wrote to Delbrück, explaining the idea and the experiment, which came to be known as the 'fluctuation test'. (The idea of the fluctuation test later led J. Goldie and A. J. Goldman to develop a more rational chemotherapeutic treatment of cancers which also arise by mutation.)

Another serendipitous finding was made by Luria in 1952 as a result of a broken test tube, a finding which presaged the discovery of restriction enzymes made many years later, for which W. Arber and H. O. Smith received the Nobel Prize.

Luria, then at the University of Illinois in Urbana, was studying the process of phage infection in bacteria. It was already known that following the entry of the phage DNA into the host bacterium, this DNA would be replicated into hundreds of new copies and would also instruct the synthetic machinery in the host to produce and assemble the protein coat of the phage according to the genetic instructions present in the phage DNA. At the end of the process the fully structured progeny phages, made of DNA and protein coat, would explode the bacteria and be released into the environment.

Luria found a mutant phage which would 'infect' its suitable bacterial host, but would not multiply in it. One day the tube of the bacterial cultures of *E. coli*, which Luria wanted to use to explore this phenomenon of 'non-productive' infection, broke and the culture was lost. 'I have never been a neat laboratory worker, and this time the breakage proved to be a lucky break', Luria remembers.[12] His colleague Gio Bertani gave Luria a culture of related bacteria *(Shigella)*. To Luria's surprise, when this culture was infected with his mutant phage, it produced a rich yield of phages that were not able to infect the original host cells (*E. coli*). Luria discovered the phenomenon of *restriction* and *modification*. As it later turned out, the restriction meant that the DNA of the mutant phage, upon entering the host bacterium, was broken up into pieces by bacterial enzymes and so could not be used for the replication and assembly of new phages: 'The *E. coli* bacteria restricted the modified phage.'[13] On the other hand, in *Shigella* the enzymes would not recognize the suitable breaking points in the phage DNA and the host would permit the DNA to replicate.

This phenomenon of restriction may be compared to the use of credit cards for obtaining cash from automated machines in banks. When the proper code is used, the machine disburses the required sum, but when the wrong code is punched, the card is rejected and no money is produced (in the case of bacteria the wrongly coded 'modified' DNA is cut up into pieces).

Since then over 700 'restriction enzymes' have been isolated from bacteria, yeast and fungi and have become the main tool of the recombinant DNA technology and the bio-technological revolution.

Luria sums it up: 'My finding was completely serendipitous. I was trying to explain a minor observation and the answer proved to be totally unexpected, not reasoned out in advance.'[14]

It is worth while relating the story of a missed opportunity concerning recombinant DNA.

In September 1969 Professor Waclaw Szybalski (of the McArdle Laboratory for Cancer Research at the University of Wisconsin), an expert on the lambda phage and its genetics, attended a seminar given by Vittorio Sgaramella (a post-doctoral fellow in H. G. Khorana's laboratory in Madison) where the latter described his discovery that T1 phage ligase can join two blunt ends of DNA. At that time ligase was known as an enzyme that was able to join two pieces of double stranded DNA.[15]

This information at the seminar stimulated Szybalski's imagination to write a letter to Sgaramella in which he suggested using this new blunt-end ligase in an experiment with lambda phage in order to produce 'deletion mutants'. At that time Szybalski had a collection of asymetrically broken lambda DNA molecules, the breaks producing short and long arms (see figure 4) which could be separated by suitable manipulation. If, instead of rejoining the short and long arms together to recover the original fragment of DNA, the connection (or ligation) was made between the two short arms, one from the 'left' and the other from the 'right' side of the respective breaks, a new DNA molecule would be obtained lacking the 'long arm' piece in the centre, or in the language of molecular biology, an artificial 'deletion mutant'. Szybalski's suggestion to Sgaramella was to produce these short-arm pieces of DNA and to join them by the new ligase. Such a deletion mutant, if able to multiply in bacteria, could be produced in sufficient amounts to be used in another experiment in which a piece of similarly cut DNA with blunt ends, perhaps from another species, could be inserted instead of the deleted part, with the help of the new ligase. Szybalski wrote: 'Such an experiment would permit us to put any piece of DNA into the central region of lambda. Wouldn't that be exciting! It would permit to purify human genes and produce their DNA in quantity.'[16]

At the time Szybalski wrote this letter, Khorana was in the process of moving to the Massachusetts Institute of Technology. When Sgaramella consulted Khorana about Szybalski's proposal, he was told first to finish the research he was then doing before moving. Sgaramella therefore excused himself from collaborating, and, since his findings about the ligase had not yet been published, he was not able to provide Szybalski with his enzyme. Thus nothing came of Szybalski's proposal.

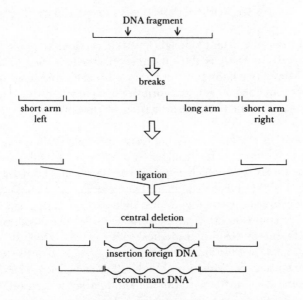

Figure 4　The experiment proposed by W. Szybalski
A DNA fragment of lambda phage is asymetrically cut by a restriction enzyme; the short, left and right, ends are separated, ligated and then a foreign DNA fragment (gene) is inserted in the deleted part to form 're-combinant' DNA.

The irony of the case was that another post-doctoral fellow in Khorana's laboratory, Hans vande Sande, independently and simultaneously also discovered a blunt-ended ligase and reported it in another seminar (which Szybalski did not attend). Had Szybalski contacted vande Sande then, the story might have finished differently. Several years later, when Szybalski visited vande Sande (at that time professor in Calgary, Canada), he found what he had missed in 1968. Vande Sande said that he. would certainly have joined Szybalski in his proposal to construct a recombinant DNA. In January 1986 vande Sande wrote to Szybalski: 'I read with interest your note to Vittorio dated September 1969. I must have presented a seminar very early after that and it certainly is a pity that we missed the opportunity in front of us then.'[17]

The forgotten transformation

There were two important, though mostly forgotten, stepping stones to the discovery that DNA is the substance of heredity. One of these was Friedrich Miescher's finding in 1869 that cell nuclei contained nuclein, a finding that remained a chemical curiosity for many decades. The second discovery was that of the transformation of pneumococci by Frederick Griffith.

Pneumococcus is a bacterium that causes pneumonia in humans and is very pathogenic to mice. Its virulence is conditioned by the presence of a polysaccharide capsule which protects the bacterium from the defence mechanisms of the infected animal. The colonies of pneumococci with such capsules have a glistening appearance and are called 'smooth' (S). Mutants of pneumococci that have lost the capsule are called 'rough' (R).

In 1928 Frederick Griffith, a Medical Officer in the Ministry of Health in England, published his discovery that infecting mice with the R mutants of one serological type, which would not kill mice by themselves, became lethal to them when mixed with the *heat-killed* pathogenic strain (S) of the same or a different type of these bacteria.[18] He coined the expression that the R bacteria were *transformed* by the dead S ones. He thought that 'the attenuated organism actually makes use of the products of the dead culture for the synthesis of their S antigen.' A few years later Alloway showed that transformation could be achieved even by cell-free extracts made of these dead bacteria. Dawson and Sia[19] also found the conditions for transformation of pneumococci *in vitro*. In the decade that followed Griffith's discovery a number of researchers at the Rockefeller Institute in New York unsuccessfully tried to shed more light on pneumococcal transformation.

It was not until 1944 that a team of scientists from the same Institute, Oswald T. Avery, Colin MacLeod and Maclyn McCarthy, described an experiment in the *Journal of Experimental Medicine*,[20] showing that desoxyribonucleate (DNA) was the substance that changed the genetic properties of a rough strain by endowing it with the ability to produce an S capsular material.

Avery began his experiments in autumn 1940, trying to fractionate the extract of the heat-killed pneumococci in order to isolate the transforming principle and to determine its chemical nature. In 1943 he wrote to his brother: 'For the past two years I have been trying to find out what is the chemical nature of the substance in the bacterial extract which induced the specific change.'[21] The fractionation involved growing pneumococci of S, type III, killing them by heating them at 65°C and lysing them with bile salts, and their extraction with chloroform and amyl alcohol. Such extracts retained the transforming capacity, but they still contained polysaccharides. In 1941 McCarthy used an enzyme recently discovered by Dubos to break down the polysaccharide, and in 1942 it became clear that the transforming principle was DNA. In the crucial experiment it was shown that breaking down the DNA by an enzyme, DNAse, abolished the transformation. In another letter to his brother Avery wrote in 1943: 'Sounds like a virus — maybe a gene'[22] and he says in the 1944 paper:

> If it is ultimately proved beyond reasonable doubt that the transforming activity of the material described is actually an inherent property of the nucleic acid, one must still account on a chemical basis for the biological specificity of its action.[23] These changes are predictable, type specific and heritable.[24]

Avery's luck in finding DNA as a transforming principle and equating it with a gene lay in the coincidence that pneumococci were the only suitable material at that time for such manipulation. No other bacterium was transformed for the next thirty years.

It took another eight years for the conclusion of Avery's group that DNA was the genetic material to be accepted. This happened when Alfred Hershey and Martha Chase[25] showed that during an infection of bacteria by bacteriophage only the bacteriophage DNA entered the host, leaving the protein coat outside, and that this was sufficient for the production of hundreds of identical complete bacteriophages. Then Watson and Crick proposed the revolutionary model of DNA.[26]

The finding of bacterial transformation and DNA's role in it led to the idea that the transfer of genetic properties should also be possible in mammalian cells. It was no simple matter. In bacterial cells the DNA is naked in the cytoplasm and readily accessible to any other DNA penetrating the bacterium. In the mammalian cells, on the other hand, the DNA is organized into chromosomes in the nucleus. Thus the entry of DNA into a mammalian cytoplasm is only the first step, which has to be followed by penetration of the nucleus before transformation can occur. In addition, mammalian cells are diploid and so even when the foreign DNA is integrated into one of the DNA strands, it will not be expressed as a phenotypic property unless it is dominant.

Early studies on mammalian transformation led to the determination that DNA is in fact adsorbed on to these cells. This was established by the use of radioactive DNA. The next series of steps required the optimization of conditions and in this way substances such as spermine and DEAE-dextran were found to be beneficial. Biochemical, but not genetic, evidence accumulated that intact DNA could be integrated into murine cells. The first genetic experiments were not done until the sixties. When intact DNA from cells resistant to a drug azaguanine was added to azaguanine-sensitive cells, it induced in them resistance at a rate of 213 per million cells, but since in the controls with degraded DNA, resistance appeared at a rate of 100 per million, the evidence was only quantitative and not really convincing.[27] Similar experiments with a property involving the enzyme inosinic acid phosphorylase showed that D98/AH-2 cells lacking this enzyme could be transformed by DNA from normal cells (D98/AG) at a frequency of 1/10,000. In this study DNAse-treated DNA did not induce early transformation.[28]

However, a more unequivocal experiment was needed to demonstrate that a totally new property could be introduced into cells by adding to them a foreign DNA from a cell that had that property. Indeed, in 1961 L. M. Kraus[29] showed that human bone-marrow cells producing only haemoglobin S (sickle-cell anaemia trait) would synthesize normal A chains of haemoglobin, when exposed for ten days to DNA from bone-marrow cells that were making haemoglobin A. Unfortunately, in this experiment the important control – of DNAse treatment – was omitted and thus the matter remained unresolved.

The first unequivocal demonstration of transformation was carried out by Elena Ottolenghi-Nightingale in 1969. She extracted DNA from tissues of C57 black mice and mixed it with skin cells of albino mice embryos. The pigment in black mice (melanin) is produced by melanoblast cells and is genetically coded. These albino cells were then implanted in the neck of young albino mice. After two weeks their melanoblasts synthesized melanin, indicating that transformation had indeed occurred. DNAse completely prevented this transformation.[30] Thus Ottolenghi found incontrovertible qualitative evidence of transformation: DNA extracted from differentiated cells would endow embryonal cells of the same species with the new property carried genetically by the DNA.

This first demonstration went unnoticed, probably because Ottolenghi did not use the words 'genetic' or 'transformation' in her paper.[31] The title 'Induction of melanin synthesis in albino mouse skin by DNA from pigmented mice' did not indicate its true genetic meaning. Since Ottolenghi then married and had a family, she did not have the opportunity to follow up her 1969 paper, and thus missed the opportunity of being recognized as a first discoverer. In the next two years, however, several other well-designed experiments in this field were carried out and later, in any case, the recombinant DNA technology rendered that type of experiment obsolete.

It would be interesting to follow the tortuous path that led to the discovery of the structure of DNA by Watson and Crick. This is amply described in Watson's own book *The Double Helix*, as well as in many reviews (at least fifteen) of it and in another book edited by Gunther S. Stent.[32] Jerry Donohue, who was in the Cambridge laboratory at the time of the discovery, reviewed Stent's book,[33] indicating that several myths still existed about the discovery, such as the myth of the invention of base pairing, generally attributed to Chargaff, the myth of the competition with Pauling, the 'spying' on him by Pauling's son Peter (who was at that time in Cambridge) and the myth of data filched from Rosalind Franklin. A rather original description of the discovery was published by J. Field in the *Journal of Irreproducible Results* in 1968.

> Hear the song of how the spiral
> Complex, twisted, double chiral
> Was discovered. Its construction
> Following some shrewd deduction
> Was accomplished. From all sides 'Oh
> Tell it as it was' they cried so
> Then he took his pen and paper
> And composed the helix caper
> Writing out the Cambridge popsy
> Turned the word of science topsy
> Turvy like had not before been
> Done. The story is no more than
> How the structure was discovered
> Secret of the gene uncovered
> Biological prediction
> Better than a work of fiction
> Stylistically breezy
> Everything appeared made easy
> And it was. The base's pairing
> Found at last — a small red herring
> Notwithstanding. How he found them
> And the hydrogens that bound them
> Was a stroke more accidental
> Than a work experimental

Chemistry was not his calling
He had read *one* book by Pauling
Models of the bases he'd made
With them on his desk top he'd played
Shuffling them and putting like with
Like he made no lucky strike with
Guanine, thymine, adenine. A
letter came from Pasadena
Horrors! then the day was won for
Pauling's model was quite done for
Extra atoms he had set in
Where no atoms should be let in
With some phrases less than modest
Pauling's model called the oddest
Back now to the basic pairing
How's the structure building fairing?
Faster, faster goes the race, then
Everything falls into place when
Tautomers which nature chooses
Are the ones our author uses
Two chains (but here we can't be sure)
Plus this extra structure feature:
Pauling's outside bases inside
Pauling's inside phosphates outside
Now they all were quite ecstatic
Soon became they quite dogmatic
Having nature's secret later
Checked against the X-ray data
This was difficult, for Rosie
Found our scientist rather nosey
Bragg compares the book with Pepys.Is
This the verdict of Maurice? His
Thoughts alas we cannot gainsay
Trumpet blowing's not his forte
Tales like this do have a moral
Whether printed whether oral
Find the right man to advise you
Then you'll get a Nobel prize too.[34]

Hydrogen bromide and the genetic code

An unexpected recollection which helped in an important discovery has been described by Michael Sela of the Weizmann Institute. In his personal memories on molecular immunology he wrote:

. . . shortly after my arrival at NIH in 1960, Marshal Nirenberg came and asked me whether I had some poly-L-phenylalanine and whether I knew its solubility properties. I did not have the polymer in Bethesda, but I did ask Nirenberg why he was interested. Through these conversations I became one of the first to know about the breaking of the genetic code, UUU leading to Phe [Phenylalanine]. While I was somewhat sceptical of the story, I immediately looked and found, hidden somewhere in an experimental section of a paper in the *Journal of the American Chemical Society*, that poly-L-phenylalanine was insoluble in all the solvents he had tested, with the exception of a saturated solution of anhydrous hydrogen bromide in glacial acetic acid. Since on that very day I was preparing just such a solution in the lab, I gladly gave the reagent to Nirenberg and was touched and surprised when he acknowledged this in the classical paper that resulted in his receiving the Nobel Prize. But the real point of the story lies elsewhere: Why did we try to use such a peculiar solvent [in the first place]? The truth of the matter is that years earlier, together with the late Arieh Berger in Rehovot, we were investigating the mechanism of polymerization leading to linear and multichain polyamino acids. One day I had two test tubes – one with polyphenylalanine and one with polycarbobenzoxylysine – stuck in an ashtray on my desk. Arie [entered the lab in order] to decarbobenzoxylate the lysine polymer, a reaction with hydrogen bromide in glacial acetic acid during which carbon dioxide is released. He took the wrong test tube away with him and then returned, puzzled because the material had dissolved and he could not see any carbon dioxide evolution. At once we realized the mistake, and I noted in my lab book that, at long last, we had found a solvent for poly-L-phenylalanine[35]

A mistaken tube helps to find a solvent for a material that many years later became a corner stone of the crucial experiment to break the genetic code.

Polymorphism: Australia antigen and hepatitis

Hepatitis B, or serum hepatitis, is still a widely spread infectious viral disease, caused by a minute DNA virus, transmitted mostly by blood and blood products. Up to about twenty-five years ago nothing was really known about the aetiology of this disease, except the suspicion that it was caused by a virus. The chance discovery, that led to the identification of the virus as a causative agent of hepatitis was made in 1966 by Baruch Blumberg at the Institute of Cancer Research in Philadelphia.

The story begins with Dr Anthony C. Allison from Oxford who came to Blumberg's laboratory at the National Institute of Health in the summer of 1960. The common project was to study sera in patients who had received many transfusions for the presence of antibodies against poly-morphic serum proteins. In fact, in the serum of one of the patients studied, there appeared a precipitin band in gel (by the so-called Ouchter-lony technique) against a lipoprotein, which they called 'Ag system'. Later, in 1963, in the serum of one out of twenty-four haemophilic patients Blumberg observed a similar precipitin reaction with proteins present in the serum of an Australian Aborigine. He called the antigen in the Aborigine's serum 'Australia antigen' or *Au* for short. In his Nobel Prize lecture in 1976 Blumberg said:

> In preparing this 'history' of the discovery of Au, I constructed an outline based on a hypothetico-deductive structure, showing the actual events which led to the discovery of the association of Au with hepatitis. From this it is clear that I could not have planned the investigation at its beginning to find the cause of hepatitis B. This experience does not encourage an approach to basic research which is based exclusively on specific-goal-directed programs for the solution of biological problems.[36]

Blumberg continued to test human sera for the presence of the *Au* antigen. He found it was quite high in transfused leukaemia patients, and this led him to hypothesize that people with *Au* are prone to develop leukaemia, i.e. that *Au* predisposed people to become 'infected' with a leukaemia agent.

In 1964 Blumberg moved to the Institute for Cancer Research in Philadelphia where he continued his studies on the *Au* antigen. Sur-prisingly it was quite frequent in children suffering from Down's syndrome (mongolism) (about 30 per cent). In 1966 one of these children, James Bair, who was *Au*-negative, was found to be positive on a second test, and liver tests indicated that he had developed chronic hepatitis. On the patient's chart, Blumberg's associate Dr Alton I. Sutnik, wrote: 'SGOT slightly elevated! Prothrombin time low! We may have an indication of his conversion to *Au*+.'

Thus at this stage the correlation between the *Au* antigen and hepatitis was suspected and later confirmed by additional tests. In April 1967, Miss Barbara Werner, a technician in Blumberg's laboratory, was working on the isolation of *Au* antigen from blood. She did not feel well and, testing her own serum, found *Au* antigen in it; she soon developed icteric hepatitis, from which she eventually recovered. This, then, was the first case of hepatitis diagnosed by the Au test. Blumberg and his four associates wrote as follows:

Most of the disease associations could be explained by the association of Au(1) with a virus . . . The discovery of the frequent occurrence of Au(1) in patients with virus hepatitis raises the possibility that the agent present in some cases of this disease may be Australia antigen or be responsible for its presence. The presence of Australia antigen in the thalassemia or hemophilia patients could be due to virus introduced by transfusion.[37]

Soon, Professor Kazuo Okochi from Tokyo, who was also independently involved in a study of anti-Ag (lipoprotein), found that its precipitation was associated with hepatitis and liver damage. When compared, Blumberg's *Au* and Okochi's *Ag* turned out to be identical and it was agreed that transfusions were involved in the transmission of this antigen. Once this was established, all blood containing *Au* antigen was excluded from transfusion services and the incidence of post-transfusion hepatitis dropped from 18 to 6 per cent.

Thus the search for polymorphisms in human sera led, via the chance discovery of the Australia antigen, to the identification of the virus of hepatitis. Later it was shown that the *Au* antigen was the surface (HB(s)) antigen of the virus that was present in abundance in the blood of hepatitis patients.

NOTES TO CHAPTER 4

1 Dubos, R. *Pasteur and Modern Science*. New York: Anchor Books, Doubleday and Company: 26–7.
2 Ibid.: 28.
3 Ibid.: 131.
4 Nicolle, C. J. H. 1932: *Biologie de l'invention*. Paris: Alcan.
5 Slaughter, F. G. 1950: *Immortal Magyar. Semmelweiss, Conqueror of Childbed Fever*. New York: H. Schuman.
6 Semmelweiss, I. 1861: On the etiology, the concept and prophylaxis of puerperal fever. Translated from German in H. Thom: *Selected Topics in Obstetrics and Gynecology*. Springfield, Ill.: C. C. Thomas: 186.
7 Sinclair, W. J. 1909: *Semmelweiss, His Life and Doctrine*. Manchester: Manchester University Press.
8 Semmelweiss, On the etiology, the concept and prophylaxis of puerperal fever: 187.
9 Luria, S. E. 1985: *A Slot Machine – A Broken Test Tube*. New York: Harper and Row (Colophon edn): 75.
10 Ibid.: 76.

74   *Chance and Disappointment in Microbiology*

11 Ibid.: 77–8.
12 Ibid.: 99.
13 Ibid.: 99.
14 Ibid.: 100.
15 Rodriguez, L. and Tait, R. C. (eds) 1983: *Recombinant Techniques: An Introduction.* London: Addison Wesley: XIV.
16 Letter from W. Szybalski to Sgaramella, 2 Sept. 1969.
17 Letter from vande Sande to Szybalski, 28 Jan. 1986.
18 Griffith, F. 1929: The significance of pneumococcal types. *Journal of Hygiene,* 27: 113.
19 Dawson, M. H. and Sia, R. H. P. 1931: In vitro transformation of pneumococcal types. *Journal of Experimental Medicine,* 54: 681.
20 Avery, O. T., MacLeod, C. M. and McCarthy, M. 1944: Studies on the chemical nature of the substance inducing transformation of pneumococcal types. Induction by a desoxyribonucleic acid fraction isolated from Pneumococcus type III. *Journal of Experimental Medicine,* 79: 139.
21 McCarthy, M. 1980: Reminiscences of the early days of transformation. *Annual Review of Genetics,* 14: 1.
22 Ibid.: 14.
23 Avery *et al.* Studies on the chemical nature . . .: 153.
24 Ibid.: 154.
25 Hershey, A. D. and Chase, M. 1952: Independent functions of viral proteins and nucleic acids in growth of bacteriophage. *Journal of General Physiology,* 36: 39.
26 Watson, J. D. and Crick, F. 1953: A structure of deoxyribonucleic acid. *Nature,* 171: 737.
27 Ottolenghi-Nightingale, E. 1974: DNA mediated transformation in mammalian cells. In P. Cox (ed.), *Cell Communications.* New York: John Wiley & Sons: 233.
28 Szybalska, E. and Szybalski, W. 1962: Genesis of human cell lines. IV. DNA mediated heritable transformation of a biochemical trait. *Proceedings of the National Academy of Science,* USA, 48: 2026.
29 Kraus, L. M. 1961: Formation of different hemoglobins in bone cultures of human bone marrow treated with human deoxyribonucleic acid. *Nature,* 192: 1055.
30 Ottolenghi-Nightingale, DNA mediated transformation: 245.
31 Ottolenghi, E. 1969: Induction of melanin synthesis in albino mouse skin by DNA from pigmented mice. *Proceedings of the National Academy of Science,* USA, 64: 184.

32 Stent, G. S. 1981: *The Double Helix*. Commentary, Reviews, Original Papers. London: Weidenfeld and Nicolson.
33 Donohue, J. 1981: Old twists to an old tale. *Nature*, 290: 648.
34 Field, J. 1968: Book review. *Journal of Irreproducible Results*, 17/1: 53.
35 Sela, M. 1987: A peripathetic and personal view of molecular immunology for one third of the century. *Annual Review of Immunology*, 5: 4.
36 Blumberg, B. 1977: Australia antigen and the biology of Hepatitis B. in *Les Prix Nobel en 1976*. Stockholm: Imprimeries Royales, P. A. Norstedt: 139.
37 Blumberg, B., Gerstley, B. J. S., Hungerford, D. A., London, W. T. and Sutnick, A. I. A serum antigen (Australia antigen) in Down's syndrome leukemia and hepatitis. *Annals of Internal Medicine*, 66: 924.

5

The Discovery of Penicillin: Design or Chance?

As with many other important discoveries, the road to penicillin was a story of frustration, insight, discovery and triumph and the hero of the story, as everyone knows, was Sir Alexander Fleming. Or was he?

His name certainly became a household word, but perhaps the case was not as clear as the layman may imagine.

Fleming was born in Lochfield, Ayrshire in Scotland, in 1881, one of four children of his father's second marriage. At the age of thirteen he was sent to London, where he lived with his three brothers and his sister, working for a while in a shipping company. When the Boer War broke out in 1900 he enlisted in the London Scottish regiment, but was not sent overseas. He practised shooting and even won a competition to bring honour to his own company. Army service did not prevent him from successfully passing the examinations necessary for admission to medical school. Fleming had a choice of twelve medical schools in London, but he chose St Mary's because he liked swimming and there was a water-polo team at that hospital. He excelled as a student because of his fantastic memory and powers of observation, and because he was good at sport. Fleming completed his studies in 1905, receiving the title of Member of the Royal College of Surgeons, and in 1908 took his final medical examination, winning the Gold Medal at the University of London. In spite of these achievements, Fleming did not want to become a surgeon because he disliked operating on living bodies. So instead, he was persuaded to join the Inoculation Service at St Mary's Hospital, directed by Almroth Wright. Wright accepted Fleming because he was recommended to him as a good shot. So instead of going into surgery, Fleming landed in a bacteriological laboratory.

Many years later Fleming said: 'Had I not taken an interest in swimming in my young days, I should probably not have gone to St Mary's hospital. I should not have had Almroth Wright as a teacher, and it is more than likely that I should never have become a bacteriologist.'[1]

From 1902 Almroth Wright was the most brilliant member of the teaching staff at St Mary's. He was a physician and a bacteriologist and he created the hospital's Inoculation Service. He was well known even outside medical circles because, thanks to an outstanding classical education and his gift of rhetoric and paradoxical eloquence, he was able to fascinate his interlocutors. He knew by heart parts of the Bible, Milton, Dante, Goethe, Browning and Kipling. He had a wealthy practice at 6 Park Crescent, popular with members of the British aristocracy and plutocracy. He used the income from his practice to finance the operation of the hospital laboratory which he directed in the spirit of enlightened despotism. This description is important in order to understand the pressures and the atmosphere in the laboratory which later affected Fleming.

Fleming's initial encounter with Wright was not encouraging. Wright was convinced that the only means of defeating an infection was immunization, which was achieved by having a disease, by vaccination or by the use of immune serum. He firmly believed that the doctors of the future would treat their patients by immunization. He disliked those who did not support this view, and no member of the laboratory would dare to argue with this concept.

Wright's interest in immunization led him to discover 'opsonization'. He found that bacteria treated with immune serum directed specifically against them, but not against any other bacteria, would facilitate the swallowing and the destruction of the 'opsonized' bacteria by white blood cells. ('Opsonized' means 'prepared for eating'.) Recovery from any bacterial infection had to be due to some sort of opsonization, which could even be quantitatively determined, by counting the average number of bacteria swallowed by the white blood cells in the presence or absence of immune serum.

So when Fleming discovered lysozyme,[2] an enzyme present in tears and the nasal mucus, and hoped to use it as a curative agent, he encountered opposition from Wright, who did not believe in any sort of chemotherapy. Henry Dale described this situation in his obituary of Fleming:

> Those of us who belong to the community of medical research are apt to find more interest in what has seemed something of a puzzle — in the fact that Fleming, having discovered penicillin, having recognized its special properties as an antibacterial agent harmless to leucocytes, and having, apparently, made a tentative observation on the application of crude medium containing it as an external antiseptic, left the discovery there and took more interest in the value of penicillin as a selective constituent of a culture medium than as potentially an internal antiseptic.

I think that the main clue, at least, is to be found in the fact that neither the time when the discovery was made, nor perhaps, the scientific atmosphere of the laboratory in which he worked, was propitious to such further enterprise as its development would have needed. Repeated failure had caused opinion then to harden, almost into a steeled conviction against the possibility of a successful chemotherapy of the common bacterial infections. Sir Almroth Wright himself had no belief in such a possibility. Even when some years later the introduction of sulphanilamide and its derivatives had removed grounds for such scepticism, Wright, as Dr. Leonard Colebrook tells in his biography, was not impressed by the tremendous change which their coming has produced . . .[3]

Fleming turned out to be a very skilled technician, to the extent that his colleagues considered his experiments a work of art. Fleming had artistic inclinations, he drew very well, and he invented a technique of painting with bacteria. Colonies of various strains of bacteria develop vivid colours: *Serratia* (also called at that time *Bacterium prodigiosum*) produced a vivid red colour, *B. violaceus* (violet), *Staphylococcus aureus* (golden orange), etc. Fleming would amuse himself and his friends by drawing a pattern on nutrient agar with an inoculation needle dipped in suspensions of suitable bacterial-broth cultures. After incubation for a day or so, the bacteria grew to colonies visible to the naked eye on the surface of the agar, each line or area made up of colonies bearing the characteristic colour.

Wright once said to Fleming: 'You treat research like a game: you find it all great fun.' And although Fleming was in appearance a serious, reticent person, he liked practical jokes and appreciated humour. He was described as quiet, devoted, rather dour, but friendly. 'Fleming liked being with people, working with them, playing with them, but not talking to them.'[4] Wright said of him that he was 'oligophasic' (Greek for 'little-speaking'). Dale said that his contribution to any discussion in the laboratory was usually in the form of Scottish grunts and terse interjections. 'One of the strong points of Fleming was that though taciturn, he excelled in clarity of written exposition which shone in his reports and papers. He never showed anger or raised his voice. He had the essential humility of the true scientist and never lost it.'[5]

Wright's beliefs about opsonization and auto-inoculation (the injection of bacteria isolated from a patient into the same patient, after the bacteria had been killed by heat or chemicals) affected the work of his staff. The final thesis of Fleming's medical studies was entitled 'Acute Bacterial Infections'. In it he presented an outline of possible treatments of patients, such as surgery, antiseptics, immunization, or increasing the patient's resistance by sera and vaccines. He made an important observation, resulting from experiments on himself, that vaccination with dead bacteria was useless when given intravenously.

It is a surprising fact that in 1909, when Paul Ehrlich invented the compound 606, salvarsan, to treat trypanosomal infections and syphilis, Fleming was the first to use it successfully in England, even though Wright at that time, speaking at the Medical Research Club, said: 'The use of chemotherapy for the treatment of bacterial infections in human beings will never be possible.'

At the beginning of World War 1, when Wright went to France as a colonel to establish a diagnostic and research laboratory there, he took Fleming with him with the rank of lieutenant. Wright was responsible for vaccination of the army against typhoid, which at that time was a most serious and lethal disease. Fleming was very worried about gas gangrene developing in lacerated wounds in the soldiers at the front. He found that their wounds healed better when, rather than being treated with antiseptics, they were first surgically excised to remove necrotic tissue. He noted that, once the wounds were surgically cleaned, the white blood cells and blood exudate had better access to the wounds to eliminate the infecting bacteria. In 1919 he wrote:

> It is very difficult for the surgeon not to be deluded into the belief that he has in the antiseptic, a second string to his bow, and, consequently, it will tend to make him less careful in his surgical treatment of the wound . . .
>
> All the great successes of primary wound treatment have been due to efficient surgery and it seems a pity that the surgeon should wish to share his glory with a chemical antiseptic of more than doubtful utility.[6]

While Fleming was in No. 8 hospital at Wimereux in 1918, dealing with lacerated fractured femurs, he wrote:

> Surrounded by all those infected wounds by men who were suffering and dying without our being able to do anything to help them, I was consumed by the desire to discover, after all this struggling and waiting, something which would kill these microbes, something like salvarsan . . .[7]
>
> What we are looking for is some chemical substance which can be injected without danger into the blood stream for the purpose of destroying the bacilli of infection . . .[8]

At the end of the war Fleming returned to the routine of the St Mary's laboratory and in 1921 he became the Assistant Director of the Department, with his own small laboratory overlooking the Fountain Abbey pub. In 1922 he made his first discovery. Observing that bacterial colonies, growing on agar plates to which he added a drop of his nasal mucus (he had a cold), became translucent and glassy, he realized that the mucus contained some anti-bacterial substance. He then inoculated neighbouring colonies that were not affected into nutrient broth until they grew into a turbid suspension. When he now added nasal mucus to the tubes, the broth cleared and became 'clear as gin'. The lucky chance in this case was that the bacterium that lysed upon the addition of nasal mucus or tears was *Micrococcus lysodeikticus*, one of the few bacteria that can in fact be lysed by the active material that Fleming named lysozyme (a lysing enzyme). In the next few weeks there was a lot of crying in the laboratory because Fleming made all his colleagues, technicians and visitors weep by putting lemon drops into their eyes (the technicians were paid 3*d.* for each batch of tears). In the ensuing experiments Fleming found that active lysozyme did not harm the white blood cells, that it was present not only in mucus and in tears, but also in the sperm of all animals, in woman's milk and even in the leaves of tulips, buttercups and peonies. The richest source of lysozyme, however, was egg-white. Unfortunately it was quite obvious that egg-white could not be injected into the blood stream. Soon it was also found that, with the exception of diphtheria and meningococci, lysozyme was helpless against other pathogenic micro-organisms. It should be stressed perhaps at this point that though Fleming's finding of lysozyme was a major discovery, he referred to it as 'my observation'.

One would have liked to think that the discovery of lysozyme would evoke some interest and excitement in medical circles. However, though Fleming published five papers on lysozyme between 1922 and 1927, he was met with indifference. Lysozyme nevertheless not only prepared the way for Fleming's discovery of penicillin, but later was the key that led Chain to penicillin. By 1950 some 2,000 papers had been published about lysozyme.

Fleming discovered penicillin in 1928. He was writing a chapter on staphylococci for *System in Bacteriology*, to be published by the Medical Research Council, for which he was studying staphylococcus variants growing on Petri dishes. He was about to leave for a vacation at the end of July 1928, so he left a stack of inoculated plates on the end of a bench. He returned to the laboratory at the end of August.

Fleming described the discovery as follows:

> While working with staphylococcus variants a number of culture-plates were set aside on the laboratory bench and examined from time to time. In

the examinations these plates were necessarily exposed to the air and they became contaminated with various micro-organisms. It was noticed that around a large colony of contaminating mould the staphylococcus colonies became transparent and were obviously undergoing lysis [see figure 5]. Subcultures of this mould were made and experiments conducted with a view to ascertaining something of the properties of the bacteriolytic substance which had evidently been formed in the mould culture and which had diffused into the surrounding medium. It was found that broth in which the mould had been grown at room temperature for one or two weeks had acquired marked inhibitory, bactericidal and bacteriolytic properties to many of the more common pathogenic bacteria.[9]

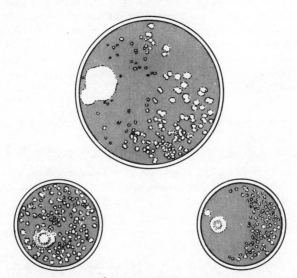

Figure 5   Comparison of Fleming's and Hare's experiments with *Penicillium* and staphylococci

Top: Fleming's photograph of his original penicillin plate. The area around the mould colony (large white blob on the left) is free of the scattered group of small staphylococcus colonies (on the right).

Bottom left: When *Penicillium* is grown after the formation of staphylococcal colonies, they are not inhibited or destroyed.

Bottom right: When the mould and the staphylococci are seeded together, but the agar plates are incubated at low temperatures (below 20°C) the mould grows into a colony. When the plate is then incubated at 37°C, staphylococci that start dividing at a rapid pace are inhibited by penicillin which had in the meantime diffused into the agar.

Source: R. Hare (1970): *The Birth of Penicillin and the Disarming of Microbes.* London: Allen and Unwin Ltd.: 74; Fleming photograph in A. Maurois (1959): *The Life of Sir Alexander Fleming.* London: Jonathan Cape: 192.

(Note the use of 'it was noticed, it was found', rather than 'I noticed, I found'.)

In Fleming's obituary in 1955, Robert Cruickshank quoted Fleming as having said:

> A mould spore, coming from I don't know where, dropped on the plate that did not excite me. I had often seen such contamination before. But what I had never seen before was staphylococci undergoing lysis around the contaminating colony. Obviously something extraordinary was happening. With the background that I had, this was far more interesting to me than staphylococcal research, so I switched promptly. I am now glad that for years my interest had been directed to antiseptics and that some years before, I had found in a somewhat similar manner another naturally occurring antiseptic, lysozyme. But for the previous experience it is likely that I should have thrown the plate away as many bacteriologists must have done before me. . . . Instead of casting out the contaminated culture with some appropriate language, I made some investigations.[10]

H. T. Herrick, writing in 1949, described the discovery thus:

> Fleming . . . was using a culture of the pathogenic organism *Staphylococcus aureus* in some of his studies, when a stray, an airborne spore of a mould, fell into the open Petri dish which contained this culture. Several days later, when Dr. Fleming had occasion to return to the dish, he noticed a remarkable phenomenon. A mould was growing *in the middle* of the Staphylococcus cuture and, as a result, the colonies of bacteria were gradually disappearing.[11]

In 1946, in a book on the history of penicillin, Fleming said: 'The name "penicillin" was given by me in 1929 to an antibacterial substance produced by a mould of the genus *Penicillium*.'[12] He described the sequence of events and then wrote: 'This was an extraordinary and unexpected appearance and seemed to demand an investigation.'

In the biography of Ernest Chain, written in 1985 by Clark, Chain is quoted as having said:

> Most of you are familiar with the story, innumerable times repeated of the stroke of good luck which Fleming experienced and exploited, which consisted of the fact that a spore of a rather rare mould *Penicillium notatum* had accidentally floated through his laboratory window [please note that the window in Fleming's lab could not be opened at all!] and settled on his Petri dish to produce the phenomenon which led to the discovery of penicillin.[13]

What was the good luck that Chain referred to? It consisted in the extraordinary chain of circumstances. *Penicillium* contaminant must have had time to grow, it needed a suitable (room) temperature to reach a suitable size, and at the same time the staphylococcus colony had to be quite young to be affected. The lucky coincidence was that at room temperature the mould grew well, while the growth of staphylococci was delayed.

Nevertheless Chain said elsewhere: . . . 'It is petty and irrelevant to try to detract from the importance of Fleming's discovery by ascribing it entirely to good luck.'[14]

It is noteworthy that in his original publication Fleming never mentioned luck or chance, though in later years he admitted the role of luck in the discovery. Twenty years after the discovery – in October 1951 – Fleming was elected by the students of Edinburgh University as their rector. The post was honorary and did not involve residence: rectors of this type were chosen as a symbol of recognition and admiration for eminent men. One of the duties of the elected rector was to deliver a rectorial address. In it Fleming spoke of success in discovery. He mentioned that Pasteur's success was due to hard work, careful observation, clear thinking, enthusiasm and a spot of luck. 'Plenty of people work hard and some of them make careful observations, but without the clear thinking which puts these observations in proper perspective, they get nowhere.'[15]

Fleming attributed his discovery to luck. It was lucky in that not only was he working in the bacteriological laboratory of Wright, but of thousands of known moulds just the one that produced penicillin settled on a plate with a culture of a sensitive bacterium. But even 'if the right mould had come in contact with the right bacteria at the wrong moment, there would have been nothing to observe. Further, if, at that precise moment, his mind had been occupied with other things he would have lost his chance . . .'[16] However, Fleming said in his speech, 'Fate ordained that everything happened right and penicillin appeared.'

So there was penicillin. What was it good for? Fleming used the mould broth, which was active even at a dilution of 1:800, for the elimination of bacteria sensitive to this drug, and as the title of his paper indicates, for the isolation of *Haemophilus influenzae* from throat swabs heavily contaminated by penicillin-sensitive cocci. This was the practical part of the discovery. He wrote: 'In addition to its possible use in the treatment of bacterial infections penicillin is certainly useful to the bacteriologist for its power of inhibiting unwanted microbes in bacterial cultures so that penicillin-insensitive bacteria can readily be isolated.'[17] Thinking of the possible therapeutic uses of penicillin, Fleming tested the penicillin broth for toxic effects. He injected 20 millilitres of mould-culture fluid into rabbits and half a millilitre into mice and noted that, even in that impure state, penicillin was not toxic. 'Penicillin was the first substance ever encountered which destroyed the bacteria without any apparent destructive action on leucocytes.'[18] He continued his research into penicillin by testing the best conditions for the growth of the mould, for its diffusibility and for lytic properties against a variety of micro-organisms. He found that pneumococci, streptococci and staphylococci were sensitive, whereas the pertussis and influenza bacilli were not. He established that penicillin could be heated to 65° C without losing potency, but would lose its active potential through prolonged storage.

Having established that penicillin was not toxic, Fleming tried it out in the form of a dressing for the treatment of a woman who had developed septicaemia after the amputation of a leg, as a result of contamination of her wound. But this did not help. In his paper Fleming wrote: 'Experiments in connection with its value in the treatment of pyogenic infection are in progress.'[19]

Fleming considered the purification and concentration of penicillin, but he was not a chemist. His two assistants, Ridley and Craddock, did some interesting work on the extraction of penicillin in various organic solvents, but it seems that Fleming was not really well acquainted with their work because he later stated, contrary to notes entered by the two assistants, that penicillin was not soluble in ether or acetone, and that it was insoluble in chloroform (which they did not try at all). Fleming did not pursue the matter.

Independently, however, the study of penicillin was taken up by Dr Harold Raistrick of the London School of Hygiene. He tried for a few years to purify and to concentrate penicillin, and became discouraged by its lack of stability during any treatment used to purify it: 'Penicillin is an extremely labile substance very readily inactivated by oxidation, evaporation in vacuo, in acid and in alkali.'[20] Even when he extracted it successfully in ether and then evaporated it, nothing remained: 'Such a thing was never known to a chemist before. It was unbelievable. We could do nothing in the face of it, so we dropped it.' However, Raistrick succeeded in devising a synthetic growth medium for the mould, made of glucose and inorganic salts and, with the help of the American mycologist Charles Thom, he identified the mould as *Penicillium notatum*.

Why did Fleming not perform a therapeutic experiment on mice with his crude penicillin preparation which he knew was not toxic? This is an intriguing question, considering the desires and beliefs he had so often expressed in the past. Surely it is one of the most staggering facts in the history of science that it was given to Fleming, the man who, helpless and compassionate among the dying soldiers of the First World War, had written 'I was consumed by the desire to discover a substance which would be injected without danger into the bloodstream . . . to destroy bacteria',[21] in fact to discover just such a substance, and that he then made no effort to propel it forward to clinical application.

There may have been several reasons for this. According to Fleming's notebooks, he was worried by the instability of penicillin, by its rapid disappearance from blood (to which it was added), and that it took rather a long time to kill off a bacterial culture. He reasoned therefore that it was not even worthwhile performing a therapeutic test of this kind upon animals.

Ernest Chain (who shared the Nobel Prize in 1945 with Fleming and Florey for the discovery) explains:

> No chemical knowledge was required for such an experiment. The reason why Fleming did not even attempt to carry out this simple experiment, is, in my opinion, that the whole atmosphere in . . . the Inoculation Department of St. Mary's was not conducive to this approach; it was, in fact, positively unsympathetic to experiments of this kind.[22]

This statement is not easy to understand in view of the reality of those times. After all, Fleming knew of the therapeutic successes of salvarsan in syphilis and of Bayer 205 in trypanosomal infection, he also knew that penicillin did not harm white blood cells, his boss's 'heroes'. But Wright's disbelief in the possible efficacy of chemotherapy must nevertheless have affected the communal thinking in his laboratory.

According to MacFarlane,[23] Fleming failed to perform therapeutic tests because he was very rational in his thinking. From his experiments he knew, first, that it took penicillin many hours to kill off bacteria, and second, that when mixed with blood or injected into the circulation, penicillin disappeared within half an hour. His conclusion therefore was that penicillin had not enough time to exert its action when injected, and so there was no sense in injecting it into an infected animal.

In this respect, Fleming's thinking was diametrically opposed to that of Florey, who used to say that if you did the experiment it was not certain that you would get an answer, but that if you did not do it, it was certain that you wouldn't get one.

Fleming successfully used penicillin as a selective agent for the isolation of Pfeiffer's bacillus *Haemophilus influenzae*, but during the decade after his discovery he never wholeheartedly thought of developing penicillin as a systemic therapeutic agent. So it was not modesty, but a lack of conviction, that kept him silent on the therapeutic possibilities of pencillin during this period. In view of Fleming's chief biographer, Robert Mac-Farlane,[24] his argument that he did not have a biochemist or the biochemical facilities to purify penicillin does not stand up to criticism. His extracts, which he himself had shown to be non-toxic on injection, were sufficiently potent to abort a lethal infection of streptococci in mice. Fleming did not really believe in penicillin during this interim period. When he gave a lecture in 1931 on the 'Intravenous Uses of Germicides'[25] he did not even mention penicillin. Among his twenty-seven papers and lectures, published during the decade after the discovery, he only once mentioned penicillin as a potential therapeutic agent.[26]

In a letter written to Lady Fleming after her husband's death, Chain again stressed his belief that

> in the Wright atmosphere of St. Mary's the mere thought of replacing immunotherapy by chemotherapy was considered absolute blasphemy. I think if this atmosphere could have been a little less despotic and people less prejudiced against the new concepts, Fleming could not have resisted the temptation to repeat his toxicity tests on infected animals with the crude culture liquid, without any chemical purification whatsoever.[27] He would — Chain continues — have observed a sufficiently dramatic curative effect.

Chain also believed that

> . . . no one in that Department, and least of all Almroth Wright would have prevented Fleming from carrying out the simple experiment of injecting crude penicillin-containing culture medium into a mouse infected with a penicillin-sensitive bacterium if he had wanted to. He did not perform it because he did not think it was worthwhile trying.[28]

Chain sums up this situation by saying it is 'a good example of how preconceived ideas in science can stifle imagination and impede progress . . . It is always dangerous when any generally accepted theories or any kind of central dogmas are taken too seriously.'[29]

Before the discovery of penicillin Fleming was a candidate for the Royal Society five times between 1922 and 1927, then again in 1930 and 1934, but he was not elected. It was not until 1943, at the age of sixty-two, that he became a Fellow of the Royal Society.

Research on penicillin languished until 1938–9, when Florey and Chain in Oxford resumed it and brought it to successful completion, as we shall see below. They succeeded in concentrating penicillin a thousandfold by acid ether extraction and rapid drying. At the end of May 1940 Professor A. D. Gardner, Miss Jean Orr-Ewing and Chain carried out a crucial animal experiment. Eight mice were infected with a lethal dose of 100 million haemolytic streptococci; four of them were then treated with five doses of 5 (or 10) micrograms of the penicillin concentrate, and four were left as controls. All the infected controls died within seventeen hours. The penicillin-treated mice survived.[30] In the next experiment, using forty-five and seventy-five mice infected with staphylococci and *Clostridium septicum* respectively, they confirmed the previous observation. These results were published in August 1940 in the *Lancet*[31] and caused a sensation. Fleming immediately went to Oxford. Chain, hearing of the visit, is supposed to have said: 'Good God! I thought he was dead.'[32] On his arrival Fleming is quoted as saying possessively: 'I have come to see what you've been doing with *my* old penicillin.'[33] Though this was not very well received, the hosts Florey and Chain shared their information about penicillin production with Fleming and gave him a sample of the purified substance to take to London.

In order to obtain sufficient quantities of penicillin for human experiments, heroic efforts were made at the Dunn School of Pathology. By unbelievable efforts the penicillin group in Oxford (seven graduates, two professors and ten assistants) managed to accumulate enough purified penicillin by January 1941 to treat a number of patients with doses of 30–50 units per milligram. First they tried the drug for toxicity in a terminal-cancer patient; there was some feverish reaction, which was attributed to pyrogens, but otherwise the penicillin was judged to be innocuous. The first real patient was Albert Alexander, a forty-three-year-old policeman who developed staphylococcal and streptococcal infection of the head after scratching his face on a rose bush, necessitating the removal of one of his eyes. Five days of penicillin treatment improved his state markedly, but then there was a relapse. There was no more penicillin to continue the treatment and the patient died. The other four cases of nearly fatal infections (a man with a 4-inch carbuncle on his back, a boy of four and a half with staphylococcal infection, a boy of fourteen with staphylococcal osteomyelitis and a baby boy of six months old) were successfully cured with penicillin.

By the summer of 1942 enough penicillin had been produced in the United States to be used for the armed forces on the front, and in some desperate civilian cases like that of Mrs Ogden Miller of Yale University who had haemolytic streptococcal septicaemia. She was given 5.5 grams of penicillin made by Merck (27 million units) and recovered. (When she met Fleming on his trip to the United States in summer 1945, he was overheard to make the rather presumptuous remark about Mrs Miller as 'my most important patient'.)

Fleming could now reap the harvest of his discovery. He wrote in 1946:

> My first experience of treating a patient with concentrated penicillin was in 1942. Middle aged man [a family friend, Harry Lambert] with streptococcal meningitis appeared to be dying in spite of sulfonamide treatment . . . After a few days of treatment with intramuscular and intrathecal injections [of penicillin] the patient was out of danger and made an uneventful recovery.[34]

These dramatic results led to a leading article in *The Times*, published on 27 August 1942 and headed 'Penicillium', which mostly referred to the work done at Oxford. On 31 August Sir Almroth Wright wrote to *The Times*:

> In the leading article on penicillin in your issue you refrained from putting the laurel wreath for this discovery round anybody's brow. I would, with your permission, supplement your article by pointing out that, on the principle *palmam qui meruit ferat* it should be decreed to Professor Alexander Fleming of this laboratory. For he is the discoverer of penicillin and was the author also of the original suggestion that this substance might prove to have important applications in medicine.

Sir Robert Robinson, however, gently remarked the next day that if a laurel wreath was due to Fleming, 'a bouquet at least, and a handsome one, should be presented to Professor H. W. Florey.'[35]

Fleming, feeling that Wright exaggerated a bit, wrote the same week to Florey: 'I was very glad to see Robinson's letter in the *Times* this morning. Although my work started you off on the penicillin hunt, it was you who have made it a practical proposition and it is good you should get the credit'; and again on 7 September, 'I do hope that the people who matter do not think that we are in opposition. I will certainly do what I can to dispel this idea.'[36]

Let us discuss the role of chance in Fleming's discovery. First we have to remember that Fleming's mind was prepared for lytic effects on bacteria by his discovery of lysozyme. He once said that success comes '. . . by hard work, careful observations, clean thinking, enthusiasm and a spot of luck.'[37] The unusual element in Fleming's discovery, however, was not that a mould spore settled in his Petri dish, but that he left the dish long enough for the mould to develop before the bacterial colonies had a chance to grow beyond the right age and physiological state to lyse under the influence of penicillin. We now know that the bacteria are sensitive to the killing effects of penicillin only when they divide. If a student wanted to repeat Fleming's discovery now by purposely arranging the conditions, he would probably fail. D. B. Colquhoun and Ronald Hare failed when trying to repeat Fleming's experiment as described.[38] The inhibition of staphylococci only occurred if the mould had been grown first. Florey's collaborator, Margaret Jennings, actually demonstrated that penicillin would not lyse already grown staph colonies. Ronald Hare, the historian of the work on penicillin, who studied the problem in detail, concluded that the only way to obtain the results Fleming observed was by first having the mould grow for several days at room temperature before the simultaneously seeded staphylococci had a chance to develop into colonies[39] (see figure 5). An examination of the weather records for the summer of 1928 reveals that during the last week of July (when Fleming left for his vacation) there was a cold spell of about ten days (the temperature ranging from 16° to 20°C); this was followed by a warm spell. So if Fleming sowed the staphylococci before leaving for his vacation and left the plates on the bench, the mould spore of a rather rare *Penicillium* species (probably coming from the mycological laboratory just beneath Fleming's room) would have a ten-day start to develop at the lower temperature before the warm spell allowed the staphylococci to grow.

MacFarlane, listing the sequence of the seven chance events leading to Fleming's discovery likens it to drawing the winners of seven consecutive horse races in the right order from a hat containing all the runners.[40]

Why was penicillin not discovered earlier? By the end of the last century Tyndall saw the inhibitory effects of *Penicillium*. Bacteriology at that time was in its infant stage, so perhaps the whole concept of antibiosis had not yet penetrated the communal mind. Since the beginning of this century, however, one of the main reasons for the failure to discover penicillin is that any bacteriologist working in a diagnostic laboratory would not use agar plates contaminated by a colony of mould, but would discard them, and second, at the end of any diagnostic test he would have thrown the plates out rather them keeping them stored, since their diagnostic usefulness would have been exhausted.

Today, when we know of the wealth of literature concerning past observations on antibiotic effects, it is difficult to understand why Fleming was not aware of them, and why he only mentioned Emmerich and his pyocyanase in the references in his paper of 1929, although in 1928 an extensive review on this subject had appeared by Papacostas and Gate (see chapter 6 below).

In the second half of the penicillin story, as recounted briefly above, the important dramatis personae are Florey and Chain.

Ernest Chain, born in Berlin in 1906, arrived in Britain in 1933 as a Jewish refugee from the Nazi regime. He defined himself as a 'temperamental continental'. His first job was at University College London in the Department of Chemical Pathology directed by Charles Harrington. Within a few months Chain got into a dispute with his chief and left for Cambridge to work under Gowland Hopkins (of vitamin fame). In 1935 he moved to Oxford to work with Howard Florey, the new director of the Sir William Dunn School of Pathology. There he first worked on the action of snake venom (with Epstein) and on the analysis of lysozyme from duodenum (with E. S. Duthie). He showed that the substrate of lysozyme, isolated from *Micrococcus lysodeikticus*, was a polysaccharide.

As a result of a casual conversation between Chain and Florey, Chain started a systematic search of the literature for antibacterial substances. Among the 200 papers he reviewed he came across Fleming's paper and thought that penicillin was a sort of mould lysozyme.

It is perhaps ironic that the path leading to the development of penicillin as a therapeutic agent started from false assumptions. As Chain himself admits, he and Florey never considered the clinical applications of Fleming's penicillin; their research problem was purely biochemical, the main point being how to overcome the instability of penicillin. They further believed that penicillin was a sort of lysozyme, and therefore an enzyme, that is, a protein, and that it should have acted on a common substrate (which Chain already knew was a polysaccharide).[41] So in order to purify and concentrate penicillin they assumed that one should apply techniques suitable for enzymes. All this was, of course, a false lead.

Chain's first experiments with the strain of the mould he had were not successful. On one occasion, while walking along the corridor, he met Miss Campbell-Renton who was working in another part of the building. She was carrying a Petri dish with a mould culture. When Chain asked her if by any chance she had any *Penicillium notatum*, she said that she was carrying a strain originally obtained from Fleming by Florey's predecessor, Professor Georges Dreyer.[42]

Chain and his student Epstein were now able to prepare good penicillin. They tried to extract it from the broth by methanol. In January 1938 the

Medical Research Council granted Chain £75 for the continuation of this work on 'penicillin actinomycetin', and in September of the same year another grant of £300 was given 'for the preparation from certain bacteria and fungi of a powerful bactericidal *enzyme* effective against staphylococci, pneumococci and streptococci'.[43] At the same time Florey asked Sir Edward Mellanby, Secretary of the Medical Research Council, for a grant of £100: 'In view of the possibly great practical importance of the above mentioned bactericidal agents [penicillin] it is proposed to prepare these substances in a purified form suitable for intravenous injections and to study their antiseptic action in vivo.'[44] Mellanby, who did not have a particular liking for Florey, approved only £25. As a result of an application to the Rockefeller Foundation, Chain obtained a large grant of about £2,500. By that time the team had been joined by Norman Heatley. He found that the growth period of the mould could be shortened, that one could harvest the same culture several times, and that the brew could be extracted with amyl acetate and then freeze dried from methanol-water extract to give a substance that was a million times more potent than the original brew.

The team also discovered that penicillin was not a protein, that it went through cellophane filters: 'It was clear that we were dealing with a chemically very unusual substance.'[45] There was still the problem of stability, because penicillin was stable only between pH 5 and 8.

As usually happens in teams made up of highly individual and competitive people, the personal relations in the group were not ideal. Chain, an ebullient and outspoken man, antagonized his British colleagues: 'Florey's behaviour to me in the years 1941 till October 1948 when I left for Rome, was unpardonably bad . . . I prefer to cover the relevant episodes with silence', he wrote.[46]

Florey, for his part, once said to Mrs Jennings, his collaborator: 'In one of my weak moments I promised this man [Chain] to test his fractions and here he comes pestering me again.'[47] Nevertheless, Florey also said of Chain: 'He has great charm of manner, is a first class musician, and can be socially very successful. As he speaks a number of languages well he is at his best at international gatherings. He is, however, somewhat egoistical and for that reason he might not be to everybody's liking.'[48] Chain, on his side, tried to mend the relations when he wrote to Florey in 1948:

I am very sorry that our personal relationship has deteriorated so much during the last years; I think the reason for it is mainly the general imperfection of human nature. I have always regretted this development and I hope that as time goes on the unpleasant episodes – which, after all, were not frightfully important when looked at from a broad viewpoint – may gradually sink into oblivion and we shall remember only the exciting and unique events of the time of our collaboration which a curious fate has destined us to experience together.[49]

The antagonistic feelings between the discoverers of penicillin also came to the surface when Chain, while on a visit to the United States with Robert Robinson and Harold King in the summer of 1945, wrote to Florey about Fleming's triumphant lecture tour in America:

The Oxford work is of course never mentioned by him [Fleming]. It will take a great deal of very considerable efforts to get things into their proper perspective, and I will do what I can though I am under no illusions about the difficulties and delicacy inherent in the present situation. I came here fully prepared to find the usual distortions of the history of the penicillin discovery but I must confess that I was staggered to see how far these distortions have gone through the systematic and carefully planned efforts of Fleming.[50]

After the successful trial of penicillin on animals, it was used in human cases. In 1941 Fleming used it with success on his dying friend. Though in Oxford the first two human cases, treated in February 1941, of a policeman and of a child with staphylococcal septicaemias, had ended in their death, as recounted above, the other trials on thirteen- and fourteen-year-old boys, a man and a six-month-old baby were all highly successful, bringing them back to life from a certain death due to bacterial infections.

The Second World War was raging, and the Americans, convinced that the British had a potent chemotherapeutic agent in their hands, stepped into the picture. Florey and Heatley went to the United States in June 1941 to meet Charles Thom, the leading mycologist at the Northern Regional Research laboratories in Peoria. There, by a stroke of luck, a new strain of *Penicillium chrysogenum* was isolated in 1943 by Miss Mary Hunt (Mouldy Mary) from a cantaloupe purchased at the local market. This new strain produced seventy times more penicillin than the Oxford strain. In addition the fermentation was now carried out in a medium containing corn-steep liquor which was much cheaper than the previous synthetic ingredients. The large pharmaceutical firms Squibb, Merck, Lederle and Pfizer joined in the effort. The mould was grown in 50,000-gallon fermentors, and because of all the improvements in media and in strains the yields of penicillin increased 20,000 fold, so that by February

1944 some 19,000 million units of penicillin were produced. In March 1944 Churchill, speaking at the Royal College of Physicians said:

> Then there is penicillin which has broken upon the world just at a moment when human beings are being gashed and torn and poisoned by wounds on the field of war in enormous numbers, and when many other diseases hitherto insoluble cry for treatment. It is a great satisfaction to be able to congratulate St. Mary's Hospital on their association with penicillin.[51]

By 1943 Chain, Abraham and Baker, who had studied the structure of penicillin, proposed that it was a thiazolidine-beta lactam, though Sir Robert Robinson, the eminent British organic chemist, believed it to be an oxazolone. Chain produced crystals of penicillin which were examined by X-ray crystallography by Dorothy Hodgkin. She proved that Chain was right.

During his stay in Oxford, before leaving for a new post in Rome, Chain co-operated with the British drug industry, especially Beecham's, on the production of new varieties of penicillin.

At that time J. C. Sheehan at MIT also tried to unravel the structure of penicillin. He said: 'On several occasions we went on ignoring the facts because we could not believe that the structure of penicillin was what the data indicated.'[52] Once the structure was finally established, efforts were undertaken to produce a completely synthetic penicillin.

Sheehan pointed out in 1982 that 1,000 chemists, biochemists, microbiologists, technicians and bureaucrats in thirty-nine laboratories had struggled in vain for years to produce synthetic penicillin. The directors of the pharmaceutical industry and academic researchers concluded that it was an impossible problem. But J. C. Sheehan did the impossible in 1956. He wrote: 'Another of the ironies of penicillin history is that a synthesis based on the avowedly wrong formula for penicillin brought the penicillin synthesis program to a close.'[53]

The research on penicillin went on. There were attempts to make the penicillin active by the oral route rather than by injection, to make it resistant to penicillinase, by which some bacteria defended themselves against the killing action of penicillin and to extend its range of activity to other pathogenic bacteria. In the late sixties a host of semi-synthetic penicillins, such as methicillin, oxacillin, diloxacillin, ampicillin, etc. were produced.

The success of penicillin during the war led scientists to search for new antibiotics, one of the first in 1942 being streptomycin, to be followed by literally hundreds of other useful antibiotics. Today, a physician has an *embarras de richesse* when he or she has to choose from this enormous armament the one most suitable to defeat a given bacterial infection. 'It is quite clear that penicillin and substances like it will only be used with maximum effect if surgeons have a real appreciation of the properties of the drugs – not only what they can do, but also what they cannot do and the reason for their limitations.[51]

Formally, the story of the discovery of penicillin ends with Fleming, Florey and Chain receiving the Nobel Prize for medicine and physiology in 1945. Fleming, who received half of the prize, was cited for the actual discovery of penicillin, while the other half of the prize went to Florey and Chain together for 'its curative value in a number of infectious diseases'. During the next ten years till his death in 1955 Fleming became world famous, a charismatic figure honoured by all. He received twenty-five honorary degrees, twenty-six medals, eighteen prizes, thirteen decorations; he obtained the freedom of fifteen cities and was made a member of eighty-nine academies and learned societies.

Florencio Bustinza from Madrid, who became Fleming's friend, said of him: 'He has an air of distinction, sweetness, bounty, sincerity which together with enchanting modesty and simplicity captivated me immediately.'[55]

Perhaps he was not a genius, but he 'had the power to see what was really there and the more mysterious flair for distinguishing between the important and the trivial.'[56] But would penicillin have been there to save the lives of thousands of World War Two soldiers and countless civilians thereafter if it hadn't been for Florey and Chain?

NOTES TO CHAPTER 5

1 Maurois, A. 1959: *The Life of Sir Alexander Fleming*. London: Jonathan Cape: 36.

2 Fleming, A. 1922: On a remarkable bacteriolytic substance found in secretions and tissues. *Proceedings of the Royal Society*, B, 93: 306.

3 Dale, H. H. 1955: Obituary, Sir Alexander Fleming *British Medical Journal*, 1: 732.

4 MacFarlane, G. 1984: *Alexander Fleming. The Man and the Myth*. London: Chatto and Windus Hogarth Press: 259.

5 Ibid.: 260.

6 Maurois, *Life of Alexander Fleming*: 108.

7 Ibid.: 97.

8 Ibid.: 93.

9 Fleming, A. 1929: On the antibacterial action of cultures of a penicillium, with special reference to their use in the isolation of *B. influenzae. British Journal of Experimental Pathology*, 10: 226.

10 Cruickshank, R. 1955: Obituary of Sir Alexander Fleming. *British Medical Journal*, 1: 734.

11 Irving, G. W. Jr. and Herrick, H. T. (eds), 1949: The story of penicillin. In *Antibiotics*. Brooklyn: Brooklyn Chemical Publishing Co.

12 Fleming, A. 1946: History and development of penicillin, in *Penicillin, Its Practical Applications*. London: Butterworth: 1.

13 Clark, R. W. 1985: *The Life of Ernest Chain. Penicillin and Beyond.* London: Weidenfeld and Nicolson.

14 Ibid.: 31.

15 Maurois, *Life of Fleming*: 249.

16 Ibid.: 250.

17 Fleming, Antibacterial action: 236.

18 Fleming, History and development of penicillin: 11.

19 Fleming, Antibacterial action: 236.

20 Clutterbuck, P. W., Lovell, R. and Raistrick, H. 1932: Studies in the chemistry of microorganisms. 26. The formation from glucose by members of *Penicillium chryso genum* series of a pigment, an alkali soluble protein and penicillin, the antibacterial substance of Fleming. *Biochemical Journal*, 26: 1907

21 Maurois, *Life of Fleming*: 97.

22 Chain, E. 1971: Thirty years of penicillin therapy. *Proceedings of the Royal Society*, B, 179: 305.

23 MacFarlane, *Alexander Fleming*: 128, 169.

24 Ibid.: 251-2.

25 Fleming, A. 1931: The intravenous use of germicides. *Proceedings of the Royal Society*, 24: 46.

26 Fleming, A. 1931: Some problems in the use of antiseptics. *British Dental Journal*, 52: 105.

27 Clark, *Life of Chain*: 30.

28 Chain, Thirty years: 305.

29 Ibid.

30 Chain, E. B., Florey, H. W., Gardner, A. D., Heatley, N. G. Jennings, M. A., Orr–Ewing, J. and Sanders, A. G. 1940: Penicillin as a chemotherapeutic agent. *Lancet*, 2: 226.

31 Ibid.

32 Clark, *Life of Chain*: 53.

33 Ibid.

34 Fleming, History and development of penicillin: 17.

35 Clark, *Life of Chain*: 76.

36 Ibid.

37 Maurois, *Life of Fleming*: 249.

38 Hare, R. 1970: *The Birth of Penicillin and the Disarming of Microbes.* London: Allen and Unwin Ltd.: 72.

39 Ibid.: 74–5.

40 MacFarlane, *Alexander Fleming*: 248.

41 Abraham, E. P., and Chain, E. 1940: An enzyme from bacteria able to destroy penicillin. *Nature*, 146: 837.

42 Clark, *Life of Chain*: 23.

43 Ibid.: 35.

44 Ibid.: 46.

45 Abraham, E. P., Chain, E. B., Fletcher, C. M., Gardner, A. D., Heatley, N. G. and Jennings, M. A. 1941: Further observations on penicillin, *Lancet*, 2: 177.

46 Clark, *Life of Chain*: 46.

47 Ibid.: 47.

48 Ibid.: 103.

49 Ibid.: 115.

50 Ibid.: 98.

51 Ibid.: 81.

52 Sheehan, J. C., 1982: *The Enchanted Ring. The Untold Story of Penicillin.* Cambridge, Mass.: MIT Press: 95.

53 Ibid.: 115.

54 Fleming, A. 1945: The Harben Lectures on penicillin, its discovery, development, and uses in the field of medicine and surgery. *Journal of the Royal Institute of Public Health*, 8: 36, 63, 93.

55 Bustinza, F. 1961: *Diez años de amistad con Sir Alexander Fleming.* Madrid: Editorial MHS: 56.

56 MacFarlane, *Alexander Fleming*: 262.

6

Antibiotics

Undiscovered antibiotics

The discovery of antibiotics followed a tortuous path ending with the discovery of penicillin by Fleming. The concept of antibiosis appeared in 1889 when Vuillemin defined it as follows: 'When two living bodies are closely united and one of them exercises a destructive action on a more or less extensive portion of the other then we can say that "antibiosis" exists.' The word was not used for several decades, until revived by Waksman.

Experimentally, quite a number of scientists observed the phenomenon of antibiosis without realizing its extraordinary potential. In 1872 Lister had written to his brother that he would try to use *Penicillium glaucum* in an infection of human tissues. No experiment of this sort was published at the time, but in 1940 a former patient of Lister's at King's College Hospital related to a Dr Fraser that in 1884 she had been injured in a street accident and her injury had become infected. Lister first tried various antiseptics, but finally only one, which she had recorded in her notebook as *Penicillium*, worked and the wound healed. The effects of *Penicillium* were also noted by John Tyndall in 1876:

> The mutton in the study gathered over it a thick blanket of *Penicillium*. On the 13th [December 1875] it had assumed a light brown colour as if by a faint admixture of clay; but the infusion became transparent. The 'clay' here was the slime of dead or dormant *Bacteria*, the cause of their quiescence being the blanket of *Penicillium*. I found no active life in this tube, while all the others swarmed with *Bacteria*.
>
> In every case where the mould was thick and coherent the *Bacteria* died, or became dormant, and fell to the bottom of the sediment . . . The *Bacteria* which manufacture a green pigment [B. pyocyaneus?] appear to be uniformly victorious in their fight with *Penicillium*.[1]

It was Pasteur who recognized the existence of antibiosis without naming it, when he said in 1877: 'In the inferior and vegetable species *life hinders life.*' He based this statement on an experiment performed with Joubert, showing that when anthrax was growing in urine in a tube and this tube was inoculated with a 'common bacterium' the anthrax bacilli would not grow: 'A liquid invaded by an organized ferment, or by an aerobe, makes it difficult for an inferior organism to multiply . . . These facts may, perhaps, justify the greatest hope from the therapeutic point of view.' Prophetically he predicted that saprophytic organisms might some day be used to combat infectious agents.[2]

In the next decade French and Italian scientists also came across antibiosis. In 1885 V. Babes described experimental studies in which bacteria of a known species produced chemical substances or modified culture medium in such a way as to harm bacteria of other species. And he predicted that . . . 'a disease caused by one bacterium could probably be treated by another'[3].

In 1885 Arnaldo Cantani worked with *Bacterium thermo* which *per se* was not pathogenic to animals. He then insufflated a culture of this bacterium into the lungs of a tuberculous patient to discover that the tubercle bacteria disappeared from the sputum of the patient, whereupon he improved considerably. Since the trial was reported in a relatively unknown journal, and concerned one patient only, these dramatic results had little consequence.[4]

The idea that the growth of one bacterium inhibits that of another caught the fancy of Richard Emmerich, who was engaged in research and teaching at the Hygiene Institute in Munich. It all started by a chance observation.

For teaching the effects of bacterial infections Emmerich used guinea pigs. These animals, when infected with streptococci (*Erysipelcoccus*) eventually recovered and appeared to be healthy and well. On one occasion, in 1887, Emmerich used one of these 'recovered' guinea pigs for an infection with some undefined soil bacteria. He also infected another, 'fresh' guinea pig with the same soil bacteria. Both animals died, the first after fifty-two hours and the second after thirty-two hours. When Emmerich dissected the corpses he was surprised that the guinea pig that had recovered from the streptococcal infection showed no evidence of the growth of the soil bacteria, while the other did.[5] 'This finding seemed to me to be most remarkable', he wrote,[6] because it indicated that the soil bacteria had been destroyed. His next experiment was to infect streptococci-recovered animals with anthrax bacilli which were known to be lethal to rabbits. He experimented with some thirty rabbits, half previously infected with streptococci, the other half serving as controls. Of the fifteen 'protected' rabbits only three died, while all the controls succumbed to the anthrax infection. To Emmerich these results meant that previous infection with streptococci made the rabbits immune to anthrax.

In the next series of experiments Emmerich attempted to cure anthrax infection by subcutaneous injection of streptococci, but in this he was unsuccessful. Out of sixteen only two animals survived. Intravenous injection of streptococci, however, gave better results. Six out of ten anthrax-infected rabbits survived. This result seemed highly promising to Emmerich and he thought that his procedure might be used as a cure for anthrax in large animals and humans.

Trying to understand the phenomenon, Emmerich eventually concluded that the streptococcal infection provided a stimulus to induce the cells of the organism to fight anthrax. 'In the battle which occurs in the animal body the streptococci are not the warriors, but diplomats, who mediate in the conflict by stimulating the animal cells to destroy the invaders.' This destruction included not only anthrax, but the streptococci themselves.[7]

An amusing sideline in Emmerich's fifty-eight-page-long paper is the sentence in which he tells his readers that the rabbits that survived the double infection 'were slaughtered two and a half months after the infection, and consumed without any untoward effect, by the Institute's charwoman and her husband.'[8]

In 1887 three publications appeared on antibiotic effects. C. Garré related his experiments in a medical journal.[9] He streaked bacteria of various types in parallel rows across jellified nutrient plates and noted that the bacteria in one row would grow, while in the adjacent row the others were suppressed. The inhibition 'is a question of antagonism caused by the secretion of a specific easily diffusible substance which is inhibitory to the growth of one species but completely ineffective against the species producing it.'[10] Garré also suggested a possible therapeutic use of this phenomenon.

In 1895 a real precursor of mould antibiotic was discovered by Vincenzo Tiberio of the University of Naples. He prepared aqueous extracts from cultures of various moulds, *Mucor mucedo, Penicillium glaucum* and *Aspergillus flavescens*, and showed that they would kill the bacteria of anthrax, typhoid, cholera, Coli and staphylococci. The most potent was the extract from *Aspergillus*. He even found that the injection of an extract of this *Aspergillus* into guinea pigs one to five days before infection with a lethal dose of typhoid or cholera would prevent their death.[11]

In the last decade of the nineteenth century several scientists in France and in Germany experimented with cultures of *Bacillus pyocyaneus* as a potential cure against bacterial infections. So, for instance, Ch. Bouchard saved the lives of twelve out of twenty-six rabbits inoculated with both anthrax and pyocyaneus,[12] but the toxicity of such cultures put a stop to the experimentation. In 1898, however, Rudolf Emmerich and Oscar Loew found that cultures of *Bacillus pyocyaneus* killed anthrax bacilli. As they put it in an extensive publication in 1899 (sixty-three pages!) 'These investigations were initiated as a result of a simple observation that many bacteriologists had certainly made before, but they either did not pay any attention to it, or interpreted it incorrectly.[13]

Emmerich and Loew assumed that the active substance in the bacterial filtrates was an enzyme and called it *pyocyanase* 'not only since it originated in *Bac. pyocyaneus*, but also because it dissolved these bacteria.' In the spring of 1898 they tested the dialysed and filtered cultures of pyocyaneus in many rabbits with great success. All the rabbits infected with lethal doses of anthrax bacilli died within two or three days, while the infected rabbits treated with pyocyanase survived for at least eight months. They concluded that the treatment of anthrax-infected animals with one or two injections of pyocyaneus enzyme was sufficient to lyse large numbers of anthrax bacilli and effect a cure.

The nature of pyocyanase was quite strange. Though it certainly had proteolytic activity (it liquefied gelatine, coagulated albumen, and fibrin), it withstood steaming at 98.5°C, as well as vacuum drying, and it was practically innocuous to rabbits (but not to guinea pigs).[11]

Because of the prevailing belief among microbiologists, Emmerich and Loew assumed that the pyocyanase effect had to do with immunity. They therefore prepared complexes of pyocyanase with some tissue proteins (presumably derived from leukocytes – though on this issue they appear to be rather secretive) and called them *immunoproteidin*. They then used these complexes for prophylactic treatment (a sort of immunization) before infection with anthrax. Indeed they found that seven to nine injections of pyocyanase, given intravenously and subcutaneously, during a period of four to eight days, would protect the experimental rabbits against a thousand-fold lethal dose of anthrax, even when the infection was carried out three to twelve days after the end of the immunoproteidin treatment.

Pyocyanase turned out to be also active *in vitro* against the bacteria of typhoid, cholera, diphtheria, streptococci and pestis, but in protective experiments carried out on rabbits infected with diphtheria or streptococci the results were not promising. Out of the six 'immunized' animals in each group four died and only two survived. Nevertheless Emmerich and Loew strongly advocated the use of pyocyanase for the treatment of diphtheria in human infections because of its detoxifying properties.

As a result of these findings, pyocyanase had actually been used quite extensively before the beginning of World War I in cases of meningitis, diphtheria, Vincent's angina, etc. Its use ceased not because it was ineffective, but because it turned out that the commercial preparations of pyocyanase contained phenol which was by itself bactericidal. Much later (in 1943) it was shown that, properly prepared, pyocyanase, would inhibit pyogenous streptococci even at a dilution of 1 : 24,000.

Thus, for a time pyocyanase was used effectively, though Emmerich's theoretical explanation for its activity was entirely wrong, but fitted into contemporary communal thinking.

An interesting development was due to a Ph.D. thesis of a student called Doehle at the University of Cologne (1889). He inoculated *Anthrax* bacilli into a nutrient medium with gelatine. When it had set as a gel, he put a paper square soaked with a *Micrococcus* on to the surface of the gel. After suitable incubation he observed that there was a clear zone of inhibition of growth of anthrax around the *Micrococcus* square. This was the precursor of a very important technique in assessing the potency of antibiotics, used up to this very day. The diameter of the inhibition zone around the pad soaked with the antibiotic correlates with the potency of the solution tested.[15]

In 1896 B. Gosio extracted from cultures of *Penicillium* a crystalline antibiotic (now known as mycophenolic acid) which inhibited anthrax. Unfortunately he did not have sufficient materials to carry out experiments on animals. In 1903 A. Lode[16] found an accidental contaminant, a gram-positive coccus *(Micrococcus tetragenus)* which inhibited the growth of *Anthrax* bacilli and of staphylococci on a nutrient plate. The active substance was not active in animal experiments. Later, in 1911, Nitsch and Choukevitch also found streptococci that inhibited the cholera bacterium in the air at Versailles.

In the second decade of this century, several scientists experimented with antibiosis against tuberculosis. Rappin injected filtered media from a cultuture of *B. mesentericus* into guinea pigs infected with lethal doses of the tubercle bacilli, and the animals survived. Similar results were obtained by Albert Vaudremer[17] with filtrates of *Aspergillus fumigatus* (it was most probably helvolic acid). From 1910 onwards, following successful results obtained with this extract in guinea pigs infected with *Mycobacterium tuberculosis*, Vaudremer went on to treat more than 200 patients with extracts of *A. fumigatus* in several hospitals in Paris. The injections were harmless, and no febrile reaction was observed. Some patients recovered completely, some improved and in some no change was observed.

Another decade passed and in 1924 André Gratia and Sara Dath found a bacterium (*B. mycoides* or *B. cytolyticus*) that produced an enzyme that dissolved other bacteria. The extract of these bacteria (mycolysate or sentocym) was used in clinical infections of the urinary tract by *E. coli*.[18] Thus Gratia was one of the first to study the production of antibiotics by *Actinomycetes*, but he did not appreciate the significance of the injurious effects the mould had upon the growth of bacteria. No wonder that his teacher, Professor Bordet, said to him: 'My boy, the trouble with you is that you don't christen your babies.'

In 1921 R. Lieske published a monograph in Leipzig on *Morphologie und Biologie der Strahlenpilze*, showing that he was aware fact that these fungi 'secreted a specific substance acting extracellularly' and inhibited other organisms to the extent that their colonies were lysed and disappeared. He suggested that this substance might be used in therapeutics.[19]

In the 1920s Ignaz Schiller from Odessa and his co-workers introduced a new idea. When yeasts are grown on a medium where the only source of nitrogen was the bodies of bacteria against which the antibiotic was to be developed, a thermolabile substance with such properties would in fact be found in the medium. Schiller called this 'induced' antagonism. In some of his experiments he demonstrated this sort of induced antagonism between *B. mesentericus, B. subtilis* or *B. anthracis* as inducers on the one hand and *Bacillus bulgaricus* and *Streptococcus lactis* as targets on the other. Later, after 1940, Schiller's idea was applied to studies involved in the isolation of new antibiotics.[20] In 1928 Papacostas and Gate published a monograph in Paris summing up all that had been known and published till then on antibiotic relationships between micro-organisms.[21]

To summarize this short historical sketch: Before the advent of penicillin a great many observations of antibiosis were recorded. The principles discerned were:

1 *Replacement* – the growth of one bacterium would replace that of another (termo instead of tubercle bacilli: staphylococcus instead of diphtheria, lactic acid bacteria instead of coli bacteria, etc);
2 *Lytic* substances produced by bacteria (sentocym, mucolysate);
3 *Parenteral applications* – pyocyanase against anthrax, *B. mesentericus* against tuberculosis, *Aspergillus* extracts against typhoid and cholera;
4 *Topical applications* – pyocyanase.

Florey sums up: 'It can be said with some truth that there is little that has been done with penicillin which was not attempted with the earlier antibiotics so far as the means then available permitted.'[22]

Why did all these experiments and observations not lead to practical and widespread use of antibiotics in clinical situations? This is understandable (even with Fleming's discovery of penicillin). No antibiotic had been unequivocally shown to possess curative properties. Even Fleming, who made the experiment to show that penicillin broth was inocuous to animals (rabbits), did not perform a proper therapeutic experiment to demonstrate that penicillin would save the lives of animals (e.g. mice) from certain death caused by a pathogenic micro-organism. All the discoveries in the golden age of bacteriology at the end of the last century were premature.

In 1945 Florey wrote: 'I cannot help feeling that Lister would be mightily amused to see the army of eager enthusiasts now stretching out suppliant Petri dishes in the hope they will receive some miraculous therapeutic manna'.[23]

Waksman's hesitations

The turning-point in the research on antibiotics came with the discovery of penicillin by Fleming in 1929 (see chapter 5). Nevertheless it took more than a decade before the 'communal blindness' to the concept of antibiotics gave way to a real understanding of the matter and paved the way to enormous research and industrial efforts in the development of a plethora of antibiotics of all kinds.

I should like to dwell on some examples of the communal blindness syndrome in the post-Fleming era. In 1932 R. Weindling found a new antibiotic, gliotoxin, in the plant *Gliocadium fimbricatum*. It was active against plant pathogenic fungi, and later was also found to be active against gram-positive and gram-negative bacteria.[24] Nothing seems to have followed this discovery.

The next example concerns the recipient of the Nobel Prize (1952) for the discovery of streptomycin, Selman A. Waksman from Rutgers University in New Brunswick, New Jersey. It might be said that he was blind to some of his own discoveries. He studied soil microbes as early as 1916, among them the producer of streptomycin, *Streptomyces griseus*. In 1932 he published the second edition of his 894-page book *Principles in Soil Microbiology*.[25] Penicillin is not mentioned there at all. The only mention of antibiotic properties of micro-organisms is of *Bacterium fluorescens* as toxic to spore-forming bacteria, and of *Bacillus subtilis* as destroying the botulinum toxin. Many years later, in 1973, Waksman said that though he had frequently observed that around *Actinomyces* colonies there was a clear zone devoid of growth of any other microbes, he had paid little attention to the significance of the phenomenon.

In 1935 Chester Rhines, a graduate student of Waksman's noticed that tubercle bacilli would not grow in the presence of a soil organism,[26] but Waksman did not think that this lead was worth pursuing: 'In the scientific climate of the time, the result did not suggest any practical application for treatment of tuberculosis . . .'[27] The same year, Waksman's friend, the poultry pathologist at Rutgers, Fred Beaudette, brought Waksman an agar tube with a culture of tubercle bacilli killed by a contaminant fungus growing on top of them. Again Waksman was not interested: 'I was not moved to jump to the logical conclusion and direct my efforts accordingly . . . My major interest at that time was the subject of organic matter decomposition and the interrelationships among soil microorganisms responsible for this process.'[28] Though Waksman knew that tubercle bacilli are rapidly destroyed in soil, he was not prepared, to make practical use of this observation or to carry the problem to a practical conclusion.[29]

It was not until the end of the thirties that Waksman embarked on an ambitious programme to search for antibiotics in the soil micro-organisms based on the suggestion that the cause of disappearance of disease producing organisms in the soil was to be looked for among the soil-inhabiting microbes, antagonistic to the pathogens and bringing about their rapid destruction.[30] In the course of the extensive screening process, Waksman and his students isolated some 10,000 cultures. Of these only about 1,000 had antibiotic properties, but only 100 excreted the antibiotic to the growth medium. Of these, ten were studied in detail and among them he found the producers of actinomycin (1940), clavicin (1941), streptothricin (1942) and streptomycin (1943). Waksman stresses that 'these findings did not come to us by mere luck or by chance discovery. They were the result of much painstaking work, after much planning and preparation.'[31]

So what occurred in the summer of 1942 was very strange indeed, when his son, Byron Waksman, then a medical student at the University of Pennsylvania, wrote a letter to his father suggesting a summer project.[32] In this letter Byron first commented on the work already going on in his father's laboratory, and on the simplicity of the methods used there for the isolation of fungi producing antibiotic substances. He continued: 'I wondered if exactly the same method could not be used with equal ease to isolate a number of strains of fungi or actinomycetes which would act against *Mycobacterium tuberculosis*.' They could be tested first against *Mycobacterium phlei* (an apathogenic cousin of tubercle bacillus) and then against the tubercle bacillus *in vivo*. 'There is no question that it [the proposed work] has a great deal of practical value or would have if successfully concluded.' Waksman senior replied: 'The time has not come yet. We are not quite prepared to undertake this problem.'[33]

How difficult it is today to understand a reply like this! After all, Byron wanted to do the project himself during his summer vacation. The elder Waksman certainly did not remember that Banting and Best had discovered insulin during their summer project! Comroe comments: 'With the solemn pronouncement "The time has not come yet" . . . vanished the possibility of a father–son Nobel Prize.'[34]

The blindness does not end here. When eventually Waksman, with Schatz and Bugie announced the discovery of streptomycin in January 1944,[35] they listed in their paper the inhibitory effects of streptomycin on nine strains of gram-positive and on twelve trains of gram-negative bacteria as well as on the tuberculosis bacterium. The table of results shows that the tubercle bacilli were in fourteenth place in the order of sensitivity after streptococci, staphylococci, salmonellae and shigellae, that is, that they could be fought with streptomycin, but nowhere else in the text is the tubercle bacillus even mentioned. 'The discovery had . . . been made, but was not discovered by the discoverers themselves!'[36] Even more aggravating is the fact that in the next paper of Waksman and his students in *Science*[37] there is no mention of streptomycin as being active against tuberculosis.

In the same year, however, Feldman and Hinshaw at the Mayo Clinic, two physicians who did understand Waksman's table and the anti-tubercular potential of streptomycin, carried out the proper clinical trials and proved its value in the treatment of tuberculosis.[38]

Frogs and magainins

As an investigator continues in his career, accident will present him with unpredicted opportunities for research perhaps in quite new directions.
Walter B. Cannon

From then on literally thousands of antibiotics have been discovered, screened and applied. They were sought among fungi, bacteria, plants

and animals, but the effort to find antibiotics in multicellular organisms
seems to have been somewhat half-hearted.

In the last two decades cecropins have been found in insects[39] and the
defensins in vertebrate white blood cells. The latest, very intriguing discovery, however, was made by Michael Zasloff, of the Human Genetics
Branch at the National Institute of Health. He isolated from the skin of
the African claw frog (*Xenopus laevis*) new polypeptidic antibiotics – the
magainins.[40]

The story of magainins is included here for the following reason: for a
number of years Zasloff's interest in the African claw frog was due to the
known fact that from these frogs large numbers of oocytes can be obtained,
such as are needed in research into eukaryotic RNA expression. Scores of
laboratories all over the world grew these frogs in water tanks, and used
them in reckless profusion as the donors of eggs. No one, including Zasloff,
thought of the possibility that *Xenopus* might be a source of antibiotics.

It was not until 1986 that Zasloff finally paid attention to what he had
been seeing for many years: in spite of the entirely non-sterile surgical
procedures required to open the abdomen of the female frog and to
remove her eggs, and then to stitch it back again with surgical thread,
the frogs, kept in contaminated water swarming with bacteria and parasites, developed no infections and their skin healed smoothly and nicely.
Medically speaking, the absence of infection under these really septic
conditions was truly remarkable. As mentioned before, what is even more
remarkable is that so many scientists working with these frogs (including
Zasloff) saw this phenomenon, but none of them drew any practical
conclusions from these observations. Here one has again a fact that is not
a fact, because everyone was blind to it.

Zasloff finally understood that this clean healing must have been associated with some sort of self-sterilizing activity of the skin. Within a short
time he isolated from the skin of his frogs two polypeptides, twenty-three
amino-acids long, of almost identical sequence (only two amino acids in
positions 10 and 21 were different), which had excellent antibiotic properties.
He named these polypeptides '*magainins*' (derived from the Hebrew word
magēn, 'a shield').[41]

These polypeptides kill various bacteria, especially the gram-negative
ones, at very low concentration (like that of streptomycin). The magainins
also killed unicellular parasites. They have been found to be totally
innocuous to humans and so they offer the promise of becoming a very
useful and important antibiotic.

When I talked with Dr Zasloff, he could not explain what was the switch that alerted him to the new possibility resulting from his observation that the frogs' skin healed so well in dirty water. Once the antibiotic properties of magainins were established, Zasloff discovered that frog-skin extracts had been extensively used for the treatment of infected wounds in China. He also learned that in South America the Indians were known to bind a living frog to an infected wound on the body's extremities and that this method accelerated healing.

When I related this story to some of my friends who had recently arrived from the Soviet Union, where they had lived in a remote rural region, they told me that they knew of a custom prevalent there to prevent milk from going sour: the farmers used to throw a living frog into the milk and keep it there for several days.

Even more amazing is the fact that in the last few decades pharmacologists have described the isolation from frog's skin of many active biogenic amines, as well as some thirty active peptides such as tachykinins, bradykinins, cerulein, bombesin, dermorphins, etc.,[42] but no one seems to have been interested in testing these substances for anti-bacterial, antiparasitic or antiviral properties.

There is nothing new under the sun, but most of us are blind to it.

NOTES TO CHAPTER 6

1 Clark, *Life of Chain*: 26.
2 Pasteur, L. and Joubert, J. 1877: Charbon et septicémie. *Comptes rendus de l'Académie de Sciences*, Paris, 85: 101.
3 Florey, H. W. 1945: The use of micro-organisms for therapeutic purposes. *British Medical Journal*, 2: 635.
4 Cantani, A. 1885: Un tentativo di batteroterapia. *Giornale internazionale delle Science Mediche*, 7: 493.
5 Emmerich, R. 1887: Die Heilung des Milzbrandes. *Archiven der Hygiene* (Berlin) 8: 442.
6 Ibid.: 447.
7 Cantani, Un tentativo di batteroterapia: 493.
8 Emmerich, 1887, *Die Heilung des Milzbrandes*: 455.
9 Garré, C. 1887: Über Antagonisten unter der Bakterien. *Centralblatt für Bakteriologie und Parasitenkunde*, 2: 312.
10 Florey, The use of micro-organisms: 636.
11 Tiberio, V. 1895: Sugli estratti di alcune muffe. *Annali d'Igiene speremintale* (Rome) 5: 91.

12 Bouchard, Ch. 1889: Influence qu'exerce sur la maladie charbonneuse l'inoculation du bacille pyocyanique. *Comptes rendus de l'Académie des Sciences*, (Paris), 108: 713.

13 Emmerich, R. and Loew, O. 1889: Bakteriolytische Enzyme Ursache der erworbenen Immunität und die Heilung von Infektionskrankheiten durch dieselben. *Zeitschrift der Hygiene und Infektionskrankheiten*, 31: 1.

14 Ibid.: 55–6.

15 Florey, The use of micro-organisms: 636.

16 Lode, A. 1903: Experimentelle Untersuchungen über Bakterien-antagonismus. I. *Zentralblatt der Bakteriologie*, Part I. Originals. 33: 196.

17 Vaudremer, A. 1913: Action de l'extrait d'*Aspergillus fumigatus* sur les bacilles tuberculeux. *Comptes rendues des Séances de la Société de Biologie* (Paris), 74: 278 and 752.

18 Gratia, A. and Dath, S. 1924: Propriétés bactériolytiques de certaines moisissures. *Comptes rendus des Séances de la Société de Biologie* (Paris), 91: 1442.

19 Lieske, R. 1921: *Morphologie und Biologie der Strahlenpilze*. Leipzig: Borntrager.

20 Schiller, I. 1924: Über 'erzwungene' Antagonisten. *Zentralblatt für Bakteriologie*, Part I. Abt. Originals, 91: 68.

21 Papacostas, G. and Gate, J. 1928: *Les Associations microbiennes*. Paris: Doin et Cie.

22 Florey, The use of micro-organisms: 637.

23 Ibid.: 641.

24 Weindling, R. 1934: Studies on a lethal principle effective in the parasitic action of *Trichoderma lignorum* on *Rhizoctonia solani* and other soil fungi. *Phytopathology*, 24: 1153.

25 Waksman. S. A. 1932: *Principles of Soil Microbiology*, 2nd edn. Baltimore: Williams and Wilkins.

26 Rhines, C. 1935: The persistence of avian tubercle bacilli in soil and in association with soil micro organisms. *Journal of Bacteriology*, 29: 299.

27 Comroe, J. 1978: Pay Dirt: The Story of Streptomycin, Part I. From Waksman to Waksman. *American Review of Respiratory Disease*, 117: 778.

28 Waksman, S. A. and Woodruff, H. B. 1940: The soil as a source of micro-organisms antagonistic to disease producing bacteria. *Journal of Bacteriology*, 40: 581.

29 Waksman, S. A. 1954: *My Life with Microbes*. New York: Simon and Schuster.

30 Ibid.: 224.

31 Ibid.: 203.

1. (left) Antoine Henri Becquerel (1852 – 1908)

2. (below, left) Wilhelm Conrad Roentgen (1845 – 1923)

3. (below, right) Arno A. Penzias and Robert W. Wilson (with beard)

4. (left) Rudolf
   Mossbauer

5. (below, left) Gerhard
   Domagk

6. (below, right)
   Christiaan Eijkman

7. (above, left) Lowell
   Hokin

8. (above, right) Salvador
   E. Luria

9. (right) Elena Nightingale

10. (above) Baruch S. Blumberg
11. (right) Waclaw Szybalski

12. (above) Sir Alexander Fleming

13. (right) Lord Florey, 1952

14. Ernest Chain

15. (above, left)
Selman Waksman

16. (above, right)
Carl Koller
(1857–1944)

17. (right) Rosalyn
S. Yalow

18. (above, left)
   John Pappenheimer

19. (above, right)
   Frederick Grant Banting
   (1891–1941)

20. (below, left)
   C.H. Best

21. (below, right)
   Ludwik Fleck

32 Ibid.: 232.
33 Comroe, *Pay Dirt*: 778–9.
34 Ibid.: 779.
35 Schatz, A., Bugie, E. and Waksman, S. A. 1944: Streptomycin, a substance exhibiting antibiotic activity against gram-positive and gram-negative bacteria. *Proceedings of the Society for Experimental Biology and Medicine*, 55: 66.
36 Birath, G. 1969: Introduction of para-amino salicylic acid and streptomycin in the treatment of tuberculosis. *Scandinavian Journal of Respiratory Diseases*, 50: 204.
37 Jones, D., Metzger, H. J., Schatz, A. and Waksman, S. A. 1944: Control of gram negative bacteria in experimental animals by streptomycin. *Science*, 100: 103.
38 Hinshaw, H. C. and Feldman, W. H. 1945: Streptomycin in treatment of clinical tuberculosis: A preliminary report. *Proceedings of Staff Meetings Mayo Clinic*, 20: 313.
39 Steiner, H., Hultmark, D., Engstrom A., Bennich, H. and Boman, H. G. 1981: Sequence and specificity of two antibacterial proteins involved in insect immunity. *Nature*, 292: 246.
40 Zasloff, M. 1987: Magainins, a class of antimicrobial peptides from *Xenopus* skin. Isolation, characterization of two active forms, and partial c-DNA sequence of a precursor. *Proceedings of the National Academy of Science*, USA, 84: 5449.
41 Ibid.: 5450.
42 Erspamer, V. and Melchiori, P. Active polypeptides: From amphibian skin to gastrointestinal tract and brains of mammals. *Trends in Pharmacological Sciences*, 1: 3915.

7
What Changes Our Behaviour?

Medical history abounds with accidental discoveries. Thus one can mention, as examples, Vogel's discovery of diuretics while he was looking for an antisyphilitic drug; Ringer's accidental finding of the role of calcium and potassium ions in physiological solutions; McLeans's discovery of an anti-coagulant, heparin, while he was looking for the opposite; the birth of a laxative following the observation that the addition of phenolphtaleine to wine (to check its acidity) caused diarrhoea; the discovery of cyclamate as a sweetener by a negligent student who put his cigarette on a spot of the bench where some cyclamate had been spilt; etc.

In this chapter I shall describe some chance discoveries in the field of anaesthesiology and neurophysiology.

From laughing gas to ether and chloroform

Anaesthesia is a term attributed to the famous Boston physician and author, Oliver Wendell Holmes, in the second half of the nineteenth century. It was actually first used by Bailey in 1721 as 'defect of sensation as in paralytic and blasted persons' and only a hundred years later it was used as 'loss of sensation'. Much later, in his book on anaesthesia published in 1871, James Y. Simpson suggested that the proper word should have been the Greek *anōdynia* (insensitivity to pain).

Who discovered anaesthesia? Before discussing the relative contributions of many contenders to this title, I shall outline a short historical sketch of the subject. In the *Odyssey* Homer (4.221) describes the use of *pharmakon nēpenthes*, presumed to be Indian hemp, as an anaesthetic. Another plant employed by ancient medicine was the mandrake (mandragora). It was described by Dioscorides in the first century AD as having its roots 'seethed in wine . . . for such as cannot sleep, or are grievously pained, and for whom, when cut or cauterized, they wish to make pain unfelt.'[1]

In the ninth century Bamberg's *Antidotum* contained a description of soporific sponge containing opium, mandragora, cicuta and hyosciamus; breathing through a sponge of this sort would induce a state in which pain was not felt.

In modern times there are many contenders to be considered as the discoverers of anaesthesiology. The credit should go first to Sir Humphrey Davy, an English chemist working with Rumford as a Professor of Chemistry. In 1813 he published the first textbook on the application of chemistry to agriculture. He became famous for using electric current to separate metals out from the solution of their salts and for being the first to isolate potassium and sodium as metals, and later (1808) of barium, strontium, calcium and magnesium.

In 1799 Davy at the age of nineteen discovered nitrous oxide. He showed that upon being inhaled NO gave rise to a feeling of intoxication, and a lowering of inhibitions. He wrote that NO is a gas 'capable of destroying physical pain, and may probably be used with advantage during surgical operations in which no great effusion of blood takes place.'[2] In spite of this prediction, the use of nitrous oxide as an anaesthetic came much later. In fact it was used in the 1840s as 'laughing gas', a social diversion, in the same way that have 'glue sniffing' and 'pot smokers' today.

In 1839 John Scoffern published a pamphlet, *Chemistry No Mystery*, in which he described the effects of breathing nitrous oxide. He attended a lecture at which this subject was discussed and the audience breathed nitrous oxide from bladders filled with this gas. The effects were dramatic:

> . . . some jumped over tables and chairs, some were bent on making speeches, some were very much inclined to fight; and one young gentleman persisted in attempting to kiss the ladies . . . As to the laughing, I think it was chiefly confined to the lookers-on . . . it is a peculiarity of this gas, that it does not act like intoxicating liquors in producing depression of spirits, disorder of the stomach, or indeed any other unpleasant effects.[3]

Next in line chronologically is Michael Faraday, who indicated in 1818 that ether had properties similar to those of nitrous oxide.[4] He stated that ether could be used to prevent surgical pain, but nobody actually used it for the next twenty-four years.

During his short life of thirty years Henry Hill Hickman was a practising physician in Ludlow, Shifnal, and Tenbury in Shropshire. In 1824 at the age of twenty-four, he performed experiments on animals involving bringing them into a state of 'suspended animation' by having them breath carbonic acid gas (CO_2). He published the results of his experiments in a letter entitled *A letter on suspended animation containing experiments showing that it may be safely employed during operations on animals, with the view of ascertaining its probable utility in surgical operations on the human subject*, in which he describes his fourth experiment as follows:

> Mice . . . confined in a glass tube a foot long, were rendered insensible by carbonic acid gas slowly introduced in small quantities, and one foot from each was taken off; no hemorrhage took place upon the return of sensation, and the wounds appeared quite healed on the third day, without the animals having apparently suffered pain, when they were given the liberty.[5]

In 1828 Hickman submitted a trial for suspended animation to the French Academy of Science. The Academy nominated a commission to check his claims, but there is no report from the commission.

Hickman was actually the first to perform planned experiments of anaesthesia in animals such as mice, cats, dogs and rabbits, and the first to use the term 'suspended animation', as well as the first to set out deliberately to abolish the pain of a surgical operation by the inhalation of a gas. It took another hundred years to confirm that carbon dioxide did have anaesthetic properties.

After Faraday there were several physicians in the first half of the nineteenth century who advocated the use of ether as an anaesthetic. The first use of ether in a dental operation was that of William E. Clarke of Rochester who in January 1842 helped the dentist Eliyah Pope to extract a tooth from a Miss Hobbie, made insensitive to pain by ether.

In March 1842 a physician in Georgia, Crawford William Long, used ether to insensitize a patient, James M. Venable, so that he could remove a tumour from his neck. Long was asked by his friends to prepare nitrous oxide for their social entertainment, but he suggested that they should use ether instead. He had already tried ether on himself and found that it, too, had exhilarating effects. His next patient was a 'Negro boy' whose toe he amputated under ether anaesthesia.[6] Long wrote in 1849: 'I noticed my friends, while etherized, received falls or blows, which I believe were sufficient to produce pain in a person not in a state of anaesthesia, and on questioning them, they uniformly assured me that they did not feel the least pain from these accidents.'[7]

Long performed further operations under ether anaesthesia, but did not publish his achievements until after Morton had announced his results.

Why did Long wait for seven years to publish his experiences with ether? He explained: 'I was anxious, before making my publication, to try etherization in a sufficient number of cases to satisfy my mind that anaesthesia was produced by the ether and was not the effect of the imagination, or owing to any peculiar insusceptibility to pain in the persons experimented upon.'[8] How many medical researchers would behave in this way today?

In December 1844 Horace Wells, himself an American physician, had his own tooth extracted under NO anaesthesia by his colleague Dr John R. Rigg. He felt no pain and he called the attention of Thomas Green Morton, a dentist at Harvard, and Charles T. Jackson, a chemist, to this finding. He then arranged for a demonstration to be given at the Harvard Medical School. Unfortunately it was not very successful, at least from a public point of view, because the patient whose tooth was being extracted groaned, though under the influence of nitrous oxide he did not feel any pain.

Morton, a very businesslike dentist, had a good understanding of Wells's idea and decided to continue it: on 30 September 1846 he arranged to extract a tooth from Eben H. First. Because he did not have nitrous oxide, he followed Jackson's advice to use 'sulphuric ether' instead. The extraction went off uneventfully and painlessly. Two weeks later Morton demonstrated the anaesthetic effects of ether in an operation performed by Dr J. C. Warren on Gilbert Abbot to remove a tumour from his neck. Morton administered the ether from a glass globe with two openings containing a sponge soaked in ether. During the following three weeks ether was used for anaesthesia in operations of the removal of a tumour from a shoulder and the amputation of a leg. When he began to use ether, Morton kept its identity secret, and even disguised it by colouring it pink. He then applied with Johnson for a patent, which was issued to them on 12 November 1846. Morton did not publish his results on the use of ether as an anaesthetic until 1849.[9]

Though Morton could have become rich, he fought Jackson over the patent and died in poverty. He was, however, honoured in 1920 by being elected to the Hall of Fame for Great Americans.[10]

Within a month of Morton's first use of ether in surgical operation, Professor Bigelow of Harvard wrote about it to his friend in London, Dr Francis Boott, and on 19 December Boott used it during the extraction of a tooth from a Miss Lonsdale. In November 1846 Dr William Fraser, a ship's doctor, who knew Morton and his discovery, was visiting an infirmary in Dumfries in Scotland. At the time of his visit, a patient was brought in with a fractured limb. When Drs James McLauchlan and William Scott decided to amputate the leg, Fraser suggested the use of sulphuric ether for anaesthesia. 'The operation was performed in a painless and satisfactory manner.'[11]

The next interesting step in the development of anaesthetic agents was taken by James Young Simpson, an Edinburgh graduate and a successful physican. In 1846 he heard of the American discovery of ether as an anaesthetic and tried to apply it in England to relieve the pains of labour. Because his patients did not like the smell of ether, and acting upon the advice of a chemist-pharmacist in Liverpool, David Walde, Simpson experimented with other volatile organic solvents such as chloride of hydrocarbon, acetone, nitrate of ethyl, benzene, iodoform and chloroform. He became convinced that chloroform was the best anaesthetic of all, because it acted more rapidly than ether and was more persistent. 'No person, so far as I am aware, has used it by inhalation or discovered its remarkable anaesthetic properties till the date of my own experiments.'[12] Simpson used chloroform in tooth-drawing, opening abscesses, the relief of neuralgia, etc., but most importantly for relieving the pains of childbirth. Though he was criticized by the clerical establishment for using anaesthesia in childbirth, he quoted the Bible to point out that God took the rib from Adam to create Eve, first putting Adam into a deep sleep. When he helped Queen Victoria in 1853 through the pain of giving birth to her seventh child (Prince Leopold) the criticism stopped. In his *Account of a new anaesthetic agent as a substitute for sulphuric ether* he described a case of childbirth in a lady in her second confinement: Three and a half hours after the birth pains commenced

> . . . I placed her under the influence of the chloroform, by moistening with half a tea-spoonful of the liquid, a pocket-handkerchief, rolled up in a funnel shape, and with the broad or open end of the funnel placed over her mouth and nostrils . . . The child was expelled in about twenty-five minutes after the inhalation was begun.[13]

The infant cried out, but the mother was 'soporose' and then the baby was removed to another room. After the expulsion of the placenta, the lady woke up

> and observed to me that she had 'enjoyed a very comfortable sleep, and indeed required it, as she was so tired, but would now be more able for the work before her.' . . . In a little time she again remarked that she was afraid

her 'sleep had stopped the pains'. Shortly afterwards her infant was brought in by the nurse from the adjoining room, and it was a matter of no small difficulty to convince the astonished mother that the labor was entirely over, and that the child presented to her was really her 'own living baby'.[14]

Another famous physician who began to use chloroform as an anaesthetic in November 1847 was Dr John Snow in London (famous for having stopped the cholera epidemic in London in 1854).

So who should be credited with the discovery of modern anaesthetics? Out of the gallery of the contenders Clarke, Long, Wells, Jackson and Morton, Clarke and Long missed the opportunity because they did not publish their experiences with ether. Wells, who consciously looked for an anaesthetic agent and chose nitrous oxide, was unfortunate because his only public demonstration did not go off well. Although the person who had the idea of using ether was Jackson, it was Morton who carried out the successful trials and therefore if only one person should be called the discoverer of general anaesthesia, the choice would fall on him.

Local anaesthesia – it all started with cocaine

This was an interesting development in the discovery of local anaesthetics. Here again the facts were staring medical practitioners in the face, but they did not draw the obvious conclusions.

In 1855 the German chemist Friedrich Gädke isolated an alkaloid from the leaves of a Peruvian coca plant (*Erythroxylum coca*) and in 1960 Albert Niemann, of the University of Göttingen, characterized it and observed that when it was taken by mouth it had a bitter taste and numbed the tongue. Professor Schroff, speaking in 1862 at the Viennese Medical Society, stressed that cocaine also narrowed the peripheral arteries and caused the widening of the pupils.

Sigmund Freud was fascinated by cocaine. He tried it on himself and the members of his family. In a review of literature on Coca, Freud wrote: 'a small dose lifted me to the heights in a wonderful fashion.'[15] Freud recommended the use of cocaine in cases of neurasthenia. One of his patients died of an overdose of cocaine, and his friend Fleisch, whom Freud tried to cure of morphine addiction, became a cocaine addict and developed delirium tremens. There is an indication that Freud was aware of the value of cocaine as an anaesthetic. In an article *'Über Coca'*, published in July 1884, he wrote that cocaine had anaesthetizing effects on the mucous membranes and therefore could be used as a local antiseptic.

'Indeed the anaesthetizing properties of cocaine should make it suitable for a good many further applications.'[16]

In 1879 Vassili von Anrep, a Russian nobleman, published a paper in Würzburg[17] describing the locally numbing effects of cocaine. He also suggested that this drug might become important in medicine. Neither he nor Freud noted that under the influence of cocaine the conjunctiva of the eye became insensitive to pain. However, this important fact was only noticed and appreciated in 1884 by Carl Koller, an ophthalmologist in Vienna. His attention was caught by a sentence in a textbook of pharmacology published at that time to the effect that because of its anaesthetizing effect upon the mucous membranes (of the tongue), cocaine 'might deserve experimental trial in quite a number of diseases.' Koller, being associated with Freud, also knew about Freud's experiments with cocaine. In her father's biography Koller's daughter, Hortense Becker, quotes what he said to her:[18]

> Upon one occasion another colleague of mine, Dr. Engel, partook of some [cocaine] with me from the point of his penknife and remarked, 'How that numbs the tongue', I said. 'Yes, that has been noticed by everyone that has eaten it'. And in the moment it flashed upon me that I was carrying in my pocket the local anaesthetic for which I had searched some years earlier. I went straight to the laboratory, asked the assistant for a guinea pig for the experiment, made a solution of cocaine from the powder which I carried in my pocketbook, and instilled it into the eye of the animal.

Koller's assistant, a Dr Gärtner, who was present at this experiment, related later in 1919:

> Now it was necessary to go one step further and to repeat the experiment upon a human being. We trickled the solution under the upraised lids of each other's eyes. Then we put a mirror before us, took a pin in hand, and tried to touch the cornea with its head. Almost simultaneously we could joyously assure ourselves, 'I can't feel a thing.' We could make a dent in the cornea without the slightest awareness of the touch, let alone any unpleasant sensation or reaction. With that the discovery of local anaesthesia was completed.[19]

Rejoicing at this discovery, Koller immediately suggested to his friend Jellinek that he should use cocaine in his experiments involving the nose, pharynx and larynx. In any case credit for the use of cocaine as an anaesthetic in ophthalmology is certainly due to Koller. His discovery completely changed medical practice in this field. Until then operations on the eye had to be performed under general anaesthetic, and this caused complications during the recovery period.

In spite of his success in anaesthesia in ophthalmology, Koller did not obtain the position he desired as an assistant in the University Hospital in Vienna, because of anti-semitism. In 1888 he emigrated to the United States and there became one of the most eminent ophthalmologists.[20]

In 1923 cocaine was chemically synthesized by Richard Willstädter.

Endorphins – Thomas Mann's prophecy

There was little really serendipitous about the road to the discovery of endogenous opiates – the endorphins. The story of their discovery, however, is presented here because of the prophetic vision of Thomas Mann in his *Magic Mountain* written some seventy years before endorphins were actually found. The setting of Mann's book was Davos, a delightful mountain resort in Switzerland with the longest ski runs in the Alps and at that time the largest number of tuberculosis sanatoria. The following conversation takes place there:

> 'Nothing different. – Oh, well, the stuff to-day was pure chemistry', Joachim unwillingly condescended to enlighten his cousin. It seemed there was a sort of poisoning, an auto-infection of the organism, so Dr. Krokowski said; it was caused by the disintegration of a substance, of the nature of which we were still ignorant, but which was present everywhere in the body; and the products of this disintegration operated like an intoxicant upon the nerve-centres of the spinal cord, *with an effect similar to that of certain poisons, such as morphia, or cocaine, when introduced in the usual way from outside* (my italics).

> 'And so you get the hectic flush,' said Hans Castorp. 'But that's all worth hearing. What doesn't the man know! He must have simply lapped it up. You just wait, one of these days he will discover what that substance is that exists everywhere in the body and sets free the soluble toxins *that act like a narcotic on the nervous system*; . . .' (my italics)[21]

In retrospect the stepping stones to the discovery of the prophesied endorphins seem amazingly straightforward and logical, though the fact of their existence came as a total surprise. One of their discoverers, Lars Terenius, said: 'The discovery of endorphins is one of those unexpected events in physiology.'[22]

The ancient Greeks knew that opium *(opion* = poppy-juice) relieved pain and produced euphoria. Early in the nineteenth century opium was shown to contain an alkaloid – morphine. Its chemical analysis indicated that it existed in two stereo-isomerical forms, of which only the lævo-isomer, but not the dextro-isomer, was active. Stereo-isomers are structures of the same compound which have an identical chemical composition, but are mirror images of each other.) This spawned the idea that the brain had to contain some very specific receptors for the lævo-isomer of morphine, and therefore it would be only a matter of suitable techniques and ingenuity to identify these 'opioid' receptors.

And indeed the path to the discovery of endorphins led through the Stanford laboratory of Avram Goldstein who experimented with radio-labelled opiates to find in 1971 a rather disappointing 2 per cent of stereospecific binding in brain homogenates, to Johns Hopkins University where in 1973 Solomon Snyder conclusively demonstrated the existence of opiate receptors by the use of radioactive naloxone, a substance known to compete with morphine for binding to the receptors.[23]

Scientists now wondered what the opiate receptors were doing in the brain. Certainly evolution would not develop them for the Greeks to use opium or for modern doctors to inject morphine to alleviate pain in their patients. Here we come back to Mann's prophecy. There must be something in our own body that would naturally bind to the receptors. One can thus predict the existence of *endogenous opioids*.[24]

The corroborating evidence that such substances existed came from the experiments of W. J. Murray and J. W. Miller at the University of Wisconsin in 1960, and of David V. Reynolds in 1969. Murray and Miller found that extracts of the pituitary gland had potentiated morphine effects,[25] and Reynolds observed that stimulation by an alternate electric current of a specific site in the brain of rats had made them insensitive to pain induced by pressure on their paws, though it did not affect their responses to other non-painful stimuli.[26]

It was only in 1974 that Lars Terenius isolated from rats' brains a factor bound to opioid receptors with very high affinity and competing with dihydromorphine.

The penultimate step was taken by Hans Kosterlitz and J. J. Hughes (in Aberdeen in Scotland) who first developed a very sensitive bioassay for opioid substances on strips of muscle from guinea pigs' intestines. Opioids inhibited the contraction of these strips induced by stimulation from electric current. In December 1975 they published their paper describing the discovery and isolation from the brain of rats of two peptides with analgesic properties, some twenty times more potent than morphine.

These peptides made of five amino acids they named enkephalins, one the leu–enkephalin and the other met-enkephalin.[27] H. R. Morris then recognized that met-enkephalin was actually a part of the lipoprotein hormone (LPH), discovered in 1964 in the pituitary by C. H. Lee, and that the five-amino acids of enkephalin were identical with the sequence of 61–5-amino acid of this hormone and were a part of what already had been named endorphins (*endo*genous-*morphine*-like substances).

The story does not end there. Avram Goldstein in Stanford identified another 17-amino acid polypeptide, dynorphin which was even 1,000 times more potent than the encephalins. He also showed that dynorphins were present not only in the central nervous system and in the pituitary, but also in the gut.[28] Thus a whole family of hormones with similar chemical structures was identified and named endorphins. Some of these endorphins alleviate pain, others control body temperature, blood pressure, etc.

From the recognition of the presence of opiate receptors in the brain to the discovery of the endorphins took only three to four years, but at least two generations had passed since the prediction of Thomas Mann.[29]

Chance and tranquillizers

The role of chance in the discovery of most of the modern drugs is very significant. Indeed, there are very few drugs that were designed with the prior knowledge of exactly how and where they would act. 'The story of most of the major therapeutic drugs presently employed in psychiatry are largely tales of serendipity.'[30]

For the last twenty to thirty years the pharmaceutical industry and the medical profession have provided us with a plethora of various tranquillizers to allay the anxieties prevalent in modern society. Chance was also instrumental in the discovery of two classes of tranquillizers, the meprobamates and the benzodiazepines (as represented by Miltown and Valium, respectively).[31]

Until the early fifties the only tranquillizers widely used were the barbiturates (such as, for example, phenobarbitol). They acted like alcohol, allaying anxiety, but inducing sleep.

Frank M. Berger, a pharmacologist who fled during World War II from Czechoslovakia to London, tried to develop anti-bacterial agents against gram-negative bacteria, since the newly discovered penicillin would not act on them. While screening a large number of chemicals, Berger observed that injected mice became paralysed, and that their paralysis was due to massive relaxation of the muscles. This was a chance observation which had a very important medical sequel. The compound was soon used as a muscle relaxant (in case of spasms or troubles with the discs in the spine) under the name of mephensin. The second chance observation was that people taking mephensin to relax their muscles were also relieved of various symptoms of anxiety. Many derivatives of mephensin were then tested and in 1955 meprobamate, under the name Miltown, was introduced into medical practice. It had the advantage over barbiturates that it did not affect the alertness of the patients, at least when used for a short time. Later it was found that after prolonged use Miltown not only induced drowsiness, but was potentially addictive.[32]

The enormous initial success of Miltown led the drug companies to search for other chemical tranquillizers. One of the scientists involved in such a search in the Roche Drug Company in Nutley, New Jersey, was a Polish-born chemist, Leo Sternbach. For two years he studied various compounds belonging to a group called quinazolines. Out of the many compounds he tested, none had any sedative effects on mice. As chance would have it, he did not test the last compound in his series at all. Two years later he gave this untested compound to Lovell Randall (also at Roche). Randall injected it into experimental animals and found that it had properties similar to those of meprobamate. The compound was named Librium. Sternbach then found that Librium was not a quinazoline at all, but belonged to another class of chemicals now called *benzodiazepines*. Thus Sternbach not only made a chemical error, he also failed to test this 'erroneous' compound. Nevertheless a very important tranquillizer, Librium, had been discovered and began to be marketed in 1960. One of the best-known derivatives of Librium is Valium (it has an additional oxygen, and the residual $NHCH_3$ is replaced by CH_3). Today there are many more drugs, members of the benzodiazepine family, and their use is staggering.

Why Valium and the like acted as they did was not understood. It took some seventeen years to uncover the molecular mode of action of these tranquillizers, when Hans Mohler (of Roche in Basel) and Claus Braestrup and Michael Squires (of Ferrosan, Denmark) discovered the benzodiazepine receptors using the procedure that had been developed for endorphins. This in turn led John Tallman of the National Institute for Mental Health (in the United States) to demonstrate that the benzodiazepine receptor was a part of a larger protein molecule, which also harboured the receptor for the inhibitory neuro-transmitter GABA (gamma amino-butyric acid). Thus it seems that the calming effects of

Valium are mediated by its binding to the receptor and the stimulation of the GABA receptor so as to inhibit neurons in various parts of the brain, especially in the so-called limbic system which regulates our emotional behaviour.

The story of the discovery of benzodiazepine 'provides another example of the important role of serendipity in science.'[33]

Psychedelic drugs and the cure of mental disturbances

One of the most dramatic discoveries occurred in the field of psychedelic drugs. They had already been described in the sixteenth century by Francisco Hernandez, the physician to King Phillip II of Spain, who on his visits to Mexico had learned from the Aztecs of the psychedelic effects of eating the peyote cactus. In 1918 this cactus was found to contain mescaline. Spanish priests also recorded rituals of the Indians in which their mushroom 'teonanactl' ('food for gods') induced visions and hallucinations in its consumers. In 1955 the mushroom was identified as *Psilocybe*.

In 1943 Dr Albert Hofmann at the Sandoz Drug Company in Basel, while synthesizing semi-synthetic derivatives of ergot (used, like ergonovine, for precipitating labour) prepared lysergic acid diethylamide (LSD_{25}). This was the twenty-fifth compound in a series that, according to the Company's policy, should not have been synthesized. On 16 April 1953, while in the process of purifying and crystallizing this compound, Hofmann felt dizziness and restlessness. He went home and then for two hours he entered a dreamlike state in which he saw fantastic pictures, colours and extraordinary shapes.

Suspecting that this state had something to do with the compound he had worked with, after a few days Hofmann intentionally ingested 0.25 milligrams of LSD_{25} (now known to be a very large dose indeed). For fourteen hours he experienced 'demonic transformation of the external world,'[34] a fear of being possessed by a demon and going insane, a feeling of being outside his body, all very terrifying. Thus LSD was born as a psychedelic drug, which in the long run brought more harm than relief: many users killed themselves or became schizophrenic.

Hofmann was alert enough to tie in the unusual trance he experienced with the compound he was working with. This association brought about the discovery of LSD.

The discovery of some of the therapeutic drugs for the treatment of mental diseases was also a combination of accident and good judgement. This was so in the case of chlorpromazine for the treatment of schizophrenia and lithium for manic patients.

John Cade, an Australian psychiatrist, was first to have the idea of administering lithium to relieve the symptoms of manic disease. In the 1940s he was working in a small psychiatric hospital where he developed a theory that mania was caused by a toxin which reached and affected the brain and was also excreted in urine. He therefore injected guinea pigs with concentrated urine from manic patients and from normal subjects. He noted that the patients' urine was more toxic than that of normal subjects.

Since Cade had no biochemical facilities, he tried to unravel the meaning of this finding by animal experiments. He reasoned that he should inject the various chemical ingredients of urine such as urea or uric acid separately to guinea pigs and the results would provide the answer. The injection of urea caused the death of the animals, but the concentration of urea in the urine of normal subjects and of manic patients was the same, so urea as a cause was out. Next he wanted to test uric acid, but he encountered the problem of solubility. In order to make uric acid soluble in water he had to convert it to a salt by reacting it with metal. Lithium urate was soluble, and blocked the lethal effects of urea. It also had a calming effect on the animals. In order to find which of the components of the compound – the lithium or the uric acid – was effective, he tried lithium carbonate in a separate experiment and found that this compound alone had a calming effect on the experimental guinea pigs.

This observation led Cade to administer lithium carbonate to manic patients. His first patient was a fifty-one-year-old man who had suffered from constant manic excitement for five years. Within five days of the administration of lithium (three times a day), the manic symptoms disappeared. The patient continued with the lithium therapy and eventually was able to lead a normal family life.

Cade's success was based on wrong reasoning. First we now know that lithium appeared to calm the guinea pigs by making them sick, and second there is actually nothing abnormal in the urine of manic patients.

After Cade had achieved good therapeutic results with ten other patients, he published his observations in 1949 in an Australian journal,[35] but no one paid any attention to his findings. It was not until 1954, when Mogens Schou in Denmark confirmed Cade's findings, that the use of lithium for mania spread through Europe. In the United States lithium therapy did not develop until the mid-sixties. In 1969 Schou had data to show that prophylactic treatment with lithium prevented mania and depression episodes in 70–80 per cent of patients.

The discovery of drugs for the treatment of schizophrenia also followed a tortuous and sometimes accidental path.[36] In 1950 the French neurosurgeon, Henri Laborit, was trying cocktails of various medications to quieten patients before administering anaesthesia and allaying their fears before surgery. Laborit thought that sudden death occurring during anaesthesia could have been due to the release of histamine. He therefore obtained promethazine as an antihistamine drug from the French drug Company, Rhône-Poulenc. When he used this drug he observed that it had beneficial effects before anaesthesia. He asked Rhône-Poulenc to provide him with other drugs chemically related to promethazine. One of these drugs given to Laborit was chlorpomazine. It proved to have a pronounced quieting effect on surgical patients. This observation led Laborit to recommend the use of chlorpromazine to his psychiatric colleagues for use in calming agitated patients.

In 1951 Jean Delay and Pierre Deniker, in Paris, started giving chlorpromazine in ever-increasing doses to psychiatric patients suffering from anxiety, hyperactivity and schizophrenia. They found that chlorpromazine had sedative effects, but, in contrast with barbiturates, it did not put patients to sleep, and thus made them more manageable without making them unconscious. They then observed that chlorpromazine in high doses had a peculiar effect on schizophrenic, but not other, patients. That is, it produced the symptoms of Parkinson's disease (rigidity, difficulty in moving, tremor of the limbs), but at the same time it improved the state of the mental patients. They deduced that the drug must have been acting on two specific locations in the brain, one connected with the site producing Parkinson's disease (*corpus striatum*) and the other associated with what was causing schizophrenia (the limbic system). They called such drugs neuroleptic (from the Greek, 'clasp the neuron'). Soon they also found that derivates of chlorpromazine, lacking their sedative effects, acted on schizophrenics.

On the other side of the ocean an American psychiatrist, Dr Nathan Kline, was experimenting with reserpine, an extract of an Indian snakeroot plant (*Rauwolfia serpentina*). In Indian folk medicine such extracts were known to help mental patients, but since 1931 the extract was known better as an anti-hypertensive drug (reducing high blood pressure).

Kline's practice showed that reserpine, when given to schizophrenic patients, relieved them of their symptoms and produced a response similar to that already known with chlorpromazine (such as Parkinson's symptoms).

At this point biochemists entered the stage and discovered that reserpine depleted the brains, and particularly the *corpus striatum*, of substances known as biogenic amines such as serotonine, norepinephrine and dopamine.

Because of the similarity in the action of reserpine and chlorpromazine in schizophrenics, Arvid Carlson in Sweden assumed that chlorpromazine would also deplete rats' brain of biogenic amines, but to his surprise this was not the case: all three amines remained at the normal levels. Concentrating on dopamine, Carlson then tested various neuroleptics and in 1963 he found that the more potent the drug was in increasing dopamine metabolites, the better was its action in relieving schizophrenic symptoms. Carlson thus faced a puzzle: reserpine caused the disappearance of dopamine from the brain: chlorpromazine raised the levels of dopamine metabolites. To resolve this apparent contradiction Carlson suggested that neuroleptics block the dopamine receptors on nerve cells in a selective way. In 1976 this proved to be true at least for one of the two types of dopamine receptors, the D2.[37] So it is now clear that dopamine neurons in the brain regulate mental processes that are deranged in schizophrenia.

The problem that now faces pychiatrists and neurophysiologists is how to devise a drug that would affect D2 receptors only in the part of the brain that is responsible for mental disarrangement (the limbic system) without affecting the *corpus striatum* or the pituitary gland.

Thus, on one hand, a wrong asumption of toxicity, followed by the accidental use of lithium in the form of a soluble salt or uric acid led to the discovery of the treatment of mania, and on the other, keen observation of the effects of an anti-hypertensive drug led to the discovery of the beneficial effects of reserpine and its derivatives in schizophrenia.

In his excellent book *Drugs and the Brain*, Solomon H. Snyder (of Johns Hopkins University) summed up this story by saying: 'The interplay of science, serendipity and sheer blunder in the development of the mood modifying and other psychoactive drugs may perplex and alarm some readers . . . One of the fascinations of the discovery process is that we often find the right answer by looking in the wrong place.'[38]

Psychoneuro-immunology

In the spring of 1974 Robert Ader, of the University of Rochester Medical School, sent a letter to the editor of *Psychosomatic Medicine*, which began with the following sentence: 'Observations made during the course of a series of parametric studies of the illness-induced taste aversion paradigm suggested that we have *inadvertently* [my italics] conditioned a suppression of the immune system.'[39] What was this 'illness-induced taste aversion' experiment? It was of the type of Pavlovian experiment, where dogs are conditioned to respond to the sound of a bell with salivation as if they were being presented with a piece of meat. In Ader's case rats were presented with a sweet solution of saccharin (conditioned stimulus (CS)) and this was coupled with an injection, thirty minutes later, of 50 mg of cyclophosphamide (unconditioned stimulus (UCS)), a drug which induces temporary nausea. The presentation of these two stimuli together resulted in the development of an aversion to saccharin. This dislike of saccharin solutions was observed when the rats were offered saccharin, at three-day intervals after the conditioning session. The rats that drank more saccharin solution at the first session disliked the sweet solution more, though on repeated trials cyclophosphamide was not used again.

Between forty-five and sixty days after the initial training some rats began to die. This death was strange because the original dose of cyclophosphamide injected was well below the level toxic to rats. Ader, however, noticed that the rats that died were those that drank most of the saccharine solution. It dawned on him that these unexpected deaths might be somehow related to another property of cyclophosphamide, aside from causing nausea, namely to the fact that it was an immunosuppressive drug. Ader then reasoned that the mortality might have been due not to a direct effect of cyclophosphamide, but to an expected conditioning of an immunosuppressive response by the consumption of saccharin.

Ader wrote in his letter to the journal: 'The potential significance of behaviorally conditioned immunosuppressive response seemed to warrant a report of this unexpected observation.[40] In his letter to me he wrote: 'The serendipitous observation of mortality in a straightforward study of taste aversion conditioning with cyclophosphamide . . . led to the establishment of a functional link between the nervous and the immune system. The "discovery" was not a "chance" event as such, but, the hypothesis did derive from a serendipitous result.' Later studies of Ader and Cohen[41] and a host of other researchers led to the development of a new burgeoning field known as psychoneuro-immunology. *Brain, Behavior and Immunity* is now the journal hosting articles in this new field.

Psycho-immunology is based on the idea that the brain influences the immune system and our resistance to diseases. Indeed, Ader and Cohn found direct proof. In their saccharin-cyclophosphamide-conditioned animals various parameters of the immune system of rats became suppressed or defective (e.g. in the production of antibodies in response to an immune challenge). The rational explanation of this phenomenon is based on the similarities between neuro-transmitters and immuno-modulators, such as the common receptor for various hormones or neuropeptides (endorphins) found both in nerve cells and in the cells of the immune system. Moreover, anatomically there are direct contacts between nerve endings and the organs of the immune system (thymus, spleen, bone marrow). The existing findings suggest the existence of a mechanism involved in complex pathogenesis of psychosomatic disease and help us to understand why a psychological stress (such as bereavement, divorce, loss of a job, loneliness, etc.) makes us more likely to fall ill.

It is also clear that immune cells can produce compounds that affect the brain. Thus a hypothesis of immune aetiology for some mental disorders becomes quite attractive.

The Portuguese man-of-war and anaphylaxis

In 1902 Charles Richet discovered anaphylaxis and in 1913 was honoured with the Nobel Prize for it.

Anaphylaxis, meaning 'protection against', is an immunological reaction which, instead of conferring protection upon the animal or person upon a repeated injection of a proteinaceous material, causes hypersensitization. Thus injection of horse serum into humans can cause an anaphylactic shock and death.

Richet stated in his Nobel Prize lecture that his discovery was 'by no means the result of profound thought, but a simple observation, almost a fortuitous one; so that my merit has only been in letting myself see facts which were plain before me.'[42]

The story began when Richet, as a guest of Prince Albert of Monaco, on his yacht, was studying the poison of *Physalia physalis* (Portuguese man-of-war), a coelenterate which floats on the surface of tropical seas and lets its 2- to 3-metre-long tentacles hang downwards. These tentacles are equipped with small sucking cups, which attach to the prey and inject a strong poison into it. Contact with *Physalia* is very painful because of the multiple injection of its poison. During his study Richet and his colleagues George Richard and Paul Portier found that the *Physalia* poison can be extracted from the tentacles by glycerol. This toxin was later found to be a small polypeptide (eight-to-ten-amino acids).

When I came back to France and had no more Physalia to study, I hit upon the idea of making a comparative study of the tentacles of the Actinia

(*Actinia equina, Actinia sulcata*) which can be obtained in large quantities, for Actinia abound on all the rocky shores of Europe.

Now Actinia tentacles, treated with glycerol, give off their poison into the glycerol and the extract is toxic. I therefore set about finding how toxic it was, with Portier. This was quite difficult to do, as it is a slowly acting poison and three or four days must elapse before it can be known if the dose be fatal or not. I was using a solution of one kilo of glycerol to one kilo of tentacles. The lethal dose was of the order of 0.1 ml liquid per kilo live weight of subject.

But certain of the dogs survived, either because the dose was not strong enough or for some other reason. At the end of two or four weeks, as they seemed normal, I made use of them for a new experiment.

An unexpected phenomenon arose, which we thought extraordinary. A dog when injected previously even with the smallest dose, say of 0.005 ml liquid per kilo, immediately showed serious symptoms: vomiting, blood diarrhoea, syncope, unconsciousness, asphyxia and death.[43]

Richet repeated these experiments several times and found that this anaphylactic reaction was conditioned by previous contact with the 'antigen', that the symptoms were entirely different from those obtained on the initial contact, and that the anaphylactic state needed three to four weeks of incubation to become established. In 1907 Richet also found that an anaphylactic state was produced by the injection of the blood of sensitized animals into a normal subject. Later others found that anaphylaxis was produced not only by poisons, but by all proteins (such as serum, milk, egg, etc.) and Sir Henry Dale independently discovered the same phenomenon 'by a stroke of luck' when he observed that a strip of the intestinal muscle of a guinea pig contracted violently in the presence of traces of horse (but not other animal) serum. This eventually led him to attribute allergic reactions to histamine.[44]

Anaphylaxis was born by chance accurate observation.

NOTES TO CHAPTER 7

1 Dioscorides, *De materia medica* 4.75. Cf. Underwood, K. A. 1946: Before and after Morton. A historical survey of anaesthesia. *British Medical Journal*, 2: 526.
2 Davy, H. 1800: *Researches, chemical and philosophical chiefly concerning nitrous oxide, or dephlogisticated nitrous air.* (Conclusions, Section III). London: J. Johnson.

128   *What Changes Our Behaviour?*

3 Underwood, 1946, Before and after Morton: 527.
4 Faraday, M. 1818: Effects of inhaling the vapours of sulfuric ether. *Quarterly Journal of Science and Arts*, 4: 158.
5 Underwood, Before and after Morton: 526.
6 Taylor, F. L., 1928: *Crawford Long and the Discovery of Ether Anaesthesia.* New York: Paul B. Hoeber.
7 Long, C. W. 1849: An account of the first use of sulphuric ether by inhalation as an anaesthetic in surgical operations. *South Medical Surgery Journal*, 5: 705.
8 Comroe, *Retrospectroscope*: 76.
9 Morton, W. T. G. 1850: Comparative value of sulfuric ether and chloroform. *Boston Medical Surgery Journal*, 43: 109.
10 Clendening, L. 1942: *A Source Book of Medical History*. New York: Dover Publications.
11 Underwood, Before and after Morton: 621.
12 Morton, Comparative value: 112.
13 Simpson, J. Y. 1847: Discovery of a new anaesthetic agent more efficient than sulphuric acid. *Provincial Medical and Surgical Journal* (10 March), reprinted in *British Medical Journal*, 1946, 2: 542.
14 Ibid.: 542.
15 Van Dyke, C. and Byck, R. 1982: Cocaine, *Scientific American*, 246/3: 111.
16 Freud, S. Über Coca. Reprinted in S. H. Snyder, 1986: *Drugs and the Brain.* New York: Scientific American Books, Inc.
17 Anrep, G. V. and Starling, E. H. 1925: Central and reflex regulation of the circulation. *Proceedings of the Royal Society*, London, (B), 97: 463.
18 Becker, H. K. 1963: Karl Koller and cocaine. *Psychoanalytic Quarterly*. Reprinted in R. Byck (ed.), *Cocaine Papers – Sigmund Freud*. New York: Stonehill.
19 Comroe, *Retrospectroscope*: 68.
20 Ibid.: 70f.
21 Mann, T. 1960: *The Magic Mountain* (translation by H. T. Lowe-Porter, Penguin Books: Harmondsworth): 188.
22 Terenius, L. 1978: Endogenous peptides and analgesia. *Annual Review of Pharmacology and Toxicology* 18: 189
23 Pert, C. and Snyder, S. H. 1973: Opiate receptor. Demonstration in nervous tissue. *Science*, 179: 101.
24 Snyder, S. H. and Bennet, J. P. Jr. 1976: Neurotransmitter receptors in the brain: biochemical identification. *Annual Review of Physiology*, 18: 153.

25 Murray, W. J. and Miller, J. W. 1960: Potency differences of morphine-type agents by radiant heat and 'cramping' analgesic assays providing evidence for a potentiating substance from the posterior pituitary gland. *Journal of Pharmacology and Experimental Therapy*, 128: 380.
26 Reynolds, D. W. 1969: Surgery in the rat during electrical analgesia induced by focal brain stimulation. *Science*, 164: 444.
27 Hughes, J., Smith, T. V., Kosterlitz, H. Fothergill, L. A. Morgan, B. A. and Morris, H. R.: 1975: Identification of two related pentapeptides from the brain with potent opiate agonist activity. *Nature*, 258: 577.
28 Goldstein, A. 1976: 'Opioid' peptides (Endorphins) in pituitary and brain. *Science*, 193: 1081.
29 Crapo, L. 1985: *Hormones: the Messengers of Life.* New York: W. H. Freeman and Co.
Snyder, S. H. 1986: *Drugs and the Brain*. New York: Scientific American Books, Inc.
30 Snyder, *Drugs and the Brain*: 110.
31 Ibid.: 158.
32 Berger, F. M. 1981: The use of antianxiety drugs. *Clinical Pharmacology and Therapeutics*, 29: 291.
33 Snyder, 1986, *Drugs and the Brain*: 159–63.
34 Ibid.: 193.
35 Cade, J. F. J. 1949: Lithium salts in the treatment of psychotic excitement. *Medical Journal of Australia*, 1: 195.
36 Snyder, *Drugs and the Brain*: 71–4.
37 Crease, I., Burt, D. R. and Snyder, S. H. 1976: Dopamine receptor binding predicts clinical and pharmacological potencies of antischizo-phrenic drugs. *Science*, 192: 481.
38 Snyder, *Drugs and the Brain*: 119.
39 Ader, R. 1974: Behaviorally conditioned immunosuppression. *Psychosomatic Medicine*, 36: 183.
40 Ibid.: 184.
41 Ader, R. and Cohen, N. 1985: CNS – immune systems interactions. Conditioning phenomena. *Behavioral and Brain Science*, 8: 379.
42 Dale, H. H. 1948: Accident and opportunism in medical research. *British Medical Journal*, 2: 451.
43 Lane, C. E. 1960: The Portuguese man-of-war. *Scientific American*, 202/3: 158.
44 Comroe, *Retrospectroscope*: 56.

8

Medical Discoveries

Night driving and discovery

Can an animal live without the pituitary gland? It has been known for a long time that the pituitary gland (*hypophysis*), suspended from the base of the brain, is an essential gland. This gland is the producer of various hormones which control the hormone productions by other glands in the body. The pituitary hormones include ACTH (adrenocorticotropic hormone, MSH (melanocyte stimulating hormone), the growth hormone, a hormone controlling insulin, oxytocin, etc.).

In the year 1940 A. V. Nalbandov became interested in the effects of hypophysectomy (the removal of the pituitary gland) in chickens.[1] For several weeks he had been trying to master the technique, but as his English colleagues (A. S. Parkes and R. T. Hill) had found earlier, the chickens died within a few weeks after the operation. So experiments could be done on such chickens only for a week or so. After a while, the chickens suddenly stayed alive after the operation not only for three weeks, but on occasion even for a few months. Nalbandov first attributed this success to his improved surgical skill, but when he started another long-term study, not only did the freshly operated chicks, but also those that had survived for several months, die. He had no rational explanation for what was happening, particularly when after a period, the hypophysectomy was again successful and the birds did not die. He said to Dr Beveridge: 'You can imagine how frustrating it was to be unable to take advantage of something that was obviously having a profound effect on the ability of these animals to withstand the operation.'[2] Nalbandov then remembered that one night, while he was returning from a party at 2 a.m., he had passed the laboratory building and noticed that lights were burning in the animal rooms. He went in to switch off the lights, but then a few days later he again found that the lights in the animal rooms had been left burning the whole night. Upon enquiry, he discovered that the lights had been left on by a substitute janitor whose task was to close the windows and lock the doors in the animal room. Not familiar with the layout of the laboratory, the new janitor preferred to leave the light on in order to find his way out. Upon further investigation, Nalbandov found that the two survival periods of the chickens coincided with the dates when the usual janitor had been replaced by the new one.

Following this 'discovery' Nalbandov was able to establish by controlled experiments that chickens with their pituitary glands removed died when kept in darkness, but if they received two one-hour periods of light per night, they would live indefinitely. He was also able to explain this strange phenomenon by finding that chickens without pituitary did not eat in the dark, and developed fatal hypoglycaemia, while those that had periods of light during the night would eat and stay alive.

What makes us sleep?

In the late 1930s John R. Pappenheimer, Professor of Physiology at the Harvard Medical School in Boston, was studying with his mentor, J. Wyman, the surface tension of aqueous solutions of dipolar ions. In the next two decades he worked on oxygen consumption and the haemodynamics of kidneys, as well as on diffusion through the peripheral capillaries. In 1965 Pappenheimer's studies involved the ionic composition of the cerebro-spinal fluid (CSF) and its relation to breathing control. For these studies Pappenheimer mastered the techniques of having small (cats) and large (goats) animals operated on so that through stereotactically positioned cannulae and tubes he had the access to the ventricles of the brain of these animals.[3]

Pappenheimer relates[4] that he used to spend Saturday mornings browsing amongst recent journals in the library. On one occasion, in 1965, he stumbled on an article by Monnier and Hossli[5] reporting the sleep-inducing properties of venous blood from the brains of animals that had been electrically stimulated in the part of the brain called the ventromedial thalamus; this area was known to be involved in the regulation of sleep. As it turned out, in 1913 Henri Pieron, experimenting on dogs, had demonstrated that dogs receiving cerebro-spinal fluid from sleep-deprived donor dogs would sleep for several hours, while the recipients of CSF from normal donors remained alert.[6] He named this sleep-inducing substance *hypnotoxin*. These experiments were later confirmed (in 1939) by Jerome C. Schneedorf and A. C. Ivy from Northwestern University. Nine out of twenty dogs, receiving CSF from sleep-deprived dogs, fell asleep within forty-five minutes and slept for two to four hours.[7]

The chance reading of a paper unrelated to his current work changed the course of Pappenheimer's research. Together with Miller and Goodrich, he embarked on sleep research. In his first experiments, reported in 1967, he corroborated Pieron's original findings that CSF from a sleep-deprived goat, when infused into the ventricles of a cat, 'made the cat torporous for several hrs.'[8]

During the next fifteen years Pappenheimer and his many collaborators tried to isolate the sleep-inducing factor from 6 litres of CSF from twenty-five goats, 15,000 rabbits' brains and 5,000 litres of human urine. The effort was finally crowned with success. In collaboration with Karnovsky and Krueger the factor was isolated and later identified as a muramyl peptide.[9] This peptide would *per se* induce the so-called slow-wave sleep into animals.

Pappenheimer and his colleagues were not alone in this effort. At the University of Tokyo Koji Uchizono independently extracted sleep-promoting material from the brains of 1,000 sleep-deprived rats: the active material extracted from 100 grams of brains amounted to a millionth of a gram![10]

Historically there are three paradigms concerning sleep-modulating factors:

(1) *Sleep deprivation* causes an accumulation of a substance in the brain that induces sleep in the animals (Pieron's substance, Pappenheimer's factor, Uchizono's sleep-promoting substance and Jouvet's paradoxical sleep factor (PS);[11]

(2) *Neurohumoral sleep mechanisms* (as proposed by Guido A. Schoenenberger in Monnier's laboratory.[12] When a cat's thalamus is electrically stimulated, the animal falls into a prolonged sleep, presumably because the electrical stimulation causes the release of a hormone that has sleep-inducing properties. This group isolated the so-called delta sleep-inducing peptide (DSIP) following an electrical stimulation of the brain.

(3) *Sleep-modulating peptides*. Some hormones may have multiple functions. Thus Jouvet discovered that vasoactive intestinal peptide (VIP) modulates sleep. He also suggested that serotonin as a neuro-transmitter interacting with neurons and receptors induces sleep. Pavel and his colleagues discovered another peptide, arginine-vasotocin (AVT) which is so potent that about 1,000 molecules of it induced a thirty-minute sleep within five minutes of administration.[13]

There is no clear answer as to what is the true sleep factor. DSIP and

AVT have different effects in different species. Only muramyl peptides have induced slow-wave sleep in all mammals tested. The activity of muramyl dipeptide (MDP) in promoting sleep would have been rather strange were it not for the interesting correlation: MDP in nature is a bacterial cell-wall product and it is known to enhance, as an adjuvant, the immune response of the infected host. Why then should a substance that enhances the immune response also induce sleep? Krueger proposes a theory saying that sleep serves as an immune function. Indeed slow-wave delta sleep may be modulated by substances induced during an infection such as interleukin -1, interferon, tumor necrosis factor, etc.[14] We all know that, on the one hand, infectious diseases are accompanied by increased sleepiness, and on the other, that in old age both the sleep requirement and the immune functions decrease. It is therefore quite surprising that 100 years before, Elie Metchnikoff, the pioneer of cellular immunity, had the idea that the type of bacterial flora might affect sleep.[15]

So on the road to the discovery of sleep factors, the missed opportunity was that of Pieron because, with the knowledge and techniques available at that time, he could not carry his research any further and so his hypnotoxin had to wait some sixty years before it was again taken up in Monnier's laboratory. Pappenheimer's research on sleep factors was the result of a chance reading of Monnier's article on the subject. From then on the ramification of the sleep research developed in the usual pattern of scientific investigation – isolation, identification, synthesis, correlative studies of various factors. In spite of the remarkable progress in the field there is still a long way to go before we truly understand which are the real sleep factors, how they work on the molecular level and what is their deeper evolutionary significance.

Schäfer did not believe it

The discovery of adrenalin as a hormone causing an increase in blood pressure was accidentally made by Dr George Oliver, a physician at Harrogate. In winter in his free time he used to conduct experiments on the members of his family. He devised a special apparatus to measure the thickness of the radial artery (the artery in the forearm and the palm of the hand). On one occasion, while the apparatus was in position on his son's forearm, he injected him with an extract of suprarenal gland which he had obtained from the local butcher. (Would a doctor today do such an experiment on his son?) He observed that the injection did cause a significant change in the thickness of the artery. He thought this observation important enough to take the vial of the extract with him and to proceed to London, to Professor Schäfer at University College. Oliver found him in the laboratory performing an experiment on a dog; the experiment involved measuring the animal's blood pressure. Oliver told the incredulous Schäfer about his observation and eventually persuaded him to inject the extract into the dog at the termination of the original experiment. 'And just so, to convince Oliver that it was all nonsense, Schäfer gave the injection and watched in amazement as the mercury mounted in the arterial manometer until the recording float was lifted almost out of the distal limb.'[16]

The discovery of radioimmunoassay

'Radioimmunoassay came into being not by directed design but more as a fallout from our investigation into what might be considered an unrelated study' on insulin.[17] In the early fifties Solomon Berson and Rosalyn S. Yalow (of the Veteran Administration Hospital in the Bronx) put the question whether the lack of insulin in the circulation of diabetic patients was due to lack of secretion of insulin, or was caused by abnormal destruction of insulin by an excess of a natural insulin-degrading enzyme. In order to be able to determine the fate of the insulin in the body they injected insulin (labelled with [131]Iodine) intravenously into diabetic and non-diabetic subjects.[18]

They found that insulin disappeared more slowly from the blood of the diabetic patients who had been previously treated with insulin than from subjects who never had received insulin before. Berson and Yalow interpreted this result as indicating that insulin-treated patients developed antibodies to insulin, that these antibodies formed soluble complexes with the injected insulin and therefore the insulin was retained in the circulation for longer. In order to verify this hypothesis, they ran plasma samples of the subjects injected with radioactive insulin in an electrophoretic set-up which, by means of electric current, separated the various blood proteins into bands travelling different distances on paper strips. At the end of the electrophoretic run the electropherograms were exposed to photographic film to find the location of the radioactive insulin and then were stained to show where the proteins were. It turned out that insulin appeared to be bound to the globulin region which contains the fractions involved in immune response.

Berson and Yalow described these results in a paper which they first submitted in 1955 to *Science*. Following its rejection, they re-submitted it to the *Journal of Clinical Investigation*, which also rejected it. The reason for the rejection was quite obvious at the time. It was then believed that although insulin was a protein, it was too small to be antigenic, and thus it should not evoke the production of antibodies. After all, millions of people were receiving insulin injections without evidence of allergic reactions and without insulin losing its efficacy in the diabetic patients. Other scientists reasoned that if the injected insulin produced antibodies, the effects would have been seen.

The rejection letter from Stanley E. Bradley, the Editor of the *Journal of Clinical Investigation* (dated 29 September 1955) and addressed to S. A. Berson stated:[19]

I regret that the revision of your paper entitled 'Insulin-I^{131} Metabolism in Human Subjects: Demonstration of Insulin transporting Antibody in the Circulation of Insulin Treated Subjects' is not acceptable for publication in THE JOURNAL OF CLINICAL INVESTIGATION . . .

. . . The second major criticism relates to the dogmatic conclusions set forth which are not warranted by the data. The experts in this field have been particularly emphatic in rejecting your positive statement that the 'conclusion that the globulin responsible for insulin binding in an acquired antibody appears to be inescapable'. They believe that you have not demonstrated an antigen-antibody reaction on the basis of adequate criteria, nor that you have definitely proved that a globulin is responsible for insulin binding, nor that insulin is an antigen. The data you present are indeed suggestive but any more positive claim seems unjustifiable at present.

The paper was eventually published in the *Journal of Clinical Investigation* in 1956 after the authors consented to remove the words 'insulin antibody' from the title and after they had shown experimentally that the binding globulin in the electrophoretic pattern met the criteria for antibody.

The fact that one can measure the binding of a radioactively labelled protein to its antibody opened a new vista for the development of an extremely sensitive and specific method for the quantitative determination of antigens or antibodies in biological fluids. The concentration of an unknown, unlabelled antigen could be obtained by measuring the extent to which it inhibited (by competition) the binding of the same radioactively labelled antigen to its specific antibody. This was based on the finding that the immunological reaction (binding) with specific gamma globulin was the same for an unknown antigen as for a known standardized antigen, provided these antigens were structurally identical. The test became known as radioimmunoassay (RIA).[20]

By means of this test Yalow and Berson could measure exactly the amount of insulin (down to 2–3 micro-units) in unextracted human plasma.[21] To popularize this method, more than 100 scientists were trained and within a few years many endocrinologists were using RIA. By 1975 4,000 hospitals in the United States alone were using RIA. Because of its sensitivity, specificity and ease of performance, RIA permitted the assay of biologically significant materials in body fluids. Not only hormones, but other substances such as drugs, enzymes and viruses could be measured by RIA. It played an important role in the discovery of new precursor forms for such hormones such as insulin, gastrin and ACTH.

In 1977 Rosalyn Yalow, together with R. Guillemin and A. Schally, received the Nobel Prize.

How to stop bleeding: from citrate to heparin

Up to 1914 the problem of blood transfusion was extremely tricky. One could not simply take a blood from a donor, keep it in a container, and then inject it into a recipient, because the blood taken from the donor would clot soon after its removal from the circulation. Direct transfusion between two people connected by artificial tubing would not work either for the same reason. The only way of direct transfusion from person to person was by the surgical joining of the artery of a donor to the vein of the recipient (anastomosing). Considering the surgical difficulties of such an operation and the dangers of infection by bacteria, blood transfusion was an extremely rare undertaking.

There was actually an anti-coagulant that had been discovered in 1896, sodium citrate, but it was not applied. In the first decade of this century it was found to be a dispersing agent which would stabilize a suspension of mastic. In 1914 a Belgian physician, A. Hustin, rediscovered the anti-coagulant properties of sodium citrate by chance, and described its use in transfusion.[22] In 1960, when he wrote an article on blood transfusion, he described again the way he had made the discovery. He said that one day he had a patient dying from having inhaled illuminating gas (carbon-monoxide poisoning). The only way to save the patient would be by withdrawing the blood, oxygenating it, and returning it to the circulation. According to the knowledge then available, the blood would clot and be useless. At that moment Hustin thought of the possibility of using citrate, remembering that this salt kept mastic in suspension. He was not daring enough to apply his idea to the dying patient, but he did some experiments. First he found that the addition of citrate to a tube containing fresh blood delayed its clotting for half an hour; next he injected a dog with citrated blood from another dog and in still another experiment he injected dogs with citrated human blood. Hustin convinced himself that the method worked and therefore on 27 March 1914 at St John's Hospital in Brussels he performed the first transfusion of glucose-citrated blood from one man to another. Hustin explains:

> The idea of citrated transfusion was then born quite naturally from a mind formed by two different disciplines; a physiological and a clinical one, the hospital environment raising the question to solve, the laboratory providing the elements for the answer. Citrate was not the best answer for clot prevention.[23]

In 1916 John McLean discovered heparin and reported the discovery in the *American Journal of Physiology*, stating that while he was studying the thromboplastic (i.e. the enhancing clotting) properties of cephalin he also examined other phosphatides derived from the liver and the heart. Having described in detail how cephalin exerts its blood-coagulating activity, he stated: 'The heparphosphatid . . . when purified by many precipitations in alcohol at 60° has no thromboplastic action and in fact shows a marked power *to inhibit* the coagulation. The anticoagulating action of this phosphatid is being studied and will be reported upon later.'[24] This statement in its terse and rather non-comittal way actually announces the discovery of heparin as an anti-coagulant. The real facts, much more dramatic and interesting, were published by McLean forty-three years later.[25]

McLean's progress in becoming a doctor was strewn with difficulties. He wanted to follow the profession of his father and uncle and to become a surgeon. During the great fire in San Francisco in 1906 his family house was destroyed. In order to be able to attend college McLean worked at all sorts of odd jobs (including mining, oil drilling, etc.). He eventually saved enough money to go to Johns Hopkins in Baltimore where his cousin was teaching anatomy. In Baltimore McLean was accepted as a student by Dr Howell. Howell presented him with a problem which McLean believed that he could solve within a year by working on his own. The problem was to define the thromboplastic substance in the brain, called cephalin. 'My problem was to determine what portion of this crude extract was the active accelerator of the clotting process and to that end, to prepare cephalin as pure as possible and determine if it had thromboplastic action. I was also to test the other components of the crude ether-alcohol extract.'[26]

While preparing for this project, McLean read a paper by Erlandsen and Baskoff describing the process of obtaining lipoids (phosphatides) from the heart and the liver. These 'lipoids' were called cuorin and heparphosphatide. With Howell's consent, McLean prepared cuorin and heparphosphatide in addition to cephalin and tested them periodically for their thromboplastic 'power'. 'If I had not saved them I would probably not have found heparin.'[27]

McLean remembers that as the time went by, a point was reached where his extracts lost their coagulating activity, and even began to retard coagulation. 'I had in mind – of course – no thought of an anti-coagulant but the experimental fact was before me': the extract of liver from which the cephalin's activity disappeared was a strong anti-coagulant!

> I went one morning to the door of Dr. Howell's office and standing there said: 'Dr Howell, I have discovered antithrombin'. He smiled and said: 'Antithrombin is a protein and you are working with phosphatides. Are you sure that salt is not contaminating your substance?' I told him I was not sure of that, but it was a powerful anticoagulant. He was most sceptical. I had the Diener, John Schweinhant, bleed a cat. Into a small beaker full of its blood, I stirred all of a proven batch of heparphosphatides, and I placed it on Dr. Howell's laboratory table and asked him to tell me when it clotted. It never did clot.[28]

At this point Howell became convinced of the discovery of a natural anti-coagulant. He joined McLean's efforts, new batches were prepared and successfully tested, and crowned by the intravenous injection of heparinized blood into a dog.

Heparin was born.

Once again we have a situation, often repeating itself, of a medical student carrying out his own project and stumbling on an unexpected or contradictory observation. Instead of ignoring it, he takes time and effort to convince his sceptical professor of the new and unusual properties of a substance.

How to freeze cells and keep them alive

One of the most important discoveries in modern biology concerns the method of freezing animal cells without injuring their viability. The freezing of sperm, ova and even embryos in their early stages has revolutionized the science and practice of reproduction. Test-tube babies, initiated from frozen sperm or embryos, have become commonplace.

It all started in 1948 by a mistake in the laboratory of Dr A. S. Parkes at the National Institute for Medical Research. At that time his colleagues Dr Anthony Smith and Mr C. Polge used the sugar fructose levulose to protect fowl spermatozoa against the injurious effects of freezing and thawing required for the long term preservation of these cells. The results of this procedure were not very promising. In the course of the study a number of samples of spermatozoa were put away in frozen storage at −79°C.

Some months later these samples were thawed and examined. Most were practically dead, except one in which the spermatozoa were not only motile, but turned out to be fertile too. The investigators interpreted this result by assuming that the chemical structure of fructose somehow had changed, perhaps as a result of contamination by a mould. Chemical analysis showed that the tube did not contain any sugar at all, but according to Dr D. Elliot, who performed the analysis, it had in it glycerol, water and a protein later identified as albumen. In fact the solution turned out to have been 'Mayer's albumen', used by histologists for the coating of glass slides.

It was soon found that next to the bottle with the fructose solution, which was standing on a shelf above the work-bench, there was also one that contained Meyer's albumen. It is most probable that the technician who was preparing the solution of fructose for freezing made a mistake and used Mayer's albumen instead. The active material preserving spermatozoa in freezing was glycerol, which is still used for freezing of cells.[29]

Parkes – speaking at the third International Congress of Animal Reproduction in Cambridge in June 1956 – said: '. . . we never found out exactly what had happened,' and in their paper in *Nature*, describing this discovery, the authors laconically reported on 'the action of glycerol and related compounds to which our attention was directed by *a chance observation* [my italics] in protecting spermatozoa against the effects of low temperatures'.

Tap water leads by mistake to discovery

Dr Sidney Ringer, a physician at University College Hospital, and one of the pioneers in pharmacological research in England, carried out experiments on the hearts of frogs outside their bodies. At the start of the experiments with these such isolated hearts, he found that they would continue to beat for a short time, when held in a solution made of distilled water and table salt (sodium chloride), adjusted to a concentration found in frogs' blood.

In one of the experiments the heart continued to beat for many hours, much beyond the expected time, although as far as Ringer knew, it was immersed in exactly the same solution as before. Since the solutions were being prepared by Ringer's laboratory boy, one Fielder, Ringer questioned him about his procedure in preparing the solutions. Many years later, Fielder, then an old man, told Sir Henry Dale that on that particular occasion, in order to simplify matters he used ordinary tap water instead of the distilled water originally used by Ringer.[30] When this fact eventually became known to Ringer, he set up an analytical test to find what there was in the tap water supplied by the New River Company of North London. The tap water contained a very low concentration of calcium and potassium ions, which, as it turned out, were essential for making an efficient 'physiological solution' that would keep the frog's heart alive and beating outside its body. Thus Ringer's solution was born, and was later improved by Locke and Tyrode to become an essential reagent in everyday use for the maintenance of living cells.[31]

A more recent chance discovery, working in the opposite direction, was made by a physician Dr M. Pras from the Sheba Medical Center in Israel. In his studies on pathological sections taken from patients with Familial Mediterranean fever he tried out many methods of extracting the amyloid bodies (characteristic proteinacous deposits in tissues of these patients) to find, by chance, that the best solvent was just distilled water.

Papain and rabbits' floppy ears

Very personal and readable stories of chance discoveries are described in a book by Lewis Thomas of the State University of New York at Stony Brook, *The Youngest Science*.[32]

When Thomas was at NYU as a fourth-year medical student, he became interested in the so-called Shwartzman phenomenon. This phenomenon is based on an observation that the injection of a small amount of bacterial endotoxin into the skin of a rabbit causes a small inflammation at the site of the injection. However, when another small dose (non-toxic) of endotoxin is injected eighteen hours after this, haemorrhages and necrosis appear in the skin. When the second injection is made intravenously, the result is the destruction of the kidneys of the injected animal.

These facts were known to Thomas. Once, at a seminar on advanced pathology led by his mentor, Professor Mallory, Thomas leaned his chair back and bumped his head against a glass jar containing some tissue specimens, knocking it over.

I picked it up to replace it and saw that it contained a pair of human kidneys with precisely the same lesion as the one in in the photograph [in a paper on the generalized Schwartzman phenomenon]. The label said that the organs were from a woman who had died of eclampsia, with severe bacterial infection as well.

. . . The intrinsically amazing effects of the generalized Shwartzman phenomenon were enough by themselves to catch my interest and make me hanker to work on it, but the human tissue in that glass jar sent me over the line, and from that day on I was resolved to turn myself, one way or another, into an investigation of that queer reaction.[33]

In 1947 Thomas was trying to prevent the Shwartzman phenomenon by injecting various drugs such as cortisone and heparin. He also experimented with papain. He thought that proteolytic enzymes might produce lesions in blood vessels associated with hypersensitivity and the Shwartzman phenomenon. He tried trypsin, ficin and papain, but only papain worked. He found that an injection into the skin of the rabbits of a small amount of papain caused the Shwartzman phenomenon by itself. He then decided to find out if a repeated intravenous injection would cause kidney necrosis. Nothing of the kind happened, but then . . . we noted that the rabbits, for all their display of good health, *looked* different and funny. Their ears, instead of standing upright at either side, rabbit-style gradually softened and within a few [18] hours collapsed altogether finally hanging down like the ears of spaniels.'[34] As Barber and Fox were to comment, 'It looked as if something important must have happened to cause this reaction.'[35]

It turns out that Thomas was not the only one to observe the phenomenon of floppy ears in rabbits injected with papain. At about the same time Aaron Kellner, Associate Professor of Pathology at Cornell University Medical College, also injected rabbits intravenously with papain and observed this funny collapse of the ears. The story of Thomas's and Kellner's observation of rabbits' floppy ears became the subject of a sociological study by Barber and Fox in 1958.[36] They interviewed the two scientists and found that the difference between the two was that one (Thomas) had used his chance observation to make a discovery ('serendipity gained'), while the other (Kellner) had not ('serendipity lost').

It took Thomas six years to understand the cause of this unusual phenomenon,[37] but in the mean time he was terribly frustrated.

I didn't do the right thing . . . I did the expected things. I had sections cut, and had them stained by all the techniques available at the time. And I studied what I believed to be the constituents of a rabbit's ear. I looked at all the sections, but I couldn't see anything the matter. The connective tissue was intact. There was no change in the amount of elastic tissue. There was no inflammation, no tissue damage. I expected to find a great deal, because I thought we had destroyed something.

So because he shared with other pathologists the conviction that cartilage in the ear (and elsewhere) was inert, Thomas did not pay sufficient attention to the microscopic aspects of the cartilage in the papain-injected rabbits.

Several years later Thomas was teaching pathology to second-year medical students. On one occasion he demonstrated to them the experiment with papain and the rabbits' ears. The students were interested, but the teacher had no explanation. This time however he did the right thing.

Well this time I did what I didn't do before. I simultaneouly cut sections of ears of rabbits after I'd given the papain *and* sections of normal ears. This is the part of the story I'm most ashamed of. It still makes me writhe to think of it. There was no damage to the tissue in the sense of lesion. But what had taken place was a quantitative change in the matrix of the cartilage. The only way you could make sense of this change was simultaneously to compare sections from the ears of rabbits which had been injected with papain with comparable sections from the ears of rabbits of the same age and size which had not received papain . . . Before this I had always been so struck by the enormity of change that when I didn't see something obvious, I concluded there was nothing.[38]

It was only such direct comparison that made Thomas realize the drastic differences in cartilage between the normal and the papain-treated rabbits, and led him to understand that papain affected the cartilage matrix in the ears (as well as in other organs such as the trachea and the bronchial tubes).

A practical use for the papain was eventually found. An injection of this enzyme helped to rid patients of a ruptured intevertebral disc without surgery.

As was stated above, at about the same time Kellner also observed the appearance of floppy ears with 'unfailing regularity' in rabbits injected with papain.[39] In an interview with Barber and Fox[40] Kellner said: 'Every lab technician we've had since 1951 has known about these floppy ears because we've used them to assay papain, to tell us if it's potent and how potent.' Again, like Thomas, Kellner did not think of cartilage as the possible site of the action of papain:

> Since I was primarily interested in research questions having to do with the muscles of the heart, I was thinking in terms of muscle. That blinded me, so that changes in the cartilage didn't occur to me as a possibility. I was looking for muscles in the sections, and I never dreamed it was cartilage.[41]

So, though the attention of both researchers was riveted to this 'bizarre' phenomenon of floppy ears, and although both initially were misled as to the possible cause by their common preconception about the nature of cartilage, it was Thomas who did not lose interest in the phenomenon and finally not only unravelled its cause, but also found some practical medical uses for it.

Another delightful 'near' discovery was that of a cure for rheumatic fever.

At the end of World War II Thomas was stationed in Guam and Okinawa, where he was engaged in the study of Japanese encephalitis. Before the end of the war he had several dozen rabbits left in the animal house for which there were no planned experiments. He became interested in the aetiology of rheumatic fever. He therefore immunized the rabbits by injecting them with a mixture of a homogenate of heart tissue and haemolytic streptococci; this procedure was supposed to evoke rheumatic heart disease.

> It worked marvellously well. Indeed, I'd never done an experiment before, nor have I done one since, with such spectacular and unequivocal results. All the rabbits receiving the mixture of streptococci and heart tissue became ill and died within two weeks, and the histologic sections of their hearts showed the most violent and diffuse myocarditis I'd ever seen. . . . The control rabbits, injected with streptococci alone or with heart tissue alone remained healthy and showed no cardiac lesions.[42]

The war ended and Thomas returned to the Rockefeller Institute. In January 1946 he decided to continue the spectacular Guam experiments using the same strain of streptococci used on the Guam and Rockefeller rabbits.

> For the next nine months I set up one experiment after another, over and over again, using several hundred rabbits, varying the doses of streptococci and heart tissue in every way possible, and I never saw a single sick rabbit,

not an instance of myocarditis, not even the slightest degree of inflammation in any animal heart . . . I have still my notebooks with those experiments, unexplainable and unpublishable, reminding me that things tend always to go wrong in research. . . . I was so sure that the experiments meant what I wanted them to mean that it never once occurred to me that I might not be able to get the same results in New York. I had all the controls I needed; I wasn't bright enough to realize that Guam itself might be a control.[43]

Had Thomas's experiments succeeded also in New York, an important step in unravelling the aetiology of rheumatic fever would have been made. Because of Murphy's Law, however, these experiments remained a missed opportunity.

Because of certain norms demanding a logical structure for methods used in research and the ideas developing within the conceptual framework of a particular field of science, published research reports omit the elements of unforeseen developments of luck or chance (see Merton)[44] and are worded in 'retrospective falsification' commanding the use of only the rational components of the reported study. Thus, as Comroe so aptly put it, only 'Retrospectroscope' analysis of past events occurring during research stored in the memories of its practitioners reveals how serendipity was the crucial element in a discovery.

NOTES TO CHAPTER 8

1 Beveridge, W. I. B. 1957: *The Art of Scientific Investigation*, 3rd edn, London: W. Heinemann Ltd.
2 Ibid.: 167.
3 Pappenheimer, J. R. 1976: The sleep factor. *Scientific American*, 235/2: 24.
4 Pappenheimer, J. R. 1987: A silver spoon. *Annual Reviews of Physiology*, 49: 12
5 Monnier, A. and Hossli, L. 1975: Humoral transmission of sleep and wakefulness II. Hemodialysis of a sleep inducing humor during stimulation of the thalamic hypnogenic area. *Pflügers Archiven der gesammten Physiologie*, 252: 60.
6 Pieron, H. 1913: *La problème physiologique du sommeil*. Paris: Masson.
7 Schneedorf, J. G. and Ivy, A. C. 1939: An examination of the hypnotoxin theory of sleep. *American Journal of Physiology*, 125: 491.

8 Pappenheimer, J. R., Miller, J. B. and Godrich, C. A. 1967: Sleep promoting effects of cerebrospinal fluid from sleep deprived goats. *Proceedings of the National Academy of Science*, USA, 58: 513.

9 Krueger, J. M., Pappenheimer, J. R. and Karnovsky M. L. 1982: Sleep promoting effects of muramyl peptides. *Proceedings of the National Academy of Science*, USA, 79: 9102 .

10 Nagasaki, H., Iriki, M., Inoue, S. and Uchizono, K. 1974: The presence of sleep promoting material in the brain of sleep deprived rats. *Proceedings of the Japanese Academy*, Series B, *Physical and Biological Sciences*, 50: 241.

11 Riou, F., Cespuglio, R. and Jouvet, M. 1982: Endogenous peptides and sleep in the rat. II. The hypnogenic properties of vasoactive intestinal polypeptide. *Neuropeptides*, 2: 265.

12 Schoenenberger, G. A. and Schneider-Helmert, D. 1983: Psychophysiological function of DSIP. *Trends in Pharmacological Science*, 4: 307.

13 Pavel, S., Psatta, D. and Goldstein, R. 1977: Slow wave sleep induced in cats by extremely small amounts of synthetic and pineal vasotocin injected into the third ventricle of the brain. *Brain Research Bulletin*, 2: 251.

14 Krueger, J., Walter J. and Levin, C. 1985: Factor S and related somnogens: An immune theory for slow wave sleep. In *Brain Mechanisms of Sleep*, ed. D. J. McGinty et al. New York: Raven Press: 235–75.

15 Ibid.: 266.

16 Dale, H. 1948: Accident and opportunities in medical research. *British Medical Journal*, 2: 451.

17 Yalow, R. S. 1978: Radioimmunoassay: a probe for the fine structure of biological system. *Science*, 200: 1237.

18 Berson, S. A., Yalow, R. S., Bauman, A., Rothschild, M. A. and Newerly, K. 1956. Insulin[131] metabolism in human subjects. Demonstration of insulin binding globulin in the circulation of insulin treated subjects. *Journal of Clinical Investigations*, 35: 170.

19 Yalow, *Radioimmunoassay*: 1238.

20 Berson, S. A. and Yalow, R. S. 1957: Kinetics of reaction between insulin and insulin binding antibody. *Journal of Clinical Investigations*, 36: 873.

21 Yalow, R. S. and Berson, S. A. 1959: Assay of plasma insulin in human subjects by immunological methods. *Nature*, 184: 1648.

22 Hustin, A. 1960: Renouveau de la transfusion sanguine au début du XX siècle. *Acta Chirurgica Belgica*, 8: 762.

23 Comroe, *Retrospectroscope*: 94.

24 McLean, J. 1916: The thromboplastic action of cephalin *American Journal of Physiology*, 41: 250.
25 McLean, J. 1959: The discovery of heparin. *Circulation*, 19: 75.
26 Comroe, *Retrospectroscope*: 91.
27 Ibid.: 91–2.
28 Ibid.: 92.
29 Polge, C., Smith, A. U. and Parkes, A. S. 1948: Revival of spermatozoa after vitrification and dehydration at low temperatures. *Nature*, 164: 666.
30 Dale, 1948, Accident and opportunities: 453.
31 Comroe, *Retrospectroscope*: 89.
32 Thomas, L. 1985: *The Youngest Science. Notes of a Medicine Watcher.* Oxford: Oxford University Press.
33 Ibid.: 153.
34 Thomas, L. 1956: Reversible collapse of rabbit ears after intravenous papain and prevention of recovery by cortisone. *Journal of Experimental Medicine*, 104: 245.
35 Barber, B. and Fox, R. 1958: The case of floppy-eared rabbits: an instance of serendipity gained and serendipity lost. *American Journal of Sociology*, 64: 130.
36 Ibid.: 128–36.
37 Thomas, *The Youngest Science*: 157.
38 Barber and Fox, The case of floppy-eared rabbits: 132.
39 Kneller, A. and Robertson, T. 1954: Selective necrosis of cardiac and skeletal muscle induced experimentally by means of proteolytic enzyme solutions given intravenously. *Journal of Experimental Medicine*, 99: 387.
40 Barber and Fox, The case of floppy-eared rabbits: 134.
41 Ibid.: 135.
42 Thomas, *The Youngest Science*: 103.
43 Ibid.: 104.
44 Merton, R. K. *Social Theory and Social Structure.* Glencoe, III.: Free Press: 103–8.

9

The Incredible Story of Insulin

The story of the discovery of insulin is a major drama, played out mainly in the last quarter of the nineteenth century and culminating in the therapeutic use of this hormone, derived from the bovine pancreas in the early twenties. As it unfolds, the study involves blind alleys, missed opportunities, crucial chance observations and their misinterpretation, and interplay of human passions and ambitions, utter dedication to the cause, with a craving for power and abject despair.

We encounter the absolute honesty of some of the heroes of the story, as well as a few who finagled their results to suit their hopes and expectations. We also find sloppy, unobservant experimentation and biased attitudes. This maze leads us to the discovery of insulin, for which Frederick Banting and J. J. R. Macleod were awarded the Nobel Prize in 1923.

Diabetes mellitus, as the disease is now known, had already been noticed around 1500 BC. In the Papyrus Ebers of that period, a disease with 'overabundant urine' was recognized. A more accurate description[1] is found in the works of Arctaeus of Cappadocia (AD 180–200) who noted that the symptoms of the disease included 'melting of flesh and limbs into urine', parched mouth, unquenchable thirst, excessive drinking, nausea and finally death. The word 'diabetes' is the same as the Greek for 'siphon', because the fluids do not remain in the body, but use it as a bladder whereby to leave it. Aretaeus was not aware that diabetic urine contained sugar and was sweet. The earliest mention of sweet urine dates back to the sixth century AD. In Vedic medicine the disease is described as *madhumea*, meaning 'sweet urine',[2] and is characterized by thirst, micturition and loss of weight. In Europe, it was not until 1674 that Thomas Willis noticed the sweet taste of diabetic urine (hence the name *mellitus*, 'sweet'), and later (in 1775) Matthew Dobson showed that this sweet taste was somehow connected to the sweetness of the diabetic blood serum.

In 1848 Claude Bernard, the famous French physiologist, demonstrated that the source of sugar in the body was the liver, although he knew that diabetic patients had a damaged pancreas. This recognition of the role of the pancreas in diabetes had to await two important observations. In 1869 a German medical student, Paul Langerhans, who was studying the pancreas, reported in his doctoral thesis that it contained two types of cell: the acinar cells lining the ducts leading from the gland to the outside, which secreted the pancreatic juice containing various digestive enzymes; and the cells scattered like islands in the body of the pancreas, with no visible connection to the outside, whose function was quite unknown. In 1893 a French histologist, Gustave Édouard Laguesse, named these mysterious groups of cells the islets of Langerhans (see figure 6). He suggested that they released some internal secretion into the blood-stream. In 1889 Oscar Minkowski and Joseph von Mering in Germany investigated whether the pancreatic juices were essential for the digestion of fats in the gut. They removed the pancreas from a dog to find out how the fats would be digested after such an operation. Here comes the unexpected observation. Minkowski was informed by his technician that the dog in question urinated frequently on the floor of the room where he was kept, although he was house trained. This observation obviously had nothing to do with

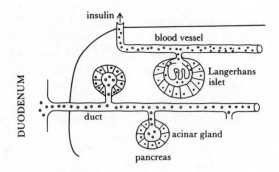

Figure 6   Diagram of the pancreas
The pancreas is a gland situated below the liver and under the stomach, between the duodenum and the spleen. A duct from the pancreas, leading to the duodenum, is lined with acinar cells which produce digestive enzymes. In the pancreatic tissue there are also the Langerhans islets (1–2% of the mass of pancreas); they secrete insulin and other hormones into the blood stream.

the problem under study. Minkowski, who was a student of Bernard Naunyn, the most outstanding diabetologist at that time, tested the dog's urine for the presence of sugar and found that it contained some 12 per cent of glucose. He wrote: 'After the complete removal of this organ [pancreas] the dogs became diabetic. This is not a case of transient glycosuria, but of a real, permanent diabetes mellitus, which, in every respect, corresponds to the most severe form of this disease in man'[3] Minkowski also showed that ligating the pancreatic duct (that is, the tube connecting the pancreas with the duodenum) and thus excluding its secretion from the intestine did not in itself produce diabetes. Nevertheless, the transplantation of pancreatic tissue from a healthy to a diabetic dog relieved the recipient animal of the symptoms of the disease. Minkowski understood that in addition to producing the digestive enzymes that the acinar cells excrete into the gut, the pancreas was also responsible for the management of glucose (sugar) in the body, and that the cells involved in this regulation were in fact the islets of Langerhans. So the chance discovery of sugar in de-pancreatized dogs established the causal relationship between Langerhans cells and diabetes, but Minkowski and von Mering did not follow this up.

Minkowski's findings were supported in 1895 by A. E. Schäfer at Stanford, who reported that normal pancreatic tissue grafted into diabetic dogs alleviated their disease. He concluded that the pancreas secretes something into the blood that prevents an excessive formation of sugar.[4]

In 1902 a Russian anatomist, Leonid Vassilyevitch Sobolev, published a review in *Virchov's Archives* in which he indicated the function of the islets of Langerhans.[5] He based his conclusions on the degeneration of the cells in these islets observed in diabetic patients, compared with those of healthy individuals who died accidentally independently. In 1901 Eugene Lindsay Opie, of the Johns Hopkins Hospital, wrote: 'Diabetes mellitus, when the result of a lesion of the pancreas, is caused by the destruction of the islands of Langerhans and occurs only when these bodies are in part or wholly destroyed.'[6] Additional evidence was provided by Édouard Hedon in 1910. He joined the blood-circulatory system of a normal dog with that of a diabetic one, and showed that such cross-circulation was sufficient to maintain a normal metabolism of sugar in both dogs.

Once the connection between the islets of Langerhans and diabetes had been established, hundreds of scientists and doctors everywhere made great efforts to isolate the elusive internal secretion from the pancreas, hoping that this secretion would cure diabetes or at least alleviate its

terrible symptoms. Among these attempts should be mentioned the work
of Georg Ludwig Zuelcer in the first decade of this century. His hypothesis
was that diabetes was caused by an excess of adrenalin (produced in the
kidneys), and that pancreatic extract neutralized this noxious effect of
adrenalin. On the basis of this assumption Zuelcer prepared alcoholic
extracts of ground pancreatic tissue, and injected it into diabetic dogs in
the hope of saving them from imminent death. Unfortunately his extracts
proved to be too toxic and his work came to an end. In a footnote to his
paper describing these results Zuelcer writes: 'This short communication
was submitted to the Editorial Office three years ago. It was not printed
according to the request of the author, because up to now his expectation
that, on the basis of theoretical research he would succeed to achieve
practical therapeutic results, has not been fulfilled.'[7]

A more successful effort was reported in a master's thesis by Ernest
Lyman Scott at the University of Chicago in 1912.[8] Scott prepared alcoholic
extracts from dogs' pancreases and used them to inject into dogs made
diabetic by the extirpation of their pancreatic glands. Three out of four of
these dogs showed a marked improvement and Scott concluded: 'There is
an internal secretion from the pancreas controlling sugar metabolism; by
proper methods this secretion may be extracted and still retain its activity.'[9]

It is noteworthy, however, that in the published version of the thesis
these conclusions were obfuscated (presumably under the influence of
Scott's supervisor, the noted physiologist Anton Carlson):

> Intravenous injection of the pancreas extract prepared as above, into dogs
> rendered diabetic by complete pancreatectomy diminish temporarily the
> sugar secretion and lower the D/N ratio in the urine. *It does not follow that
> these effects are due to the internal secretion of the pancreas in the extract.*[10]

Scott weakened his position even more by stating that 'the pancreas
extract may decrease the output of sugar from the tissues by a toxic or
depressor action, rather than by a specific regulatory action on the pancreas
secretion.'[11] As a result of this erroneous evaluation of his results, Scott
did not follow the lead dictated by his successful experiments. In 1923
Carlson apologized in a letter to Scott: 'I feel that I personally have to
shoulder a great deal of blame for discouraging you from going ahead with
that work.'[12]

Other scientists who obtained promising results, but did not follow
them through, were Israel Kleiner and S. J. Meltzer of the Rockefeller
Institute in New York. As early as 1915 they obtained good results in dogs
treated with pancreatic emulsions. In 1919 Kleiner published the results

of sixteen experiments in which the injection of saline extracts of pancreas into diabetic dogs caused a significant decline in their blood sugar.[13]

In the years 1920–1 Nicolas Paulesco in Romania succeeded in preparing pancreatic extracts that were effective not only in dogs, but also in human patients.[14] Nevertheless, he suspended his work because of the toxic effects of the extracts. Later he was to feel cheated by Sir Frederick Banting of the credit for his work. Banting in fact knew of Paulesco's work before publishing his results, but he misunderstood the text, which was written in French, and as a result ignored it. Paulesco even protested to the Nobel Prize Committee about this 'unfairness'.[15]

A convincing experiment, which might have advanced diabetes research by more than a decade, was carried out by the French physiologist, Marcel Eugène Gley (1857–1930) in 1905. Gley was aware of the current progress being made in hormone research. The concept of hormones (from the Greek *hormōn*, 'setting in motion',) as substances produced by one tissue in the body, carried by blood to another tissue and affecting its function, became acceptable at the beginning of this century. Ernest Henry Starling isolated secretin, Jokichi Takamine adrenalin and Gley himself discovered the existence of the parathyroid gland.

Gley assumed that the pancreatic excretory cells would interfere with the successful extraction of the endocrine secretion. He therefore injected denatured gelatine into the pancreatic ducts of his experimental animals so as to block and destroy the acinar cells lining the duct. These cells would degenerate. He then made an extract of what remained of the pancreas, which he injected into 'de-pancreatized' dogs. Excretion of glucose in the urine of these treated dogs ceased and Gley wrote: 'The extract injected into dogs made diabetic by removal of the pancreas greatly decreased the quantity of sugar excreted by these dogs, and at the same time it also improved all symptoms of diabetes.'[16] Gley completed his experiments in 1905, but he did not publish them until 1922, after the dramatic findings of Banting and Best had become publicly known. In one of the most baffling episodes in the history of science, Gley put the report of his successful experiments in a sealed envelope and sent it to the Société de Biologie in Paris, with instructions not to open it unless he so requested.

Here we witness a clear case of missed opportunity, actually of a deliberate missed opportunity. The use of a sealed envelope was a peculiar feature of French science. It was a way of safeguarding the priority of an investigation that had not yet been completed. It assured the scientist not only of priority, but also of relative secrecy. Thus Gley kept his excellent results dormant for seventeen years and published them too late to be given the credit. In his paper written in 1922,[17] when he was Professor of Physiology at the University of Paris, Gley added an explanation to the original manuscript of 1906. He said that at that time he had needed more experimental animals to convince himself of the validity of his results. But he did not have the means of keeping more experimental animals in his laboratory, and so he abandoned further experimentation. It seems that he was not sufficiently confident of the importance of his findings to go ahead with open publication. Nevertheless it is strange that he did not continue, even at a slower pace, to amass more important evidence with the limited means at his disposal. Although in most cases the publication of incomplete or erroneous work may delay the advancement of science, Gley's case shows the opposite. Here, the delay of publication, in spite of the fact that Gley was sufficiently influential to have his findings published in *Compte rendue des Séances de la Société de Biologie*, postponed the therapeutic application of insulin for almost a generation.

Banting and Best

Against this background of unsuccessful or inconclusive attempts to obtain an active pancreatic extract for the treatment of diabetes, the stage was now set for the momentous discovery of insulin by Banting, Best, Macleod and Collip.[18]

Frederick Banting graduated from Medical School in Toronto in 1916 and until 1918 he served with the Canadian troops fighting in Europe in World War I. He gained the Military Cross for heroism. Upon his return from the war, Banting practised medicine in London, Ontario. He became interested in diabetes, up to that time a lethal disease which was being treated by means of a severe and strict diet. Banting understood that the regulatory function of the pancreas in glucose metabolism might be connected to the production of a hormone by this gland, and that the lack of such a hormone leads to the disease. He learned from the literature that earlier attempts to extract this hormone had mostly failed. Banting believed, as did Scott before him, that this failure was due to the 'fact' that when the pancreas was ground up to obtain the extract, the extract also contained (in addition to the putative hormone) digestive enzymes that would destroy the active anti-diabetic principle.

In October 1920 Banting read a paper by Moses Barron,[19] showing that a blockage of the pancreatic duct by a stone caused the degeneration of the acinar cells lining the duct without affecting the Langerhans cells. This paper gave Banting an idea which he wrote down:

Diabetus
Ligate pancreatic ducts of dogs. Keep dogs alive till acini degenerate leaving islets.
Try to insolate the internal secretion of these to relieve glycosurea.[20]

(Note the spelling mistakes – 'diabetus', 'insolate', 'glycosurea'.) It seems that at this stage Banting had not read the paper written by Scott in 1912, which reported:

> It was hoped that the presence of the digestive enzymes could be eliminated by the atrophy of the gland which follows complete ligation of the ducts; but after several attempts in the dog which proved futile as far as complete atrophy was concerned, this method was abandoned as impractical.[21]

Had Banting read Scott's paper he might have been discouraged by this approach and instead used the technique that Scott described as successful, namely the extraction of the fresh pancreas by means of alcohol (which inactivates the enzymes). In any case, with this idea of the ligation of the duct in mind, Banting went to Toronto, to Professor John James Macleod, who at the age of forty-four was Professor of Physiology at the University of Toronto. In 1913 Macleod had written a book on *Diabetes, its Pathologic Physiology* in which he stated that the internal secretion of the pancreas was destroyed during extraction by proteolytic enzymes, and so attempts at therapy by the use of extracts would be unsuccessful. He therefore supported therapy of diabetes by diet.

When Banting presented his idea to Macleod, the latter was clearly not greatly impressed because he did not believe that Banting, a small-town surgeon, was properly equipped to undertake such an ambitious programme, or knew enough about the chemistry of blood sugar, the physiology of the pancreas, etc. Banting, however, was insistent and managed to persuade Macleod to provide him with laboratory space, a few dogs and an assistant for ten weeks. Macleod assigned a medical student, Charles Best, to help Banting in the experiments he proposed. Banting arrived in Toronto in May 1921 and performed the first operation on dogs under Macleod's supervision. Macleod monitored the experiments until mid-June, when he went off for a summer vacation in Europe, not to return until September. By that time Banting had many experiments going. His procedure was to tie off the ducts of a dog's pancreas, to wait several weeks until the gland shrivelled without affecting the Langerhans islets. The pancreas was then removed, ground up and extracted in saline. By July Banting and Best already had an extract which they injected into dogs with extirpated pancreases. The injection of the extract stopped the symptoms of diabetes and prolonged the lives of the diabetic dogs for a while. Banting first called the extract *isletin*, but later, when Macleod insisted, the extract was renamed *insulin*.

Not satisfied with the overall results of the treatment of diabetic dogs with his extracts, Banting modified his approach. He would cause the depletion of acinar secretion by the continuous stimulation of the glandular secretion by a hormone secretin (produced in the duodenum) in the hope that he would thus obtain a pancreas depleted of digestive enzymes that could harm insulin. In October he read Paulesco's report,[22] but not understanding the French, he disregarded the information. Banting also read a paper by Laguesse and Carbon stating (as quoted by Bliss[23]) that when the pancreas was removed from pregnant bitches, they did not become diabetic until after the delivery of their puppies. It was understood that the foetal pancreas served as a source of insulin to keep the pregnant diabetic bitch in health. Banting thus began to experiment with the extract of foetal-calf pancreases which were rich in Langerhans cells, but devoid of mature acinar cells.

At the end of November in 1921 Banting and Best wrote up the results of their experiments. Their paper was published in February 1922.[24] In the paper they reported the use of seventy-five doses of saline extracts from degenerated pancreases in the treatment of ten diabetic dogs. The conclusion they reached was that in all cases there was a reduction of sugar in the blood and urine of the treated dogs. In fact, an inspection of Banting's notebooks shows that out of the seventy-five doses of extract, forty-two gave favourable results, twenty-two unfavourable and eleven were inconclusive. The aqueous extracts, however, were not dependable or satisfactory in practice, partly because of the fickleness of the results and partly because of their toxicity.

In their next paper, in 1922,[25] Banting acknowledged Scott's method of · preparing insulin from the adult pancreas. In a later description of Scott's work (1929), however, he did not mention the fact that Scott's alcoholic extracts were efficacious, but instead dwelt on the lack of success of the technique of ligation of the duct and on the fact that some of Scott's extracts were toxic. Thus Banting misunderstood and misinterpreted Scott's work.[26]

In his summary *History of Insulin*, published in 1929, Banting wrote: 'E. L. Scott had the idea of ligating the pancreatic duct a long time previously, but apparently he did not get degeneration of the gland because his extracts were toxic',[27] but he failed to mention Scott's later successful methods and results. Later historians of science such as Lloyd Stevenson and S. Harris in 1946, as well as Wreshall, Hetenyiu and Feasby in 1963,[28] used Banting as a source and altered Scott's conclusions, distorting his science.

It was Banting's collaborator James Bertram Collip who was to appreciate Scott's work, as is witnessed by the statement in his paper: 'The use of alcohol in preparing pancreatic extracts by E. L. Scott in 1912 should be especially noted. Scott came so near to obtaining the active principle that it is hard to understand why he did not pursue his work further.'[29]

In December 1921 Collip joined Banting and Best. He was Professor of Biochemistry on sabbatical leave from the University of Alberta in Edmonton. Macleod and Collip advocated the use of the extraction procedure devised by Scott and Zuelcer, namely the use of alcohol as an extractor. Since they also faced the problem of how to assess the efficacy of the extracts rapidly, Collip developed a suitable test in rabbits, as well as a quick biochemical method to determine the concentration of glucose in serum and urine. It soon became clear that Collip's alcohol extracts not only were non-toxic but they were active in relieving the symptoms of diabetes.[30]

On 11 January 1922 one of these extracts was successfully used on a fourteen-year-old diabetic patient, Leonard Thompson. From then on, continuous treatment, with 85 insulin units daily, allowed Thompson to live until the age of twenty-seven. Another famous patient of Banting and his group was Elisabeth Evans Hughes, a diabetic who weighed only 45 lb. at the age of fifteen. She lived to the respectable age of seventy, having taken 43,000 injections of insulin. When she died it was of a heart attack.

An interesting sideline on Thompson is that after the first injection of insulin his blood sugar dropped from 0.44 to 0.32, and the sugar in his urine from 2.5 to 2.0 per cent. But when Banting mentioned this patient in his Nobel Prize lecture he stated that after the injection of the extracts Thompson's urine contained no sugar at all.

These dramatic improvements in the first two patients led to rapid progress in insulin manufacture and therapy. Within a year thousands of diabetic patients were brought to controllable health from the brink of death.

Remembering the exciting days of the discovery of insulin, C. H. Drinker of Stanford University wrote in 1942: 'When insulin was discovered, I can well remember that the classical experiment of Banting and Best had been proposed a year before by a third year student and

rejected by all of us in that laboratory as too much a task for a man with
no experience in animal work.'[31]

In 1923 Banting and Macleod were awarded the Nobel Prize in
Medicine and Physiology, for the discovery of insulin, the first to be given
to a Canadian. Banting was not entirely happy that Professor Macleod
alone shared the prize with him, while his close collaborator, Best, did not.
In Banting's view, Macleod just gave advice and provided the facilities for
the research. In the end Banting accepted the prize and shared half of it
with Best. Similarly Macleod shared his part of the prize with Collip.

In the years that followed Banting made Macleod's life in Toronto so
unpleasant that in 1928 Macleod, frustrated, went to Scotland to become
Regius Professor at the University of Aberdeen. Banting's animosity
toward Macleod was such that even in 1940 he was quoted by Bliss as
calling him 'a grasping, selfish, deceptive, self seeking and empty of
truth'.[32]

Banting was knighted in 1934. During the Second World War he died
in an air crash over Newfoundland. After his death the Banting–Best
Department of Medical Research was directed by Best.

Epilogue

As this chapter recounts, during the second half of the nineteenth century
and the first quarter of the twentieth, hundreds of scientists attempted to
understand the aetiology of diabetes and to find a cure for it. A few, like
Scott, Zuelcer, Paulesco and Gley, almost reached it, but only Banting
with his unshakeable faith, imagination, conviction and determination,
obtained usable insulin, or, as the Nobel award put it, 'credit for having
produced the pancreatic hormone in a practical, available form'.[33]
Banting achieved this in spite of 'wrongly conceived, wrongly conducted
and wrongly interpreted series of experiments',[34] or, as Sir Henry Dale
more generously stated: 'The discovery of insulin proved to have resulted
from a stumble into the right road where it crossed the course laid down
by faulty conception.'[35]

It is interesting to compare Banting's notes and the results of his
experiments with the record published in the scientific literature. In his
first paper[36] Banting proved to have misread Paulesco's work and
misinterpreted the results of an experiment in which Paulesco successfully
used an extract of fresh, untreated pancreas. Internal discrepancies may
be found between the published figures and charts and those found in the

notebooks. In the last experiment described, while the charts show one set of figures for the volumes of extract injected and for the duration of the ligation of the duct, the text contains a second set of data and the notebook still a third set. The summary was not true to the findings. Although Banting and Best stated that the extracts always reduced sugar levels, in fact, only forty-two out of seventy-five injections brought about this reduction.

Banting's work was criticized as early as 1922, soon after the publication of the discovery of insulin. Roberts pointed out[37] that Banting's research (supported by Macleod) was based on a wrong hypothesis, namely that the digestive enzymes of the pancreas should be destroyed in order to isolate the active hormone. In fact, in the pancreas there is an inactive precursor of trypsin, trypsinogen, which is activated only upon its arrival in the intestine. Second, in their experiments of 18 August 1921, Banting and Best used an extract of a fresh, whole gland. In their paper describing this experiment,[38] they observed that this extract was more active than an extract of the degenerated pancreas, a finding which would indicate that their hypothesis of proteolytic enzymes in the pancreas destroying the internal secretion was wrong. Nevertheless they concluded that the extract of the intact pancreas was weaker, and therefore that their hypothesis was right. Third, the experiments entailing the exhaustion of the pancreatic juices by secretin was meaningless. The correct experiment would have been to show that an extract of normal, non-exhausted pancreas was active. Fourth, when they switched to alcoholic extracts, they did not make any comparison *in the same experiment* with aqueous extracts and thus had no real controls.

In 1954 Banting's work was criticized[39] in that he did not test for toxic effects from the extracts – for instance testing for a rise in temperature in the injected animals. It was pointed out that Banting and Best did not actually go beyond what Scott and Zuelcer had achieved, and that it was essentially Collip who, by producing the first non-toxic alcoholic extract, went beyond the earlier workers. The successful commercial production of insulin required certain necessary steps which were mostly contributed by others. These steps were:

(1) The use of alcohol for extraction was advocated by Zuelcer in 1907 and rediscovered by Collip.

(2) The method of quick determination of sugar in small volumes of blood was the contribution of Lewis and Benedict in 1913.[40]

(3) The discovery that insulin was insoluble in 95 per cent alcohol and could thus be precipitated from aqueous extracts was the result of team

work by Banting, Best and Collip. This was the step needed to produce non-toxic extracts;

(4) The discovery that an extract of normal pancreas injected into dogs reduced hyperglycaemia and glycosuria was made by Kleiner and Meltzer in 1910.[41]

(5) The development of a physiological assay for insulin based on the production of convulsions in rabbits was due to Collins.

(6) The precipitation of insulin at 'isoelectric point' was the work of Doisy, Somogyi and Shaffer in 1923.[42]

To sum up, Banting and Best did not discover insulin on their own. Nevertheless they made an essential contribution to the discovery by beginning a process that led without interruption to the successful commercial production of insulin. Banting's great idea that duct ligation was an essential part of the discovery was simply not correct, but it led him to stumble in the right direction.

According to Darwin, credit goes not to men who discover things, but to those who convince the world of the importance of their discovery.[43] This situation is even more strikingly exemplified by Fleming's discovery of penicillin, which did not become a true discovery until Florey and Chain had produced penicillin on a scale that permitted a successful human experiment.

The story of diabetes and insulin does not end here. Insulin is now not the only remedy available for the treatment of diabetes.[44] During the first half of this century scientists and physicians were looking for chemical alternatives to treat diabetes. In 1918 C. K. Watanabe[45] noticed that guanidine derivatives affected the levels of blood sugar. He thought, therefore, that it might be useful to control the level of blood sugar in diabetes with this compound. Unfortunately the guanidine derivatives were toxic, causing liver and kidney failures, and were abandoned. In 1930 the findings of Argentinian doctors[46] that sulfonamides caused a drop in the blood sugar of rabbits were ignored until World War II. In 1942 M. Janbon and his colleagues in Montpellier treated undernourished typhoid patients with the sulfonamide isopropyl thiodiazo-derivative (IPTD). They noticed that some of the patients died in coma with neurological disorders that resembled those of patients dying of diabetes. They measured the blood glucose in the patients they had treated and concluded that there was a connection between hypoglycaemia and sulfonamide treatment.[47] Little action was taken following this observation until four years later Auguste Loubatières continued the studies on hypoglycaemia in IPTD-treated dogs and rabbits, and came to the conclusion that IPTD affected the Langerhans cells.[48] He therefore suggested using IPTD in human diabetics, but again nothing was done about these suggestions until 1955, when two German scientists, Franke and Fuchs, independently noticed hypoglycaemia in pneumonia patients treated with the sulfa derivative B255. They proposed its use for the treatment of diabetes.[49] On the basis of this information another sulfonamide compound, D860, the tolbutamid (N-p-toluyl-sulfonyl N'n butylurea) began to be used for diabetic patients. Since then, hundreds of other analogues have been produced and tested, but tolbutamid remains an important drug for the treatment of certain forms of diabetes. In 1980 in the United States alone 1.8 million diabetic patients were treated with tolbutamid, compared with 1.3 million insulin users. In Europe 30 per cent of diabetics are treated with tolbutamid and other sulfanylurea derivatives.

An intriguing postscript to the insulin story may be found in a report from China dating from 1966, in which Kung-Yueh-ting and his colleagues in Shanghai and Beijing wrote:

> The first total synthesis of [insulin] was accomplished in 1965 in the People's Republic of China. Holding aloft the great red banner of Mao Tse-tung's thinking and manifesting the superiority of the socialist system, we have achieved, under the correct leadership of our party the total synthesis of bovine insulin . . . Throughout the various stages of our investigation, we followed closely the teachings of Chairman Mao Tse-tung: eliminating superstitions, analysing contradictions, paying respect to practice, and frequently summing up experiences . . . The total chemical synthesis of insulin is a piece of work which stems directly from the big leap forward movement.[50]

NOTES TO CHAPTER 9

1 Poulsen, J. E. 1983: *Features of the History of Diabetology*. Copenhagen: Munkgaard: 13.
2 Clendening, *A Source Book of Medical History*: 54–6.
3 Von Mering, J. and Minkowski, O. 1890: *Archiven für experimentelle Pathologie und Pharmakologie*, 26: 371.
4 Schäfer, A. E. 1985: *Lancet*, 2: 321.
5 Sobolev, L. V. 1902: Zur normalen und pathologischen Morphologie der inneren Sekretion und Bauchspeicheldrüse. *Virchovs Archiven*, 48: 168.
6 Opie, E. L. 1910: *Disease of the Pancreas*, Philadelphia.

7 Zuelcer, G. L. 1907: Experimentelle Untersuchungen über den Diabetes. *Berliner klinische Wochenschrift*, 44: 475.

8 Richards, D. 1966: The effect of pancreas extract on depancreatized dogs: Ernest L. Scott's thesis of 1911. *Perspectives in Biology and Medicine*, 10: 84.

9 Ibid.: 88.

10 Scott, E. L. 1912: On the influence of intravenous injections of an extract of pancreas on experimental pancreatic diabetes. *American Journal of Physiology*, 29: 306.

11 Ibid.: 309.

12 Sawyer, W. A. 1966: Frederick Banting's misinterpretation of the work of Ernest L. Scott as found in secondary sources. *Perspectives in Biology and Medicine* 29: 617.

13 Kleiner, I. S. 1919: The action of intravenous injections of pancreas emulsions in experimental diabetes. *Journal of Biological Chemistry*, 40: 153.

14 Paulesco, N. C. 1923: Quelques réactions chimiques et physiques appliquées à l'extrait aqueaux du pancreas pour le débarasser des substances protéiques en excès. *Archives Internationales de Physiologie*, 21: 71.

15 Bliss, M. 1982: *The Discovery of Insulin*. Chicago: Chicago University Press: 233.

16 Gley, E. 1922: Actions des extraits de pancréas sclérose sur des chiens diabétiques (par extirpation de pancréas). *Comptes rendus des Séances de la Société de Biologie*, 87: 1322.

17 Ibid.: 1324.

18 Banting, F. G. and Best, C. H. 1922: The internal secretion of the pancreas. *Journal of Laboratory and Clinical Medicine*, 7: 256.
Banting, F. G. and Best, C. H. 1922: Pancreatic extracts. *Journal of Laboratory and Clinical Medicine*, 7: 464.
Banting, F. G., Best, C. H., Collip, J. B. and MacLeod, J. J. R. 1922: The effect of pancreatic extract (insulin) on normal rabbits. *American Journal of Physiology*, 62: 162.

19 Barron, M. 1920: The relation of islets of Langerhans to diabetes with special reference to cases of pancreatic lithiasis. *Surgery, Gynecology and Obstetrics*, 31: 432 .

20 Bliss, *The Discovery of Insulin*: 50.

21 Scott, On the influence of injections on diabetes: 310.

22 Paulesco, N. C. 1921: Action de l'extrait pancréatique. *Comptes rendus des Séances de la Société de Biologie* (Paris), 85: 555.

23 Bliss, *Discovery of Insulin*: 92.
24 Banting and Best, Internal secretion: 256f.
25 Banting and Best, Pancreatic extracts: 484ff.
26 Sawyer, Frederick Banting's misinterpretation: 611.
27 Banting, F. 1929: The history of insulin. *Edinburgh Medical Journal*, 1: 18.
28 Stevenson, L. G. 1946: *Sir Frederick Banting*, Toronto: Ryerson.
   Wrenshall, G., Hetenyi, G. and Feasby, W. R. 1963: *The Story of Insulin*, Bloomington: Indiana University Press.
   Harris, S. 1946: *Banting's Miracle. The Story of the Discovery of Insulin*. Philadelphia: Lippincott.
29 Collip, J. B. 1923: The history of the discovery of insulin. *New Medicine* (Seattle), 22: 267.
30 Bliss, *Discovery of Insulin*: 116–17.
31 Drinker, C. K. 1942: *The Lymphatic System*. Lane Medical Lectures. London: N. Milford: Oxford University Press: 30.
32 Bliss, *Discovery of Insulin*: 202.
33 Nobel Lectures. Physiology and Medicine 1901–1921. Amsterdam: Elsevier, 1967: 474.
34 Roberts, F. 1922: Insulin (letter) *British Medical Journal* (16 Dec.), 2: 1194.
35 Dale, H. H. 1922: Insulin (letter) *British Medical Journal* (23 Dec.), 2: 1241.
36 Banting and Best, Internal secretion: 256f.
37 Roberts, *Insulin*: 1193.
38 Banting and Best, Pancreatic extracts: 464f.
39 Pratt, J. H., 1954: A reappraisal of researches leading to discovery of insulin. *Journal of History of Medicine*, 9: 281.
40 Myers, V. C. and Bailey, C. B. 1916: The Lewis and Benedict method for the estimation of blood sugar. With some observations obtained in disease. *Journal of Biological Chemistry*, 24: 147.
41 Kleiner, I. S. and Meltzer, S. J. 1914: The influence of depancreatization upon the state of glycemia following the intravenal injections of dextrose in dogs. *Proceedings of the Society for Experimental Biology and Medicine*, 12: 58.
42 Doisy, E. A., Somogyi, M. and Shaffer, P. A. 1923: Some properties of an active constituent of pancreas (insulin). *Journal of Biological Chemistry*, 55: 31.
43 Mackay, A. L. 1977: *The Harvest of the Quiet Eye*. London: The Institute of Physics: 43.

44 Clarke, R. F. and Duncan, L. J. P. 1977: Harnstoff Therapie. In K. Oberdise (ed.), *Diabetes mellitus B. Handbuch der inneren Medizin*, vol. 7, 5th edn, Part 2B. Berlin, New York: Springer Verlag.

45 Watanabe, C. K. 1918: Studies in the metabolic changes induced by administration of guanidine base. I. Influence of injected guanidine-HCl upon blood sugar content. *Journal of Biological Chemistry*, 33: 253.

46 Ruiz, C. L., Silva, L. L. and Libenson, L. 1930: Contribución al estudio sobre la composición quimica de la insulina. Estudio de algunos cuerpos sinteticos sulfurados con acción hypoglycemiante. *Rivista de Societá Argentina Biologica*, 6: 134.

47 Janbon, M., Chapal, J., Vedel, A. and Schaap, J. 1942: Accidents hypoglycémiques graves par un sulfanidothiodiazol (le VK57 ou 2254RP). *Montpellier Medecine*, 441: 21.

48 Loubatières, A. 1946: Étude physiologique et pharmacodynamique de certains dérivés sulfamides hypoglycemiantes. *Archives Internationales de Physiologie*, 54: 174.

Loubatières, A. 1955: Action curative du p-amino-benzène-sulfamido-isopropylthiodiazol dans le diabète sucré humain. *Comptes rendus de l'Académie des Sciences* (Paris) 241: 1422.

49 Franke, H. and Fuchs, J. 1955: Ein neues antidiabetisches Prinzip. Ergebnisse klinischer Untersuchungen. *Deutsche medizinische Wochenschrift*, 80: 1449.

50 Klotz, I. M. 1986: *Diamond Dealers and Feather Merchants*. Boston: Birkhaeuser: 36.

10

What Do We Call a Fact?

A scientific statement that speaks about reality must be falsifiable.

Karl Popper

In precisely controlled experiments the scientist will observe what he damn well pleases.

N. S. Hellerstein

We see only what we know.

J. W. von Goethe

The thought collective and a scientific fact

'Seeing is believing' is an old proverb. Seeing and believing led people to accept as facts the notion that the sun rotates around earth, that maggots originate from decaying flesh and mice from stored grains of wheat. In modern times seeing also means using microscopes, telescopes, physical laws, chemical analyses, etc. But what we see or perceive instrumentally: is it a fact, a reality?

'Science is built up with facts, as a house is with stones. But a collection of facts is no more science than a heap of stones is a house.'[1] Science is built upon observation, measurement, inference, verification and deduction.

Consider Frank Herbert's story of the 'Hidden Wisdom' in his book *Heretics of the Dune*:[2]

There was a man who sat each day looking out through a narrow vertical opening where a single board had been removed from a tall wooden fence. Each day a wild ass of the desert passed outside the fence and across the narrow opening – first the nose, then the head, the forelegs, the long brown back, the hindleg and lastly the tail. One day, the man leaped to his feet with the light of discovery in his eyes and he shouted for all who could hear him: 'It is obvious! The nose causes the tail!'

What we see, conceive or understand depends very much on what we expect to see. Our understanding depends on what we were taught to see, as well as on our cultural predisposition and previous training. A layman, looking for the first time into a microscope at a slide with a stained tissue section, discerns only colours, but not the structure of the tissue. Our brains add information to the image we see in order to complete a pattern. There exists a whole field of investigation concerned with the determination of the minimal amount of information necessary for the recognition or understanding of a pattern. Redundant information often obscures the pattern, which escapes the notice of the observer. In figure 7 we see an enigmatic arithmetical series.

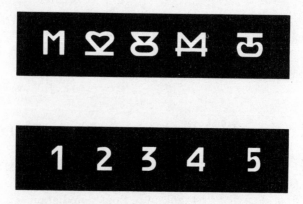

Figure 7   An enigmatic arithmetical series

Very few observers guess that it is a series 1, 2, 3, 4, 5, 6, etc. Each number is combined with its mirror image and is thus camouflaged. We are well aware of camouflage in nature. It makes the shape, the colour or the surface pattern of an animal look like something else and is generally exploited in the struggle for survival in nature.

In psychology books there are examples of how ambiguous patterns lead to a different interpretation of the image presented to the observer. Well-known examples include the drawing of a cube which, depending on the observer, can be perceived tridimensionally as seen from below or from above. The image of a stylized goblet changes imperceptibly into human faces (figure 8), a picture of an old woman may be perceived with proper instruction as that of the profile of a young girl (figure 9) and a duck changes into a rabbit.

Figure 8   Two faces in profile or a wine glass?
Source: J. V. McConnell (1974): *Understanding Human Behavior.* New York: Holt, Rinehart and Winston: 287.

Figure 9   An old lady or a young girl?
Source: J. V. McConnell (1974): *Understanding Human Behaviour.* New York: Rinehart and Winston: 288.

Even more difficult is the observation of transient phenomena, when the time element, the sequence of events, has to be considered, especially when what occurs is not expected. It is not enough to look *at* events in a changing scene – one has to look *for* each detail to be able to record it consciously.

W. H. George relates a story[3] from a psychology congress in Göttingen. During one of the meetings two men, running after each other, burst into the conference room. One of them fired a shot from a revolver and then the two rushed out. The chairman of the meeting, who actually was the author of the 'happening', asked the audience to write down what they had witnessed. (Unknown to those present, the whole event had been recorded.) At the end of the session forty reports were collected and monitored for the accuracy of the description. Only one person made fewer than 20 per cent mistakes about the main events, fourteen had up to 40 per cent and the remaining twenty-five had more than 40 per cent. In half of the accounts there were elements of pure imagination: that is, things were described that did not happen at all. So in spite of the fact that the audience was composed of trained psychologists and that they were given the opportunity to record what they had witnessed immediately after this unexpected 'happening', and though none of those present was personally involved in the events, most either missed, misinterpreted or even invented the factual parts of the whole story. The recorded facts were thus made up not only of what really happened, but also of illusions and errors supplied by the onlookers' minds. When the witnesses to the 'happening' were confronted with an unexpected event, their readiness for accurate observation may have been impaired. Are we really ready to observe and to record the details when something unexpected happens? It is not enough for an observer to keep his or her eyes open unless he or she has an idea what is being looked for.

Ronald G. Stansfield of the Department of Industrial Sociology at the City University in London carried out an experiment with freshers who were science and engineering students. They were simply asked to watch a dripping tap and to report their observations.[4] The experiment involved seventy-five students in nine separate groups. The instructions the students received were: 'Look at a tap slowly dripping water into a bowl. Write a description of what you see as you watch the water coming out of the tap and joining the water in the bowl below. . . . The tap should be set to drip roughly once a second.' From the analysis of the reports, the students, when tested, could be divided into several groups: twenty-five who wrote the report while watching the tap, eighteen who recorded their observations immediately afterwards, seven who did it one hour later, and still others who based their description on the general idea of how a tap drips, by simply relying on their memory. The actual descriptions comprised twenty-six that were purely imaginative assays and thirty-nine containing some sort of description of the events. In this combined group, twenty-eight described what could not have been observed. For instance, among the unobservable statements were: 'the droplet assumes a spherical shape, surface tension providing an elastic bag, to contain the water as it falls', 'the falling drop retained a somewhat streamlined spherical shape' or 'the droplet falls through space with an ever increasing speed.' In fact, what one can see is a blurred impression. One cannot see the falling of the drop; one cannot make out its shape; one cannot judge its speed or acceleration.

Experiment should be the sole interpreter of the artifices of Nature. Experiment, however, involves the hand and the eye as well as the mind. In addition to performing an experiment and noting its outcome, there is also the problem of its description in words. Not all scientists find it easy to translate into words what they have experienced in the laboratory – and so their reports are often inadequate and their historical description may not be entirely truthful.

Stansfield's experiment indicates that even students who had had some schooling in science were not familiar with the process of observing and writing a description of what they had seen, or, to use a psychological term, they suffered from 'trained incapacity'. 'The initial grounding in science which people receive today conditions them to report what from teacher and textbook they have learnt to be right and proper, and inhibits them from direct observation and description.'[5]

Einstein said: 'I find it difficult to understand particularly in periods of transition and uncertainty, how much fashion plays a role in science, scarcely inferior to the one it plays in women's dress.'[6] Examples of fashions in experimental psychology are provided by English associationism, the introspection of the Würzberg school, Watsonian Behaviourism, Gestalt theory, Neo-behaviourism, etc. Swift had predicted this when he said: 'Now systems of Nature were but new fashions which would vary in every age; and even those who pretend to demonstrate them from Mathematical Principles would flourish but a short Period of Time and be out of Vogue when that was determined.'[7]

Discoveries are made when the time is ripe and are then readily accepted as filling the available gaps in knowledge. In 1868 John Tyndall wrote of Faraday:

> Before any great scientific principle receives distinct enunciation by individuals, it dwells more or less clearly in the *general scientific mind* (my italics). The intellectual plateau is already high, and our discoverers are then those who like peaks above the plateau, rise a little above the general thought at the time.[8]

For discovery a different attitude of mind is required than that required for proof. According to Claude Bernard, the famous French physiologist, observations are of two types: one involves passive or accidental observation (usually labelled as chance) and an induced or active observation following a hypothesis. In both cases observation is not a passive watching, but involves an active mental process. The idea of untheoretical sense data is mistaken. We can never free observation from the theoretical element of interpretation. Our observational knowledge is theoretical and fallible.

The Göttingen experiment indicates that witnessing an unexpected or unpredictable event led to a misleading observation. As teachers, we know that students often ignore the results of their experiments when they do not coincide with their expectation or their teacher's explanation. 'More discoveries have arisen from intense observation of a very limited material than from statistics applied to large groups, for only by being familiar with the usual can we notice something as being unusual or unexplained.'[9]

Claude Bernard therefore advocated the use of a hypothesis in order to plan an experiment, but he insisted that once the experiment had been started the hypothesis should be forgotten. Scientists who are emotionally involved in their hypotheses are not found among the discoverers. Karl Popper stated: 'We are not observers, we are thinkers.' Science is an argumentative debate in which experiment plays a vitally important role.[10]

In his book, *Genesis and Development of a Scientific Fact*, Ludwik Fleck stressed the importance of 'thought collective' (*Denkkollektiv*), defined as 'a community of persons mutually exchanging ideas or maintaining intellectual interaction'.[11] Such a community, irrespective of content or logical justification, affects the perception of scientific 'facts'. Fleck distinguished paradigm from thought style, the former being a social product formed within the collective as the result of social forces, and the latter as that which sociologically affects cognition in the thought collective. 'A fact is supposed to be distinguished from transient theories 'as something definite, permanent and independent of any subjective interpretation by the scientist.'[12]

Truth is neither relative and subjective nor absolute and objective, but essentially determined and measured by a given thought style. Thus truth in science is a function of the particular style of thinking that has been accepted by the thought collective. It can therefore vary with time and culture. For Fleck reality was a 'systematic harmony of illusion which is acceptable because it is coherent'.[13] Every era and age has its own thought style, and cognition is a social process.

A fact begins with a signal of resistance from the collective. This signal, this indication, becomes gradually stylized, then consolidated and eventually it emerges as an accepted fact, on condition that it does not stand alone, but is interwoven into an existing system of ideas that fit the given thought style. Knowledge based on such facts is therefore not only the result of the interaction of the scientist with the subject studied, but also includes the collective, conditioned by the ruling thought style. 'Between the subject and the object there exists a third thing, the community.'[14] Scientific knowledge is culturally conditioned. Salvador E. Luria concurred with this view in his autobiography when he said: '. . . in science the speed of acceptance of new theory may depend on the dominant thought of a specific time.'[15]

According to Fleck, a scientific fact may be defined as a 'connection of concepts in a particular style of thought which, although it may lend itself to be examined from individual or social psychological standpoints, can never adequately be reconstructed from such standpoints alone'.[16]

There is a myth about observation and experiment.We tend to believe that first we make an observation which may perhaps be inaccurate or imprecise, then we adjust our experimentation so as to obtain more precise 'facts'. This may be true of classical mechanisms, but not in the modern rather confused and rapidly advancing fields of science. We have to learn to see with an idea of what we are looking for and to ask questions. Only then do education and tradition pave the way to our readiness for a 'style-adequate', directional perception. Only then can we ask questions that can be answered by 'yes' or 'no', or apply methods of measurement that will provide us with the answer, to be considered as fact. Actually, so-called scientific evidence cannot confirm that a theory is true; it can only confirm that it is more true than other theories.[17]

A different idea about the nature of scientific fact was expressed by Walter H. Seegers, Professor of Pharmacology at Wayne State University (known for having unravelled details of the process of blood coagulation). He wrote:

A 'scientific fact' is a product of my life's creation no more unique in principle than writing with a pen. For me, a laboratory discovery is a manifestation of my own creativity induced with the use of special instruments. Science is based on observation; but the process of observing depends on my readiness to give meaning to my sensory experience with light, sound, smell, warming, cooling, muscle movement, tasting, pain, delight, unhappiness, anger, hunger, enthusiasm, anticipatory reward, humoral activation and the whole bundle of my universal being of which my mind in one of the essentials.[18]

According to Seegers, the individual, the unique, is at the basis of the concept of 'fact'. 'One is compelled to ask if philosophy drives the man to great scientific achievement or if in the more or less accidental process of scientific discovery a man is driven to develop a philosophy about his place and relationship in the natural world.'[19]

Albert Einstein, in conversation with Niels Bohr, said: 'If a person, such as a mouse, observes the universe, does that change the state of the universe?' This in the context that quantum theory is incompatible with any reasonable idea of reality. And according to Eddington, the symbols physicists use to describe reality have as much resemblance to the real qualities of the material world 'as a telephone number has to a subscriber'.[20]

Speaking of discoveries, Fleck stated:

An important discovery originates, after numerous errors and detours from false presuppositions and irreproducible experiments. The heroes of the drama cannot tell us how it happened, they rationalize, idealize the course of events. A few of the eyewitnesses speak of lucky coincidences, and the sympathetic ones of intuitive inspiration.[21]

Poincaré defined a mathematical discovery thus:

It does not consist of making new combinations with mathematical entities already known. That can be done by anyone and the combination that could be formed would be infinite in number and the greater part of them would be absolutely devoid of interest. Discovery consists precisely in not constructing uselesss combinations but in constructing those that are useful, which are an infinitely small minority. Discovery is discernment, selection.[22]

On the other hand, R. W. Weisberg's view is that 'scientists do not make great inductive leaps into the unknown independently of what has come before, but even in its most impressive manifestation, scientific discovery develops incrementally, and is firmly based on the past', or in other words, 'detailed past experience is crucial in determining how efficiently an individual solves a novel problem.'[23] This is obviously true in discoveries made by Fleming, by Waksman, by Pasteur and many others.

The role of lateral or divergent thinking

In the process of problem-solving a logical step-by-step procedure represents what Edward de Bono[24] calls 'vertical thinking'. He compares it to digging a hole which may be made increasingly deep and wide, but it may be dug in a wrong place. To find the right place one needs *lateral thinking* which is based on haphazard, unlikely combinations of thoughts, results, conclusions taken often from different disciplines. When a solution to a problem is arrived at by lateral thinking it is found to be amazingly simple in retrospect – ('Why didn't I think of it before?) In retrospect, a lateral-thinking solution can be shown possibly to have been reached by vertical thinking, that is, by a logical sequence beginning at the problem and leading to solution. The trouble is that one cannot think ahead of such a sequence of rational steps. Vertical thinking can lead to 'snowblindness', a term Koestler used to described 'that remarkable form of blindness which often prevents the original thinker from perceiving the meaning and the significance of *his own* discovery'.[25] Koestler gives the example of Kepler who had the solution of elliptical orbits in his hands for three years before he recognized the truth, but 'The truth of Nature, which I had rejected and chased away, returned by stealth through the backdoor, disguising itself to be accepted. Ah, what a foolish bird I have been!'[26]

New ideas depend on lateral thinking — a low-probability thinking. 'With vertical thinking logic is in control of the mind, whereas with lateral thinking logic is at the service of the mind.'[27]

Lateral thinking seems to be an important ingredient in creativity, and is involved in the generation of new ideas. New ideas usually come from new information that requires reappraisal of old ideas. New ideas can also occur without any new information. Einstein formulated his theory of relativity without doing any experiments and without having any new information. Confirmation of his theory came later. But Einstein was a unique one-time phenomenon, a genius. This sudden illumination is often called a 'hunch': 'a unifying idea which springs into consciousness a solution to a problem in which we are intensely interested . . . A hunch springs from a wide knowledge of facts but is essentially a leap of the imagination, in that it goes beyond a mere necessary conclusion which any reasonable man draws from the data at hand.'[28]

R. W. Weisberg defies de Bono's idea that lateral (divergent) thinking, as opposed to vertical (convergent), thinking, is important in creativity. Creative problem-solving does not invoke a sudden shift to a new way of viewing, but rather it beings with playing with existing ideas and modifying them to make them more relevant to the specific problem.[29] This gradual changing of ideas is exemplified in the discovery of insulin, in the way anti-psychotic drugs were developed, but even then chance has often played an important role. A new idea emerges in the mind of one person when all the ingredients come together at a proper time.

The late Derek de Solla Price, Yale University, believed that the crucial turning-points in discoveries and new ideas came only when there was a suitable technology to find and develop them. Many of Leonardo da Vinci's inspired ideas were only paper work because at that time there was no technology to verify or to develop them. Charles Babbage at Cambridge would easily have constructed a modern computer calculator if he had today's technology at his disposal. But technology *per se* does not generate new ideas.

Once a new idea is born, it cannot be 'unthought', as a new-born baby cannot be returned to its mother's womb. But it is very difficult, nay impossible, for a new-born baby to replace a well-functioning adult professional, be he or she a statesman or a scientist. Though one might assume that an old idea could serve as a stepping-stone to something better, more often than not it hinders the acceptance and development of new ideas. Max Planck said: 'An important scientific innovation rarely makes its way by gradually winning over and converting its opponents . . . What does happen is that its opponents gradually die out, and that the growing generation is familiarized with the ideas from the beginning.'[30]

The acquisition of thorough knowledge about a subject might be detrimental to the development of new ideas. 'This has already been done and it was not successful' is the usual argument of the experts. Nevertheless it is better to have any idea, even if it is wrong, than always to be right, but not to have any ideas at all.

Ideas that are expressed in words have a problem. Words have definite meanings (unless used in an Orwellian context) and their use in speech or writing petrifies and rigidifies the ideas and what may develop from them. However, when one thinks in wordless images, their plasticity and fluidity permit a much better grasp and projection of concepts.

The role of humour in lateral thinking should also be considered. After all, humour depends on an unexpected, sudden change of frame of mind for two situations that are fully plausible in their own context, but become incompatible in a changed frame of reference. This sudden switch at the end of a plausible story is the key to laughter. The same applies to some of the Hitchcock's or Roald Dahl's stories. The reader is led along a logical and perfectly plausible path to a solution which is surprising or unexpected, although perfectly reasonable once he grasps the facts. It seems to me that the ability to operate such switches as in humour or in these mystery stories helps the scientist to look from a different perspective at a set of facts so they may lead him to a discovery.

Creativity often involves semantic re-definition – that is, the ability to shift the function of an object or of its part and to use it in a new way, an ability called by Koestler *bissociation*[31] – connecting previously unrelated levels of experience or frames of reference, or thinking on more than one plane of experience.

In creative thinking a person thinks simultaneously on more than one plane of experience, whereas in routine thinking he follows the paths worn by past associations. When two independent matrices of perception or reasoning interact with each other, the result is 'either a collision ending in laughter or their *fusion* in a new intellectual synthesis, or their *con-*

frontation in an aesthetic experience'.[32] Indeed, there is an important aesthetic ingredient in creativity.

J. H. Hildebrand quotes Poincaré:

> The scientist does not study nature because it is useful; he studies it because he delights in it and he delights in it because it is beautiful. Of course, I do not speak here of that beauty which strikes the senses, the beauty of qualities and appearances, not that I undervalue such beauty, far from it, but it has nothing to do with science; I mean that profound beauty which comes from the harmonious order of the parts and which a pure intelligence can grasp.[33]

NOTES TO CHAPTER 10

1 Newman, J. R. 1956: Commentary on an absent-minded genius and the laws of chance. In *The World of Mathematics*. New York: Simon and Shuster: 1378.

2 Herbert, F. 1964: *Heretics of the Dune*. London: New English Library: 390.

3 George, W. H. 1936: *The Scientist in Action. A Scientific Study of His Methods*. London: Williams and Norgate Ltd.

4 Stansfield, R. C. 1975: The new theology? The case of the dripping tap. *British Association for the Advancement of Science*, 2 Sept. 1975; Guildford.

5 Ibid.: 7.

6 De Broglie, L. 1962: *New Perspectives in Physics*. New York: Basic Books.

7 Koffka, K. 1935: *The Growth of Mind*. New York: Harcourt and Brace.

8 Tyndall, J. 1868: *Faraday as a Discoverer*. London: Longman, Green and Co. (quoted by Beveridge (9: 109).

9 Beveridge W. I. B. 1957: *The Art of Scientific Investigation*. London: W. Heinemann: 105.

10 Koffka, *Growth of the Mind*: 244.

11 Fleck, L. 1979: *Genesis and Development of a Scientific Fact*, ed. T. T. Trenn and R. K. Merton, Chicago: Chicago University Press: 158.

12 Ibid.: xxvii.

13 Ibid.: 156.

14 Fleck, L. 1960: Towards a free and more human science (unpublished paper at the Israel Institute for Biological Research, Ness Ziona, Israel).

15 Luria, S. E. 1984: *A Slot Machine – A Broken Test Tube. An Autobiography*. New York: Harper and Row (Colophon edn).

174   *What Do We Call a Fact?*

16 Baldamus, W. 1977: Ludwik Fleck and the development of the sociology of science. In P. R. Gleichmann, J. Goudsblum and H. Korte (eds), *Human Figurations*. Essays for *Festschrift für Norbert Elias*, Amsterdam: 135–56.
17 Koestler, *Art of Creation*: 240.
18 Seegers, W. H. 1977: How I got started in science. In W. R. Klemm (ed.), *Discovery Processes in Modern Biology*, Melbourne, Fla: R. E. Krieger: 247.
19 Ibid.: 243.
20 Koestler, *Art of Creation*: 253.
21 Fleck, *Genesis of a Scientific Fact*: 76.
22 Poincaré, H. 1914: *Science and Method* (translated by F. Maitland). Walton-on-Thames: T. Nelson and Sons, Ltd.
23 Weisberg, R. W. 1986: *Creativity, Genius and other Myths*. New York: W. H. Freeman: 90.
24 De Bono, E. 1967: *The Use of Lateral Thinking*. London: Jonathan Cape.
25 Koestler, *Art of Creation*: 217.
26 Ibid.: 218.
27 De Bono, *Lateral Thinking*: 18.
28 Platt, W. and Baker, R. A. 1931: The relationship of scientific 'hunch' to research. *Journal of Chemical Education*, 8: 1975.
29 Weisberg, *Creativity, Genius*: 138.
30 Mackay, A. L. 1977: *The Harvest of the Quiet Eye*. London: The Institute of Physics: 119.
31 Koestler, *Art of Creation*: 45.
32 Ibid.: 45.
33 Hildebrand, J. H. 1981: A history of solution theory. *Annual Review of Physical Chemistry*, 32: 1.

11

Personal Epilogue[1]

I have navigated in this book through the history of science and its various fields, showing how some scientists were lucky enough to make important discoveries while others missed their chance on the road to discovery.

As an author and scientist myself, I should like to share with the readers some of my own missed chances in my endeavour to advance science.

I came to Israel in 1937 as a student at the Hebrew University in Jerusalem. In 1940 I interrupted my studies to join the British Army in Palestine. After serving in the Jewish Brigade in Palestine, North Africa and Italy for six years, I returned to my studies at the University, obtained my M.Sc. and began to work on my Ph.D. thesis in 1947. The subject was a search for soil bacteria that would produce an antibiotic against typhoid and dysentery bacteria. At that time the only two known useful antibiotics were penicillin and streptomycin. I got off to a rather successful start by isolating from the soil of Galilee a bacillus whose colonies had the peculiar property of rotating synchronously on agar plates. An extract of the broth in which these bacteria grew inhibited the growth of typhoid bacteria. (My rotating bacillus was later found to produce polymyxin.) By force of circumstances during Israel's war of independence in 1948, I had to give up my project because the laboratories on Mount Scopus were evacuated and I went to war again. The cultures of the bacteria perished. When I resumed my scientific career in 1951, I started a new Ph.D. thesis on the aerosol immunization of chickens against the dreaded Newcastle disease, which appeared in epidemics and killed off or paralysed whole flocks. It was therefore important to protect the chickens by vaccination. At that time this was done by intramuscular injection of an attenuated 'vaccine' strain of virus. In the early fifties a vaccine strain of this sort had been developed by Dr A. Komarov, then Director of the Veterinary Institute of Israel. His strain, derived from India, was not entirely innocuous: it caused about 1 per cent mortality in the inoculated chicks, but this was an acceptable price to pay for the protection.

In preparation for the study of the Newcastle disease virus I spent the year 1951 at the Harvard Medical School where I acquired expertise in producing and measuring bacterial and viral aerosols. Equipped with this experience, I returned to Israel and started laboratory experiments on the aerosol vaccination of chicks, using the Komarov strain. Under properly controlled conditions, the experiments did in fact demonstrate that the vaccination was efficient and that the aerosol-vaccinated chicks were resistant when challenged with lethal doses of a virulent Newcastle virus.

Komarov learned of my results and accepted my proposal to try out the aerosol vaccine in the field. We selected a suitable flock of a few hundred two-week-old chickens at a kibbutz. The experiment was scheduled for the end of December 1952. This was at the height of the cold and rainy season. We went to the kibbutz, atomized the vaccine in the chicken pen and hoped for the best. Rains set in and continued for a week, flooding the countryside so that that there was no access to the kibbutz. When we finally got there the picture was one of calamity. More than half of the chickens were dead or paralysed. It turned out that under conditions of cold and humidity Komarov's strain was lethal when the birds inhaled it rather that receiving it by intramuscular injection.

These discouraging results very much dampened Komarov's enthusiasm for further field experimentation and the project languished. But concomitantly, as I learned later, Ray Bankowski in California was getting good results with aerosolized vaccine, using the much more attenuated B-1 strain of the Newcastle disease virus (NDV). Today aerosol vaccination is an accepted practice worldwide. In my youthful optimism I had hoped that a mesogenic (moderately virulent) strain of virus such as Komarov's, would do the trick. It did so in a controlled laboratory environment, but not, alas, under harsh field conditions.

My interest in the Newcastle disease did not decrease. I began to study the pathogenesis of this viral infection. During the next five years I unravelled the sequence of events leading from infection acquired by inhalation, food or injection, through the spread and multiplication of the virus in various internal organs, to its secretion in the faeces of the infected birds.

With this expertise I went on sabbatical in 1958 to Robert Huebner at the Institute of Infectious and Allergic Diseases at NIH in Bethesda, Maryland. There I intended to study the pathogenesis of avian leucosis, known at that time as visceral lymphomatosis, because of lymphomatous tumours in the intestinal organs of the affected birds. This disease had been extensively studied for more than a decade by Ben Burmester at East Lansing in Michigan. I thought that the experience I had gained from my NDV studies would be useful in my proposed study.

Until 1957 the only test for the presence of avian leucosis virus (ALV) in the environment or in any biological material was to inject a sample of the suspected material into chickens and then to wait for six to nine months for the results, namely the development of lymphomatous tumours in the visceral organs. Using this procedure, Burmester was able to elucidate the natural path of transmission of the virus from the affected hen through her egg to the hatched chick, and then through the air from one chick to another. But this procedure was cumbersome and protracted and required the maintenance of specially isolated, genetically selected birds. There was a rather urgent need for a more rapid test.

To develop such a test – one that would take a few days instead of the better part of a year – I combined in my thinking two tests known to me. There was known to be some connection between the Rous Sarcoma Virus (RSV) and visceral lymphomatosis. In 1956 Vincent Groupé at Rutgers and Harry Rubin in California independently discovered that the infection of chick embryo cultures in Petri dishes produced characteristic cell agglo-merates, pocks (also named foci), in the infected cultures. Another finding I was familiar with was that rubella virus infection, not directly detectable in infected cell cultures, was nevertheless demonstrable by the so-called heterologous interference test, namely by superinfection of the rubella-infected cells with an enterovirus ECHO 11. In such a test, normal cells, not infected by the rubella virus, would be destroyed by the ECHO 11 virus, while rubella-infected cells would survive.

I therefore wrote to Rubin seeking his advice and co-operation in developing a similar interference test for ALV, using RSV as the challenging virus. His answer was disappointing: He did not believe there was much chance of success for such a test. I dropped the idea and switched my attention to a chicken adenovirus.

About two years later Howard Temin and Harry Rubin developed an interference test for ALV. Their work was based on a chance observation that not all cultures of chick embryos responded equally well to an infection with RSV; they then prepared cultures, each from an individual embryo, and demonstrated that only embryos coming from eggs laid by lymphomatous hens were resistant to RSV infection. This finding enabled them to develop a quick convenient test for the isolation and quantitation of the AL virus. Nine years later, when I spent another sabbatical at

Rubin's laboratory at Berkeley, I asked him about his negative attitude to my original proposal. Rubin, the most honest and straightforward scientist I have ever met, had no recollection of my letter and of his response. On a minor scale this course of events once more demonstrates the basic truth of Fleck's dictum about the community of thought and the readiness to accept or to incorporate a new, unusual idea or technique into the accepted mode of thinking or experimentation.

As we scientists navigate in the stormy seas of scientific research, some of us, like Columbus, find a new continent, believing it to be something else, while others explore it and find hidden treasure by chance or by design. The lucky ones acquire fame and recognition in their lifetime and later adorn the pages of scientific history. Others, who missed their chance, are forgotten by posterity. Only from time to time is some light shed on their unrecognized contribution to the advancement of science.

In his book on the *Art of Scientific Investigation* W. I. B. Beveridge stressed the fact that great discoveries had been made 'by means of experiments devised with complete disregard of well accepted beliefs'.[2] So, for instance in chemotherapy, nearly all the discoveries were made as a result of false hypotheses or chance observations. Beveridge's advice is that scientists should train their powers of observation, so as to be able to take account of the unexpected and pay suitable attention to it.

For most scientists, the motto 'It is better to travel hopefully than to arrive' might be the guide to a very fulfilling career.

NOTES TO CHAPTER 11

1 Kohn, A. 1987: Missed chances on a hopeful road. *The Scientist*, 1 (October 5): 14.
2 Beveridge, W. I. B. 1957: *The Art of Scientific Investigation*. London: W. Heinemann: 89.

Table of Missed Discoveries

Name of credited discoverer	Year	Discovery	Follow up Agent	Year
Ibn-al-Nafis	1242	small blood circulation	Servetus	1553
Steinhauser	1840	cod-liver oil		1930
Mayer	1842	mechanical equivalent of heat	Joule	1847
Mayer	1842	law of conservation of energy	Helmholtz	1856
Waterston	1845	molecular theory gases	Joule	1890
Mendel	1860	genetics	DeVries	1900
?	1873	DDT	Müller	1939
McMunn	1886	cytochrome	Keilin	1924
Landsteiner	1901	blood groups		1914
T. Smith	1903	O. H. antigens	Weil and Felix	1917
Hörlein	1908	sulfonamides	Domakg	1936
Fleming	1929	penicillin	Florey	1939
Atanaseff	1939	electronic computer	Mauchly and Eckert	1945

Additional Reading

Cannon, W. B. 1945: *The Way of an Investigation*. New York: W. W. Norton.

Glasser, O. 1958: *Dr. W. C. Röntgen*. 2nd edn, Springfield: C. C. Thomas.

Hadamard, J. *The Psychology of Invention in the Mathematical Field*. Princeton: Princeton University Press.

Hanson, N. R. 1958: *Patterns of Discovery*. London: Cambridge University Press.

Hughes, H. W. 1974: *Alexander Fleming and Penicillin*. London, Priory Press Ltd.

Knight, D. 1986: *The Age of Science*. Oxford: Basil Blackwell.

Kuhn, T. S. 1970: *The Structure of Scientific Revolutions*. 2nd edn, Chicago: Chicago University Press.

Lowes, J. 1927: *The Road to Xanadu. A Study of the Ways of Imagination*. Boston: Houghton Mifflin.

Ludovici, L. J. 1952: *Fleming. Discoverer of Penicillin*. London: Andrew Dakers, Science Book Club.

Masters, D. 1946: *Miracle Drug*. London: Eyre and Spottiswode.

Montmasson, J. M. 1931: *Invention and the Unconscious*, London: Kegan Paul.

Nicholson, M. 1956: *Science and Imagination*, New York: Cornell University Press.

Planck, M. 1933: *Where is Science Going?* London: Allen and Unwin.

Ratcliff, J. D. 1945: *Yellow Magic: The Story of Penicillin*. New York: Random House.

Sinclair, W. J. 1909: *Semmelweiss, His Life and Doctrine*. Manchester: Manchester University Press.

Name Index

Abel 8
Abbot, G. 113
Abraham, E. P. 93
Adams, J. C. 37–8
Ader, R. 124–5
Allison, A. 71
Airy, G. B. 37–8, 63
Alpher, R. A. 27
Ampère, A. M. 12–14
Anderson, K. D. 5, 38
Arago, D. 38
Arber, W. 63
Archimedes 3
Aretaeus 147
Atanasoff, J. V. 6, 7, 179
Avery, O. T. 66–7
Aurelius, Marcus 4
Aurivillius, C. 5

Babbage, C. 171
Babes, V. 98
Bankowski, R. 176
Banting, F. G. 105, 147, 151–8
Barber, B. 142
Barron, M. 152
Basov, H. 30
Beaudette, F. 104
Becker, H. K. 116
Becquerel, H. 22–4
Bennett, W. R. 30
Berger, A. 71
Berger, F. M. 119
Bernard, C. 15, 149, 167–8

Berry, C. E. 6
Berson, S. A. 134, 136
Bertani, G. 63
Berthelot, C. L. 7
Berzelius, J. J. 45–6
Best, C. H. 105, 151–8, 229, 230
Beveridge, W. I. B. 130, 178
Bigelow 113
Blackett, P. M. S. 38
Bliss, M. 154
Blumberg, B. 71–2
Böhringer, C. H. 49
Bohr, N. 169
Bolyai, J. 3
Boott, F. 113
Bordet, J. J. 102
Bothe, A. 38
Bouchard, Ch. 100
Bovet, D. 48
Boylston, Z. 7
Bradley, S. E. 135
Braestrup, C. 120
Brahe, T. 2
Brailsford, J. F. 21
Brueckner, K. A. 30
Bugie, E. 105
Burmester, B. 177
Bustinza, F. 94

Cade, J. F. J. 122
Cannon, W. B. 105
Cantani, A. 98
Carlson, Anton 150
Carlson, Arvid 124

Caro, H. 47
Carrington, T. 30
Cattel, H. 21
Cavendish, H. 5
Chadwick, J. 5
Chain, E. B. 82–3, 85–92, 158
Chargaff, E. 69
Chase, M. 67
Churchill, W. 1, 93
Clark, R. W. 82
Clarke, W. E. 112, 115
Clay, J. 8, 38
Clayton, J. H. 21
Cohen, N. 125
Colombo, R. 4, 5
Colquhoun, D. B. 89
Collip, J. B. 155–7
Compton, A. H. 8, 38
Comroe, J. H. 105, 144
Coulomb, C. A. 5
Craddock, S. R. 84
Crick, F. 3, 26, 69
Crookes, W. 15–16, 18, 21
Cruickshank, R. 82
Curie, I. 5

Dahl, R. 172
Dale, H. H. 2, 24, 77, 127, 140
Darwin, C. 158
Davy, H. 42, 111
da Vinci, L. 2, 171
Dath, S. 102
Dawson, M. H. 66
de Bono, E. 170
de la Rive, A. 13–14
de Solla Price, D. 171
de St Victor, N. 24
Delay, J. 123
Delbrück, M. 62
Deniker, P. 123
Descartes, R. 3
Devons, S. 13
Dicke, R. H. 28

Dioscorides 110
Dobson, M. 147
Doisy, E. A. 158
Domagk, G. 47–8
Donohue, J. 69
Dreyer, G. 90
Drinker, C. K. 155
Dubos, R. 67
Dumas, J. B. A. 7
Duthie, E. S. 90

Ebers 147
Eckert, J. P. 6, 179
Edison, T. A. 15
Edwards, J. H. 21
Ehrlich, P. 79
Eijkman, C. 50–1
Einstein, A. 4–6, 8, 36, 167, 169, 171
Elliot, D. 139
Emmerich, R. 98–100
Epstein 90

Faraday, M. 5, 14, 23, 25, 111–12, 172
Feldman, W. H. 105
Fermat, P. 3
Field, J. 69
Fleck, L. 168, 170, 178
Fleming, A. 76–89, 92, 94, 97, 103, 158
Flexner, S. 47
Florey, H. W. 85, 87–8, 103, 158
Fox, R. 142
Franke, H. 159
Franklin, B. 42
Franklin, R. 69
Fraser, W. 113
Freud, S. 115–16
Frölich, T. 51
Fuchs, J. 142
Funk, K. 51

Gädke, F. 115
Galen 4
Galileo 43

Galle, J. G. 38
Galvani, L. 10–11, 24
Gamov, G. 26
Gardner, A. D. 87
Garré, C. 99
Gärtner 116
Gate, J. 102
Gauss, J. K. F. 3, 5
Geissler, H. 15
Gelmo, P. 47–8, 78
George, W. H. 165
Gley, E. 151–2, 156
Goldie, J. 62
Goldman, A. J. 62
Goldstein, A. 118–19
Goodrich, C. A. 132
Goodspeed, A. W. 16
Gosio, B. 101
Goethe, J. W. von 163
Gould, G. 5, 29–31
Gratia, A. 102
Griffith, F. 66–7
Groupé, V. 177
Guillemin, R. 136

Hare, R. 81, 89
Harrington, C. 90
Harris, S. 155
Heatley, N. 91–2
Hedon, I. E. 149
Heidelberger, M. 47
Henry, J. 1
Herbert, F. 163
Herman, R. C. 27
Hernandez, F. 121
Herrick, H. T. 82
Hershey, A. 67
Herschel, W. H. 36–8
Hickman, H. H. 111–12
Hildebrand, J. H. 173
Hill, R. T. 130
Hinshaw, H. L. 105
Hittorf, J. W. 16
Hodgkin, D. 93

Hofmann, A. 121
Hofmann, A. W. 46
Hofstaedter, R. 31
Hokin, L. E. 51–4
Hokin, M. R. 53
Holmes, O. W. 59, 110
Holst, A. 51
Homer 110
Hörlein, H. 48
Hossli, L. 131
Howell, 138
Huebner, R. 176
Hughes, E. E. 155
Hughes, J. 118
Hunt, M. 92
Hustin, A. 136–7

Ibn-al-Nafis 4
Ivy, A. C. 131

Jackson, C. T. 113, 115
Jacob, F. 4
Janbon, M. 158
Jellinek 116
Jenner, E. 7
Jennings, M. 89, 91
Jennings, W. N. 16
Johnson, T. A. 38
Joliot, P. 5, 38
Joubert, J. 98
Jouvet, M. 132

Karnovsky, M. L. 132
Kekulé, F. A. 3
Kellner, A. 141–3
Kepler, J. 2
Khorana, G. 64
King, C. G. 51
King, H. 92
Kleiner, I. S. 150, 158
Kline, N. 123
Koch, P. 50
Koestler, A. 171–2

Kohn, A. 175–8
Koller, C. 116–17
Komarov, A. 175
Kosterlitz, H. 118
Krafft, L. 16
Kraus, I. M. 68
Krebs, H. 53
Krueger, J. M. 132–3
Kuhn, T. 31
Kung-Yueh-ting 159

Laborit, H. 123
Languesse, G. E. 148, 153–4
Langerhans, P. 149, 153–4, 159
Lavoisier, A. L. 43–4
Lee, C. H. 119
Leibniz, G. W. 3
Leibniz, H. M. 31
Lemaître, A. G. E. 26
Lenard, P. E. A. 16–17, 21, 23
Leverrier, U. J. J. 37
Lieske, R. 92
Light, J. C. 30
Lipkin, H. J. 33
Lister, J. 97, 103
Lobachevski, N. I. 3
Lode, A. 101
Loew, O. 100
Lomonosow, M. V. 41, 44
Long, C. W. 112, 115
Loubatières, A. 158
Luria, S. E. 60–4, 168

McCarthy, M. 66–8
McClintock, B. 6
MacFarlane, G. 85–6
McLauchlan, J. 114
McLean, J. 110, 137–8
MacLeod, C. M. 66
Macleod, J. J. R. 147, 153–4, 156
Maiman, T. H. 29
Malus, E. L. 2
Mann, T. 117, 119
Mao Tse-tung 159

Marconi, G. 15
Mauchly, J. W. 6
Maxwell, J. C. 8
Mayer, J. R. 5
Mayow 41–2
Mellanby, Sir E. 91
Meltzer, G. J. 150, 158
Mendel, G. J. 6
Merton, R. 144
Metchnikoff, E. 133
Michell, J. 53
Michelson, A. A. 4
Miller, J. B. 118, 132
Miller, O. 88
Millikan, R. A. 8, 38
Minkowski, O. 148–9
Mohler, H. 120
Monnier, A. 131
Moon, P. B. 32, 35
Morris, H. R. 119
Morton, W. T. G. 113, 115
Mössbauer, R. 31–6
Münsterberg, H. 21
Murray, W. J. 118

Nalbandov, A. V. 130–1
Naunyn, B. 149
Newman, M. H. A. 6
Newton, I. 3, 33
Nicolle, C. J. H. 58–9
Niemann, A. 115
Nightingale, E. 68
Nirenberg, M. 71
Nitti, F. 48

Oersted, H. C. 11–12
Okochi, K. 73
Oliver, G. 132–3
Opie, L. E. 149
Orr-Ewing, J. 87
Ottolenghi, E. 68

Papacostas, G. 102
Pappenheimer, J. R. 131–3

Parkes, A. S. 130, 139
Pasteur, L. 1, 56–7, 97
Pattle, P. E. 1
Paulesco, N. C. 151, 156
Pauling, L. 69–70
Pavel, S. 132
Peebles, P. J. E. 28
Penzias, A. A. 26–8
Perkin, W. H. 46
Phipps, J. 7
Pieron, H. 131–2
Pimentel, G. 30
Planck, M. 172
Poincaré, H. 5, 170, 173
Polanyi, J. C. 30
Polge, C. 139
Pope, E. 112
Popper, K. 163
Portier, P. 127
Pras, M. 140
Priestley, J. 41–4
Prokhorov, A. 30

Quastel 53
Queen Victoria 114

Raistrick, H. 84
Ramsden 7
Randall, L. 120
Rappin 101
Ratcliffe 21
Rayleigh, J. W. (Lord) 24
Reynolds, D. V. 118
Rhines, Ch. 104
Richet, C. R. 127
Richter, B. 7
Rigg, J. R. 113
Ridley, E. 84
Ringer, S. 110, 139–40
Roberts, F. 157
Robinson, R. 88, 92–3
Röntgen, W. K. 16–23
Roosevelt, F. D. 48

Rous, P. 6
Rubin, H. 177–8

Schäfer, A. E. 133–4, 149
Schally, A. 136
Schatz, A. 105
Schawlow, A. L. 29–30
Scheele, K. W. 41–2
Schiller, I. 102
Schneedorf, J. G. 131
Schoenenberger 132
Schou, M. 122–3
Schroff 115
Scoffern, J. 111
Scott, E. L. 150, 153–4, 156–7
Scott, W. 114
Seegers, W. H. 169
Sela, M. 70–1
Semmelweiss, I. P. 7, 59–60
Serendip 1
Servetus, M. 4
Sgaramella, V. 64
Shäfer 132–3
Shaffer, P. A. 158
Sheehan, J. C. 93
Shuler, K. E. 30–1
Sia, R. H. P. 66
Simpson, J. Y. 114
Smith, A. 139
Smith, H. O. 63
Smith, T. H. 179
Snow, J. 17, 115
Snyder, S. H. 118, 124
Sobolev, L. 149
Somogyi, M. 158
Squires, M. 120
Stähle, H. 49
Stahl, G. E. 41
Stansfield, R. G. 166
Steinhauser 179
Stent, G. 69
Sternbach, C. 120
Stevenson, L. 155
Stokes, G. G. 31

Index

Strutt, J. W. 24
Sutnick, A. I. 72
Swift, I. J. 167
Szent-Györgyi, A. 1, 51
Szigety, A. 15
Szybalski, W. 64–5

Takamine, Y. 151
Tallman, J. 120
Taton, R. 13
Temin, H. 177
Terenius, L. 117
Tesla, N. 14–15
Thom, C. 92
Thomas, L. 140–4
Thompson, L. 155
Thomson, J. J. 16
Tiberio, V. 99
Ting, S. C. C. 3
Townes, C. H. 27, 29–30
Tréfouel, J. 48
Tréfouel, T. J. 48
Turing, A. M. 6
Tyndall, J. 89, 97

Uchizono, K. 132

Vande Sande, H. 65
Vaudremer, A. 101
Vesalius 4
Virchov, R. 60
Vogel 110
Volta, A. 11, 24

von Anrep, V. 116
von Mering, J. 148–9
von Siemens, W. 20
Vuillemin, P. 97

Waksman, B. 105
Waksman, S. 75, 103–5
Walpole, H. 1
Warren, J. C. 113
Watanabe, C. K. 158
Waterston, J. J. 7
Watson, J. D. 3, 26, 69, 110
Watt, J. 3
Weindling, R. 103
Weisberg, R. 170–1, 256
Wells, H. 113, 115
Werner, B. 72
Wilkins, M. 3
Willis, T. 147
Willstädter, R. 117
Wilson, R. W. 26–8
Wöhler, F. 45–6
Wolf, M. 49
Woodward, R. B. 46
Wright, A. 76–9, 86, 88
Wyman, J. 131

Yalow, R. 134–6
Yukawa (Yugawa), H. 1

Zasloff, M. 106-7
Zehnder, L. 16, 20–1
Zuelcer, G. L. 150, 156–7

Subject Index

absorption 31–2
Academy of Science 12, 24, 38
acetone 114
acetylcholine 52–3
acids 84
  ascorbic 51
  benzoic 42
  citric 42, 46
  gallic 42
  helvolic 101
  hexuronic 51
  hydrocyanic 42
  lactic 42, 102
  malic 42
  mycophenolic 101
  oxalic 42
  phosphatidic 53
  tartaric 42, 56
ACTH 130, 136
Actinia 127
Actinomycetes 105
actinomycetin 91
actinomycin 105
addiction 120
adenine 70
adenylate
  cyclase 52
  monophosphate 52
adrenal cortex 51
adrenalin 133, 150–1
adrenoreceptors 49
agar 57, 80

air
  dephlogisticated 43
  fixed 43
  liquid 33
albumen 24, 100, 139
alcohol 46, 119, 150, 157
  amyl 67
alcoholic extract 150, 154–5
alizarin 46
allergy 127, 135
aluminium 16, 23
ALV (avian leucosis virus) 177
amines biogenic 107, 124
ammonia 29
  cyanate 45
  sulphate 45
ampicillin 92
amputation 114
amyl acetate 91
amyloid bodies 140
anaesthesia 110–15, 123
  local 115–17
analgesic 118
anaphylaxis 126–7
anatomy 4, 210
antagonism 99, 158
antenna 27
anthrax 57, 99
antibacterial 47–8, 90; 119
antibiosis 89, 97, 102
antibiotics 57, 67, 93, 97–109
antibodies 125, 134–5

anti-coagulant 136–8
antigens 66, 127
  Australia 71–2
anti-hypertensive 49, 123
antiseptic 77, 79, 91, 97, 115, 127
anxiety 123
arterial 45, 133
artery 133, 136
Aspergillus 99
  flavescens 99
  fumigatus 101
asymmetry 56
astronomy 3, 36–8
atomic
  absorption 32–3
  nuclei 32
  particles 16
  recoil 32–5
  weight 26
Australia antigen 71–3
aversion 125
avian leucosis 176–7
azaguanine 68
azote 42

bacillus, rotating 175
Bacillus anthraxis 98–100, 102
Bacillus bulgaricus 102
Bacillus mesentericus 101–2
Bacillus mycoides 102
Bacillus pyocyaneus 99–100
Bacillus subtilis 102, 104
Bacillus violaceus 78
bacteria 21, 50, 66, 77, 83, 97
  gram negative 105, 119
  pathogenic 66, 81, 93
  phage-resistant 61–2
  soil 98, 104, 260
bacterial
  colonies 62, 78, 80, 81, 89
  cultures 61–2, 78, 175
  flora 133
  infections, *see* infections
  mutants 61–3

  resistance 62
  virulence 66
bacterial strains
  anthrax 57, 100–1
  attenuated 56, 66
Bacteriolytic 80
Bacterium fluorescens 104
Bacterium prodigiosum 78
bacteria:
  cholera 100–1
  Clostridium 87
  diphtheria 80, 100
  dysentery 175
  Erisipelcoccus 98
  Escherichia coli 61, 63, 102
  Haemophilus 83–4, 86
  meningococci 80
  Micrococcus 101, *lysodeikticus* 80, 90;
    tetragenus 101
  Mycobacterium phlei 105
  Mycobacterium tuberculosis 101, 105
  pertussis 84
  pestis 100
  pneumococci 47, 66–7, 84
  pyocyaneus 97
  Salmonella 105
  Serratia 78
  Shigella 63, 105, 174
  Staphylococcus 78, 80–4, 87, 89, 101,
    105
  streptococci 47–8, 84, 86–7, 98–101,
    105, 143
  Streptococcus lactis 102
  typhoid 100, 174
bactericidal 81, 91, 101
bacteriolytic 81
bacteriophage 61–4, 107
  lambda 64–5
  T1 64
barbiturates 119–20, 123
bar code 31
barium 111
  chloride 22
  platinocyanide 17

Beecham 93
behaviour 110–29
behaviourism 167
Bell Laboratories 28, 48
benzene 3, 46, 114
benzodiazepines 119–21
beri-beri 50
'big bang' 26–8
biochemistry 41–54
bissociation 172
bleeding 140
blindness, communal 103
blood 5, 71, 85, 151
    cells 52, 80
    circulation 4–5, 85, 149
    citrated 137
    coagulation (clotting) 136–7, 169
    poisoning 60
    pressure 49, 119, 134
    serum 71–2, 155
    stream 80, 148
    sugar 155, 236
    transfusion 137
    venous 131
    vessels 79
Böhringer und Sohn 49
bombesin 107
bone-marrow 68
bones 18–19
bradykinin 107
brain 118, 123–5
    homogenates 118
    ventricles 131
British Research Council 91
burns 22

calcination 41, 70
calcium 53, 110, 140
calx 41–2, 68–9
Cambridge 5, 37, 69, 90, 139
camouflage 164
cancer 6, 22, 62, 87
carbon

dioxide 42, 71, 112
    monoxide 136
carbuncle 87
cartilage 142–3
cathode 15–17
cats 132
cecropin 106
cellophane 91
cells:
    acinar 148
    bone marrow 68
    degeneration of 149
    differentiation of 68
    freezing 138–9
    Langerhans 148
    mammalian 67
    melanoblasts 68
    nerve 52
    sickle 68
    white blood 77, 79
cephalin 137–8
cerulein 107
chemistry 41–54
    inorganic 45
    organic 45
    theoretical 30
chemotherapy 3, 62, 77, 85, 92, 178
chickens 50, 57, 130, 176–7
childbed fever, *see* puerperal fever
childbirth (labour) 114
chimpanzees 58
China 107, 159
chlorination 60
chlorine 42
chloroform 67, 111, 114
chlorpromazine 122–4
cholera 57, 115
cholesterol 52
chromosomes 67
citrate 136–7
clavicin 104
clonidine 49
clotting 137, 169
coal-tar 46

coca 115
cocaine 115–16
coil 13–15
  Ruhmkorff 17
cold 49
Cold Spring Harbor 6
Collège de France 12
combustion 30
comet 36
community (thought) 2, 168
compass 12
computers 7, 171
conductor 13
conditioning 125–6
contamination 82, 89
copper 13–14
cornea 116
cortisone 141
cosmology 28
creativity 171–3
Crookes' tube 15–18, 21
crystal 2, 17, 33, 35–6, 121
  fluorescent 18, 21
  lattice 35
crystallography 2, 56, 93
CSF 131
cuorin 138
cyclamate 110
cyclophosphamide 125
cytoplasm 67

Davos, Switzerland 117
degeneration 148
Denkkollektiv 168
depression 123
diabetes 135, 147ff
diarrhoea 110
diet 50, 153
digestion 148
diglycerides 53–4
diloxacillin 93
diphtheria 101
diploid 67
disease

of chickens 6, 51, 57, 82, 176–7
liver 72–3
Newcastle 176
Parkinson's 123
of silkworms 57
of wine 57
diseases
  bacterial 50
  infectious 50, 133
  mental 121
  psychosomatic 126
  viral 50
DNA 26, 63–71
  double stranded 64
  lambda 64
  model 67, 69
  radioactive 68
  recombinant 63–5
  virus, *see* hepatitis B
DNAse 67–8
dogma 5, 14
dogs 131, 134, 137, 148–51, 153, 158
dopamine 124
Doppler effect 33–5, 58
Down's syndrome, *see* syndrome
drugs 47–9, 94, 171
  antihypertensive 49
  DSIP 132
  psychedelic 121–4
Dunn School of Pathology 87
duodenum 148–9, 154
dyes, aniline 46–7
  colour fast 47
  organic 48
  textile 47
dynamo 15
dynorphin 119

eclampsia 141
École Polytechnique 37
Edison Company 15
electric
  circuit 13
  current 10–15, 118, 134

alternating 14
    direct 14
discharge 10
induction 14–15
motor 14
spark 17
switch 51–2
wire 20
electricity 10, 20, 21
    animal 10
    static 10
    'streaming' 16
electromagnetism 11–14, 35
electrons 18
electronvolt 32
electrophoresis 134
electroscope 23
electrostatics 5
elements 27, 42, 45
elliptic functions 5
embryos 139, 177
endorphins 117–19
endotoxin 140
energy, 32–3
    conservation 5, 24, 33
    free 29
    internal 35
    kinetic 35
    translational 35
enkephalin 119
enzymes 63, 134, 157
    digestive 148, 152–3
    ligase 64–5
    phospholipase C 53
    phosphorylase 68
    proteolytic 141, 153, 157
    pyocyanase 100–2
    restriction 63
epidemics:
    beri-beri 50
    cholera 115
    smallpox 7
    typhus 58–9
ergonovine 121

ergot 121
errors 5, 165–6
ether 4, 84, 111–14
    extract 53, 138
etherization 112
ethyl nitrate 114
excitation 35
    dissociative 30
    vibrational 30

fashion 167
fermentation 43, 56, 92, 145
fever, childbed, *see* puerperal fever
ficin 141
fluctuation test 63
fluorescence 17–18, 21, 31
fracture 19, 22, 114
frog 10, 105–7, 139
    eggs 165
    heart 139–40
fructose 139
fungi 105

GABA 121
galaxy 27–8
galvanism 11
galvanometer 11
gastrin 136
gelatine 100–1, 151
gene 64, 67
    jumping 6
genetics 6, 67
    code 71
geometry, analytical 3
    non-Euclidean 3
germicides 86
Gestapo 48
glands 53, 153
    adrenal 51
    pituitary 124
    salt 53–4
    suprarenal 133
    sweat 49
    thyroid 22

glaucoma 49
Gliocadium 103
gliotoxin 103
globulins 135
    gamma 135
glucose 136, 149, 158
glycerol 139, 195
glycosuria 158
Göttingen 165, 167, 249
gravitation 3, 12, 35–6
gravity 42
growth
    hormone 49
    media, *see* nutrient media
Guam 143
guanidine 158
guanine 70
guinea pigs 58–9, 98–101, 118, 122, 127

hallucinations 121
haemoglobin 68
haemophilia 72
haemorrhage 140
happening 165
heart 4–5, 137, 140, 143, 155
    ventricles 4
Heidelberg 31
helix 69–70
hemp, Indian 110
heparin 110, 136–8, 141
heparphosphatide 138
hepatitis B 71–3
histamine 123, 127
Hospital
    King's College 97
    Queen's (Birmingham) 21
    St John's 137
    St Mary's 76–7, 79, 85, 93
    Sheba Medical Center 140
    University College 139
Honeywell 7
hormones 49, 52, 132, 136, 151
Hughes Research Laboratory 29
humour 172

hunch 171
hydrogen 46, 71
    bromide 71
    fluoride 42
    sulfide 42
hyosciamus 111
hyperglycaemia 158
hypersensitivity 127
hypnotoxin 131–2
hypoglycaemia 158–9
hypophysectomy 130
hypophysis 130

IG Farbenindustrie 48
illusion 166, 168
images 164–5, 172
imidazoline 49
immune response 7, 125, 133
immunity 125
immunization 57, 77, 100, 176,
immunology 56
immuno-modulators 126
immunoproteidin 100
immunosuppression 125
immunotherapy 77
indigo 47
induction 13–14
    coil 17
    motor 13–14
infection
    bacterial 77, 79, 83, 92, 94, 143
    inapparent 58
    latent 58
    lethal 59, 87, 176
    'non-productive' 58
    pyogenic 84
    streptococcal 47–8, 87, 98
    trypanosomal 85
inflammation 144
inhalation 114
inhibition 98–9, 101–2, 105
inoculation 7, 77
inositol 53
isotope 36

Institute
  Cancer Research 71–2
  Hygiene (Munich) 98
  Max Planck 31
  National Institutes of Health 70–1,
    106, 176
  Pasteur (Paris) 4; (Tunis) 58
  Rockefeller 6, 47, 66, 143, 150
  Veterinary (Israel) 175
  Weizmann 33, 70
insulin 134–6, 147–62, 171
  radioactive 134
interference 177
interferon 133
Interleukin-1 133
inversion 29
iodine 134
iodoform 114
iridium 31
islets (Langerhans) 148–50
isletin 154
isotopes 26, 28, 31–2, 36

jackpot 61–3
Jewish Brigade 175
Journal of Irreproducible Research 69

kidney 45, 131, 140, 158
  necrosis 140–1
kinase *(see* protein kinase)

labour *(see* childbirth)
Lactams 93
laser 5, 26, 29–31
  chemical 30
  ruby 29
latency 59
lateral thinking, *see* thinking
laughing gas 110, 113
lead 18–19
Lederle 92
leucocytes 77, 80, 84
leukaemia 72–3
levity 42

Leyden jar 10
Librium 120
lice 58
ligase 64–5
ligation 64, 154–5, 158
light 29
  coherent 29
  fluorescent 31
  monochromatic 29
  polarized 57
lightning 10
Lille 57
lipids 52–3
lipoids 138
lipoprotein 72
lithium carbonate 122–3
liver 73
London, Ontario 152
London, UK 87, 115, 134
London School of Hygiene 84
luminescence 15, 22, 24
lungs 4
lymphoma 177
lysergic acid (LSD) 121
lysozyme 77, 80, 88
lytic substances 102

madder 47
madhumea 147
magainin 105–7
magnesium 111
magnet 13–14, 18
magnetic
  field 12–14
  needle 12
magnetism 12–13
maize 6
mandrake 110
mania 122
maser 26, 27, 89
Medical Council, Vienna 60
  Research Club 79
  Research Council 80, 91
melanin 68

membranes
  cell 52–3
  mucous 115
memory 166
meningitis 88
mental disorders 122–4
mephensin 120
meprobamate 120
Merck 92
Mercury (planet) 37
mercury 17, 44, 134
  oxide 42
mescaline 121
meson 3
messenger, second 52–4
metabolism
  calcium 53
  glucose (sugar) 149, 152
methanol 91
methicillin 93
Mexico 121
mice 86, 103, 109, 119
microbiology 56–75
micro-organisms 4, 50, 56–75
  pathogenic 80
  soil 103
microwaves 28–9
migraine 49
milk 107, 196
midwives 60
Miltown 119
MIT 64
momentum (recoil) 35
monkeys 56
moon 36–7
morphine 117–18
Mössbauer effect 33–5
mould 57, 80, 82–3, 89–92, 99, 139
mucolysate 102
Mucor 99
muramyl peptide 132–3
Murphy's Law 144
muscles 10, 52, 118, 120
  relaxant 120

mutants 6, 61
  deletion 64–5
  spontaneous 62
Mycobacterium, see bacteria
myocarditis 143
myths 3, 69, 169

naloxone 118
narcotic 117
nebulae 37
necrosis 140
Neptune 38
nervous system 50, 119
  sympathetic 49
neurasthenia 115
neuroleptic 123–4
neurons 123
neurophysiology 110, 124
neurotransmitter 52, 126, 132
neutron 26
Newcastle disease, *see* disease
nitrogen 42
nitrous oxide 111
Nobel Prize 4–6, 20–2, 26–7, 31, 33, 44,
    47–8, 51, 70, 72, 94, 98, 103, 105,
    131, 156
norepinephrine 124
nuclear, physics 32
  radiation 32
  resonance 31–3
nuclei, atomic 32, 35
  radioactive 31
nucleic acid 66
nucleoproteins 53
nucleus 67
nutrient medium 84, 102
  plate 82, 84, 89, *see also* Petri dish

obstetrics 59
Okinawa 143
oligophasic 78
oocytes 106

ophthalmology 116–17
opiates 119
opioids 118
opium 117
opsonization 77–8
optochin 47
oscillations 29
  harmonic 35
osteomyelitis 87
oxacillin 93
oxazolone 93
Oxford (city) 71, 87, 92
oxygen 41–4

pain 111–13, 117, 119
Palestine 175
pancreas 148ff
  degeneration 149
  foetal 154
pancreatic duct 148
  extract 150–5
  juice 148
papain 140–3
paradigm 46, 132
paralysis 59, 119
paratartrate 56
parathyroid 151
Paris 123
particles
  alpha 23
  atomic 16, 18
  charged 16, 23
  elementary 27
Pasadena, Calif. 70
patent 30
  royalties 30
pathogenesis 176
pathogens 47, 66, 103
patients
  diabetic 155
  manic 122
  pneumonia 159
  psychiatric 123
  surgical 123

penicillin 76–94, 97, 103, 158
  concentration 84
  crude 86
  extraction 84, 87
  purification 87
  sensitivity 84
  stability 85, 90
  synthetic 93
  yield 92–3
penicillinase 93
Penicillium 57, 81, 97
  chrysogenum 92
  glaucum 97, 99
  notatum 81, 84, 90
peptides 119, 132
  muramyl 132–3
  sleep-inducing (DSIP) 132
  vasoactive 132
peyote 121
Petri dish 81, 89, 103, 136, 160
Pfizer 92
phage, *see* bacteriophage
phenobarbitol 119
phenol 101
phenolphtalein 110
phenotypic 67
phenylalanine 71
phlogiston 41, 44
phosphates 70
phosphatides 136–7
phosphatidyl-inositol 52–4
phospholipase C 53
phospholipids 52
phosphorescence 22–3
phosphorus 53
phosphorylation 52, 68
photochemistry 39
photoelectric effect 5–6
photographic film 134
  plates 16, 18–19, 23
photography 21–4
photon 8
Phylloxera 57
Physalia 126

pituitary 124, 130–1
planet 36–8
plates, agar 57, 89
platinum 12, 18
  cyanide 16
pneumonia 47, 159
Poisson distribution 62
polarization 2
polio virus, *see* viruses
pollutants 31
polycarbobenzoxylysine 71
polymorphism 71, 73
polymyxin 175
polypeptides 106, 119, 195
polysaccharide 66–7, 90, 141
Portuguese man-of-war 126
positron 8, 63
potassium 29, 110, 214
  bichromate 46
precipitin 113
primates 58
promethazine 123
prophylaxis 100
prosectorium 59
proteins 72, 134
  kinase C 54
  synthesis 53
prothrombin 72
protonsil 47–8
Psilocybe 121
psychedelic 121, 123
psychiatry 123
psychology 165–6
psychoneuroimmunology 124–6
puerperal fever 5, 7, 59–60
pulmonary 4–5
pyaemia 60
pyocyanase 90, 100–1

quantum
  physics 31
  theory 35
quinazolines 120
quinine 46

rabies 57
rabbit 57, 98–101, 103, 140–2, 158
  ears, floppy 141–3
racemic 56
radar 31
radiation 15, 22, 27–8
  background 26–8
  black body 28
  cosmic 28, 43
  electromagnetic 58
  extraterrestrial 27
  infrared 61
  microwave 28
  nuclear 32
  quantum 35
  radioactive 22, 32
  sun 37
radio-
  activity 5, 16, 35, 53, 134
  astronomy 27
  graphs 21–2
  immunoassay 134–6
  noise 27
  telescope 26–8
rats 118, 124–5
Rauwolfia serpentina 123
rays
  cathode 16
  cosmic 8
  gamma 31–4
recoil 32–4
recoilless 31–4
receptors 52, 132
  adreno- 49
  benzodiazepine 120
  dopamine 124
  opioid 119
recombinant DNA, *see* DNA
relativity 5–6
reserpine 123–4
resonance 31, 49
  nuclear 31
respiration 44
restriction enzymes 63

retrospectroscope 144
rheumatic fever 143–4
Rhône-Poulenc 123
ribonucleic acid (RNA) 53, 106
ringworm 22
Roche Drug Company 120
Rockefeller Foundation 91
Rocky Mountain spotted fever 58
Royal Astronomical Society 38
Royal College of Chemistry 46
Royal College of Physicians 93
Royal College of Surgeons 76
Royal Society 8, 86
ruby, *see* laser

saccharin 125
sagacity 1, 20
St Mary's Hospital, *see* Hospital
salvarsan 84
Sandoz Drug Company 121
sarcoma 6, 177
Saturn 36
Scheele's green 42
schizophrenia 122–4
science philosophy 167–73
scintillation 16
scurvy 51
secretin 154, 157
sedatives 120
Sentocym 102
septicaemia 88, 92
serendipity 1–3, 49, 63, 119, 121, 141, 160
serotonin 124, 132
SGOT 72
Shwartzman phenomenon 140–1
sickle cell anaemia 68
sleep 119, 131–3
  delta 133
  deprivation 132
  factors 132
  modulation 132
  slow wave 132
smallpox 7

snakeroot, *see* Rauwolfia
snowblindness 170
Société de Biologie 152
soda water 42
sodium 31
  chloride 140
  citrate 136
  vapour 31
solar system 2
solenoid 12
solution, salt 140
  Locke 140
  Ringer 140
spectrum 37
spermine 68
spermatozoa 139
Sperry Rand Company 6
spinthariscope 16
spleen 125
spores 82
Squibb 92
Stanford 3, 5, 118
Staphylococci, *see* bacteria
steam engine 3
stereo-
  isomer 119
  specific 119
  tactic 131
streptococci, *see* bacteria
Streptomyces griseus 103
streptomycin 93, 103–5, 160–1
streptothricin 104
strontium 111
sugar 147, 151, 154, 157
sulfanilamide 47, 78
sulfonamide 47, 88, 158, 241
  derivatives 158–9
  para-amino-benzene 48
sulphur 43
sunlight 43
sun spots 36
surgery 31, 79, 94
surgical procedures 106, 112
suspended animation 112

syndromes:
  Down's 72
  Parkinson's 124
  Tourette 49
syphilis 85

tachykinins 107
tap, dripping 247
tautomers 70
technology 171
telescope 27, 36, 163
TELSTAR 27
tentacles 126
teonanactl 121
thalamus 131
thalassemia 73
theory 44
  Gestalt 167
  gravitational 35
  quantum 35, 169
  relativity 5–6
  sleep 133
therapeutic 86, 99, 103
therapy 84
  diabetes 153
thiazolidine 93
thinking
  communal 2, 101
  convergent 171
  creative 171
  divergent 171
  lateral 170–2
  vertical 170–1
thought
  collective 163, 168–9
  community 168
  style 168
thromboplastic 137
thymine 70
thyroid, *see* gland
tissue
  connective 142
  heart 144
  necrotic 79

Tokyo 73
tolbutamid 159
toxic 84, 154
toxin 51, 122, 126
trachea 218
tranquillizers 119–21
transducers 85
transformation 66–8
transformer 15
transfusion 72–3, 136
transplantation 149
trypsin 157, 216
trypsinogen 157
tuberculosis 101, 104–5, 151, 161, 164
tumour 12, 113, 172, 263
  necrosis factor 133
Tunis 92
typhoid 79
typhus 57–8

universe 26, 28, 48, 253
University
  Aberdeen 118, 156
  Alberta 155
  Birmingham 21
  Bologna 10
  Calgary 65
  California, Berkeley 178
    La Jolla 30
  Caltech 27
  Cambridge 6
  Chicago 150
  City (London) 166
  College, London 90, 134
  Cologne 101
  Columbia 27, 29
  Copenhagen 11
  Cornell 141
  Edinburgh 83
  Göttingen 167
  Harvard 113, 115, 131, 176
  Hebrew 175
  Heidelberg 16
  Indiana 61

Johns Hopkins 118, 148
London 76
McGill 86
New York (Stony Brook) 140
Northwestern 131
Oxford 87
Prague 15
Princeton 28
Rochester 122
Rutgers 103, 177
Stanford 118, 155
Tokyo 132
Toronto 152
Vienna 47
Wayne State 169
Wisconsin 64, 118
Würzburg 16
Yale 88
uranium 16, 22, 23
Uranus 36–8, 62
urea 45, 122
uric acid 122
urine 122, 132, 146, 151

vaccination 7, 57, 79, 175
vaccines 77
  aerosol 176
vacuum 16, 43, 84
Valium 119, 120
variola 7
vaso-constrictor 49
vasotocin 132
venom 90
vibration 29, 32
virulence 58, 66, 176

virus 6, 61, 136
  aerosol 175
  attenuated 176
  adeno 177
  avian leucosis 176–7
  cowpox 7
  hepatitis 73
  Japanese encephalitis 143
  Newcastle disease 176
  polio 59
  Rous sarcoma 177
  rubella 177
  smallpox 7
  tumour 6
  visceral lymphomatosis 176
vitamin 51
  B 50
  C 51
volt 11
voltage 16
Vulcan 37

wave, sound 18
wavelength 27–9, 32–3
  absorption 32–3
  emission 32–3
  shift 32
wireless 15
wound 79, 93

X-rays 15–22
Xenopus levis 106

yeast 57, 102

zinc-sulfide 16